VEIL

GREG RUCKA
TONI FEJZULA

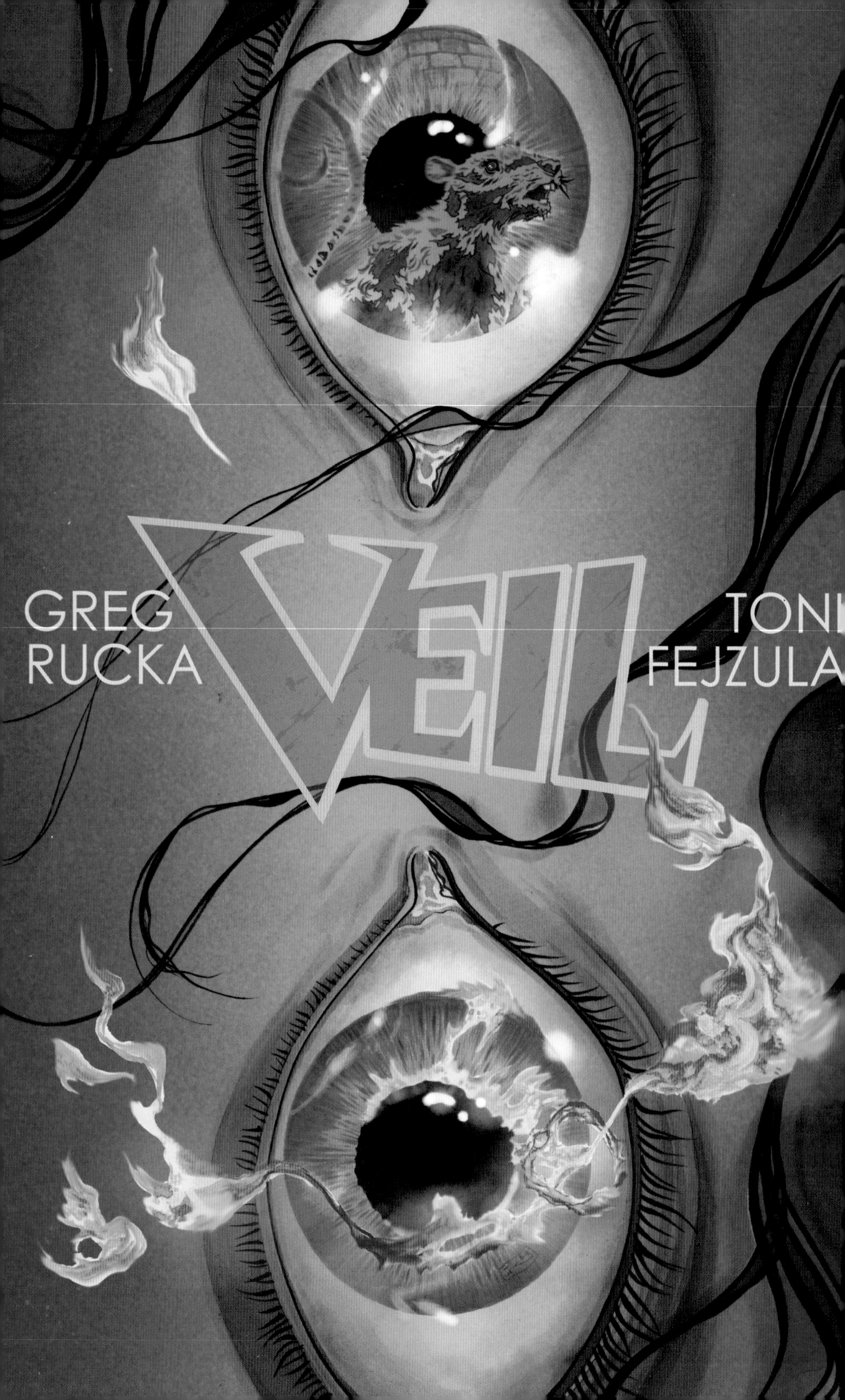
GREG
RUCKA
VEIL
TONI
FEJZULA

STORY *by* GREG RUCKA

ART AND COVER *by* TONI FEJZULA

COLORS *by* TONI FEJZULA *with* ALJOŠA TOMIĆ

LETTERS *by* NATE PIEKOS *of* BLAMBOT®

Facing: ILLUSTRATION *by* J. H. WILLIAMS III

DARK HORSE BOOKS

Production Tech CHRISTINA McKENZIE
Designer KAT LARSON
Assistant Editor SHANTEL LaROCQUE
Editor SCOTT ALLIE
Publisher MIKE RICHARDSON

Special thanks to IVANA DRAGICEVIC, TALON KELLEY, DAVE STEWART, and CHRISTINA McKENZIE

Published by Dark Horse Books, a division of Dark Horse Comics, Inc.
10956 SE Main Street, Milwaukie, OR 97222

First edition: January 2015 | ISBN 978-1-61655-492-7

10 9 8 7 6 5 4 3 2 1
Printed in China

International Licensing: (503) 905-2377 | Comic Shop Locator Service: (888) 266-4226

President and Publisher MIKE RICHARDSON | Executive Vice President NEIL HANKERSON
Chief Financial Officer TOM WEDDLE | Vice President of Publishing RANDY STRADLEY
Vice President of Book Trade Sales MICHAEL MARTENS | Editor in Chief SCOTT ALLIE
Vice President of Marketing MATT PARKINSON | Vice President of Product Development DAVID SCROGGY
Vice President of Information Technology DALE LaFOUNTAIN | Senior Director of Print, Design, and Production DARLENE VOGEL
General Counsel KEN LIZZI | Editorial Director DAVEY ESTRADA | Senior Books Editor CHRIS WARNER
Executive Editor DIANA SCHUTZ | Director of Print and Development CARY GRAZZINI | Art Director LIA RIBACCHI
Director of Scheduling CARA NIECE | Director of Digital Publishing MARK BERNARDI

This volume collects issues #1–#5 of Veil.

CHAPTER ONE

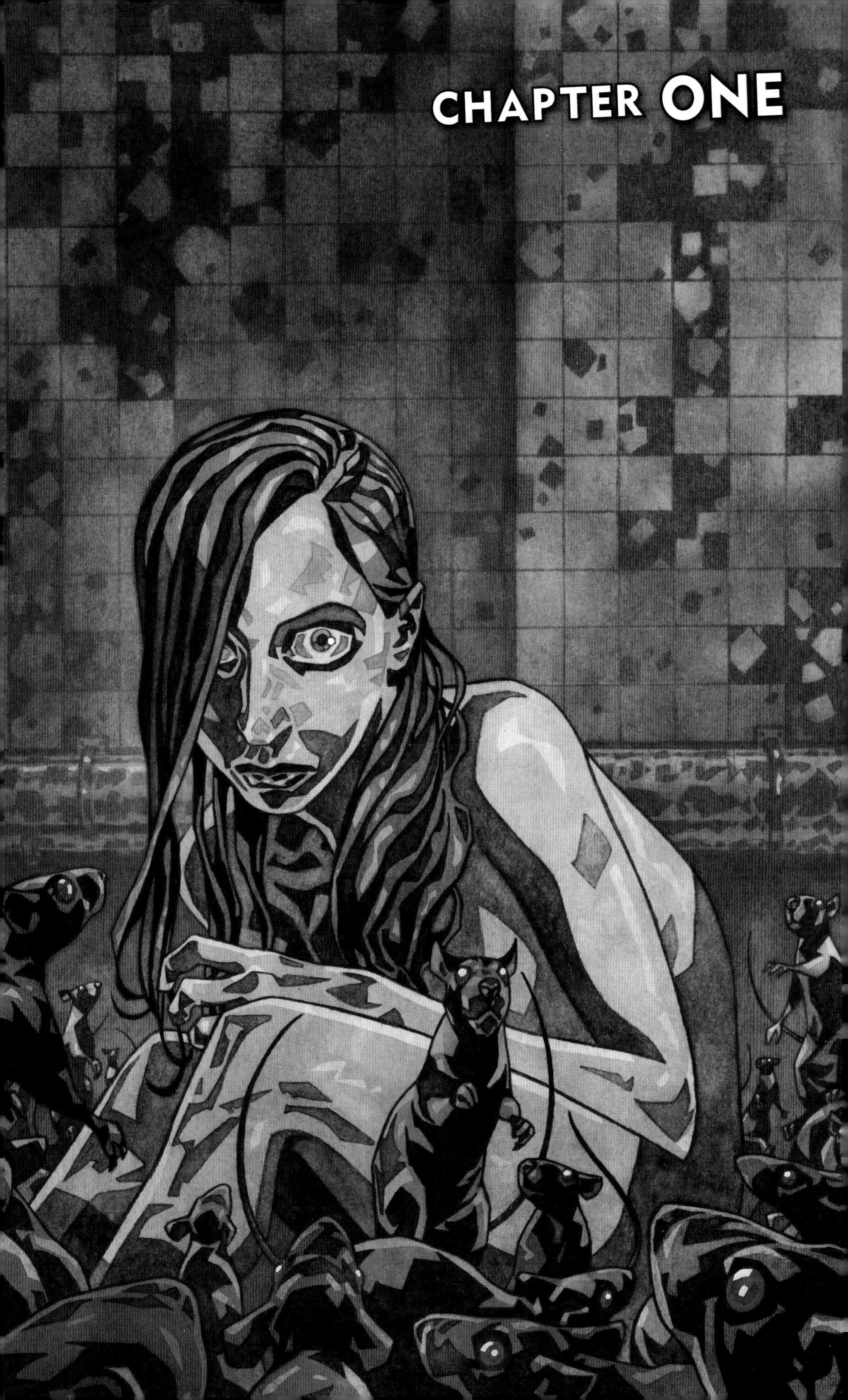

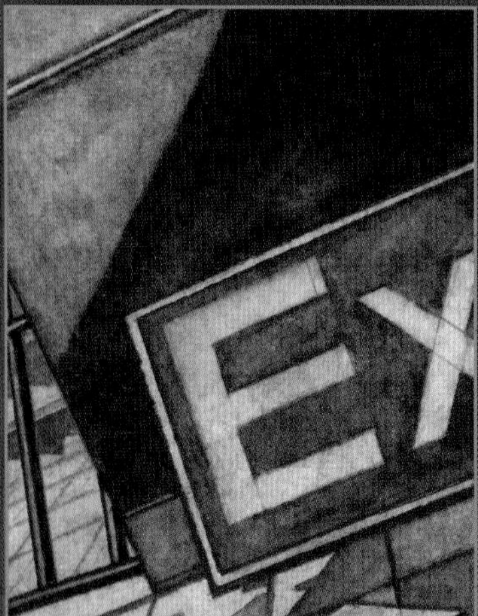
EX

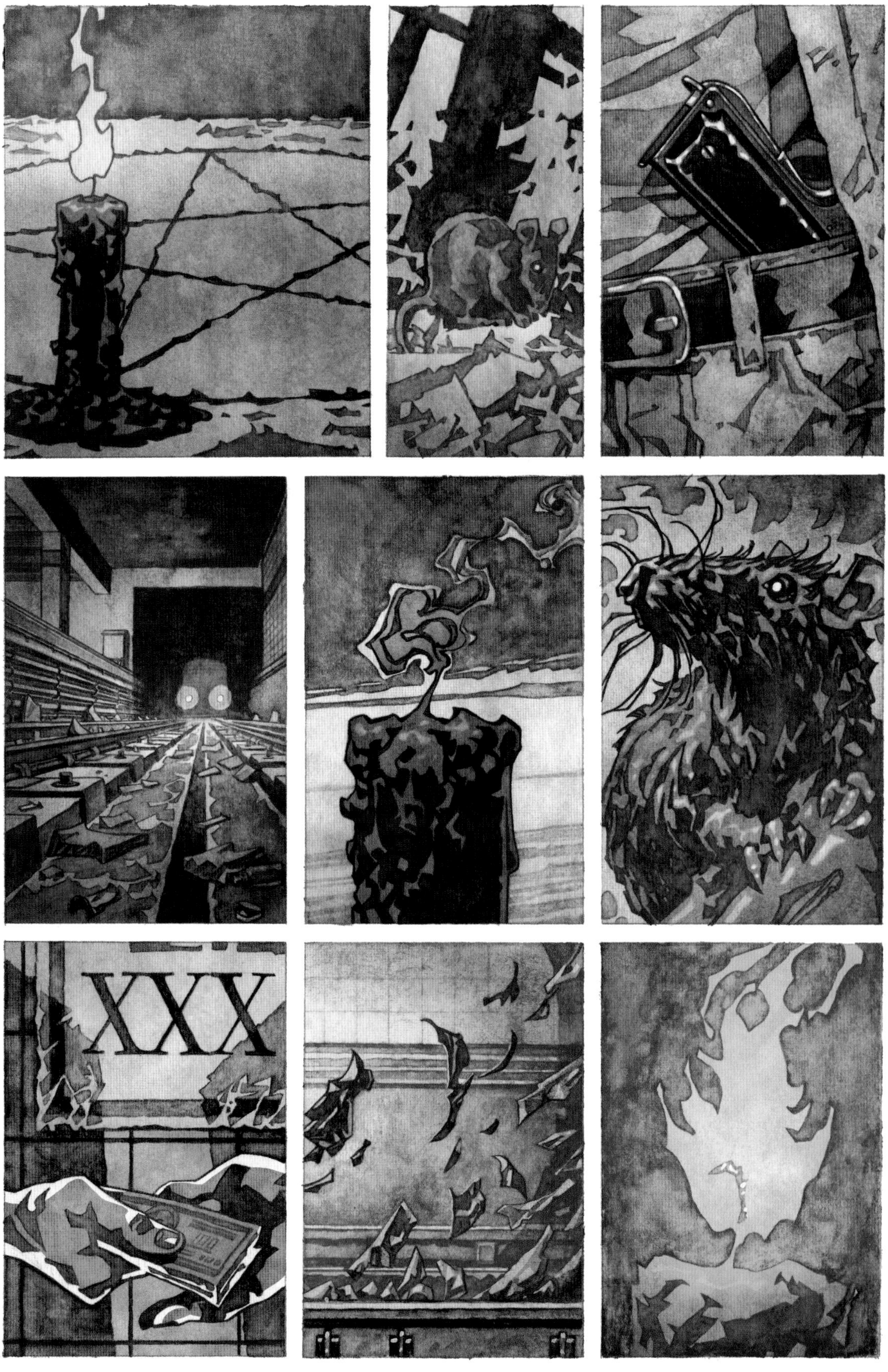
XXX

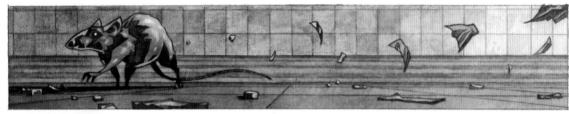

UH...
HNHH...
HNNH!
HNN
NHNN
HU-HUH
HURTS...
...IT...
...HURTS...?

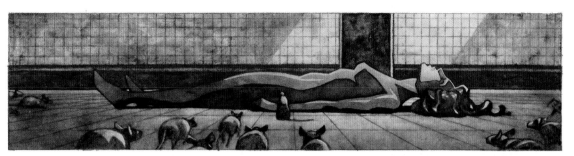

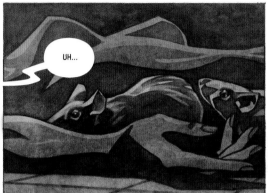

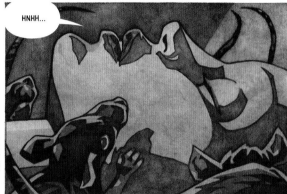

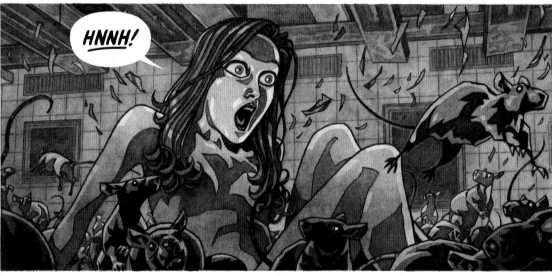

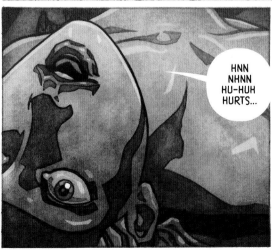

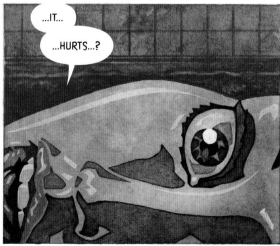

RRR...

...RRRAT!

YOU'RE A *RAT!*

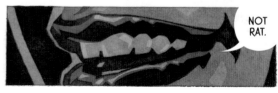

NOT RAT.

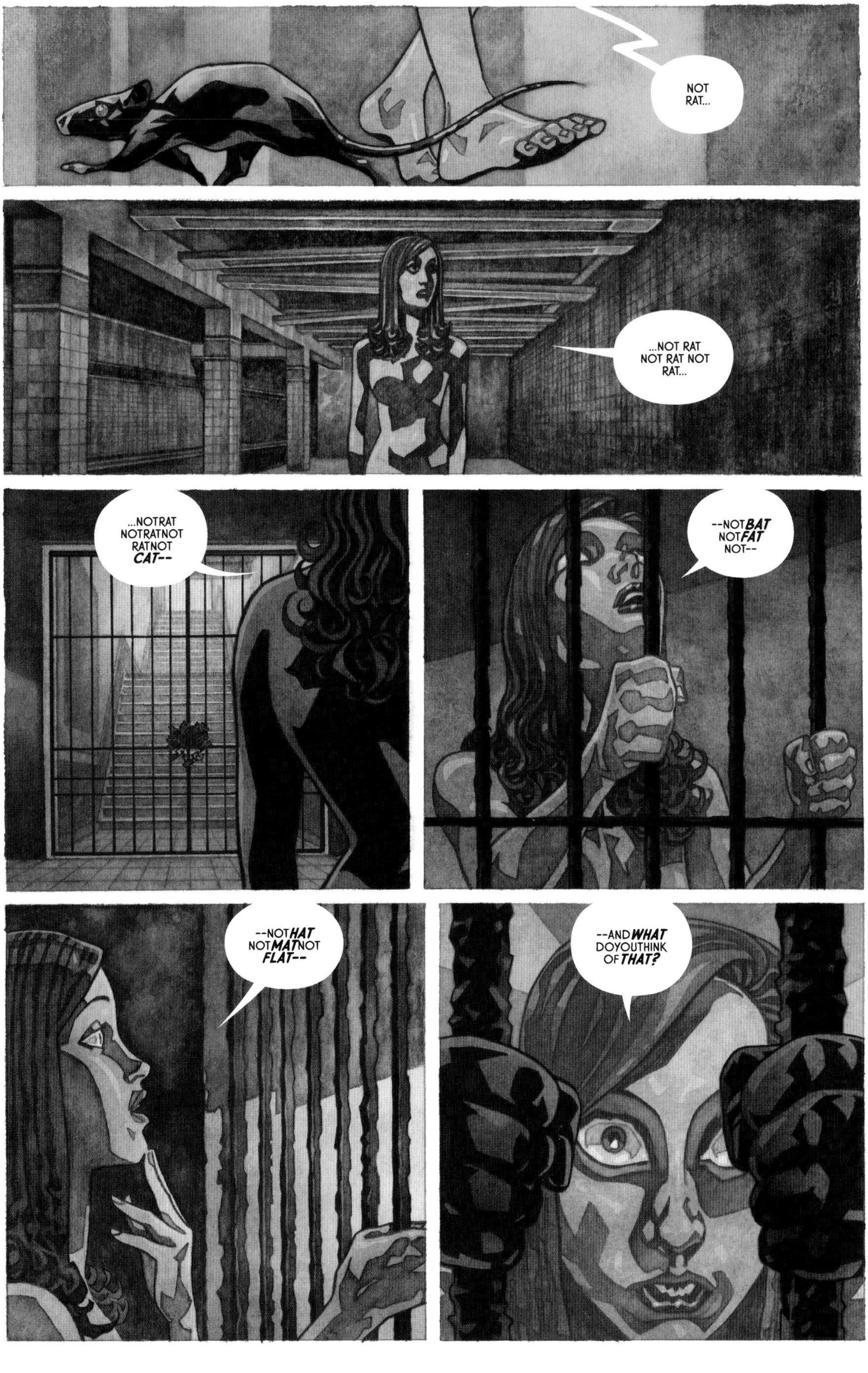
NOT RAT...
...NOT RAT NOT RAT NOT RAT...
...NOTRAT NOTRATNOT RATNOT CAT--
--NOTBAT NOTFAT NOT--
--NOTHAT NOTMATNOT FLAT--
--ANDWHAT DOYOUTHINK OFTHAT?

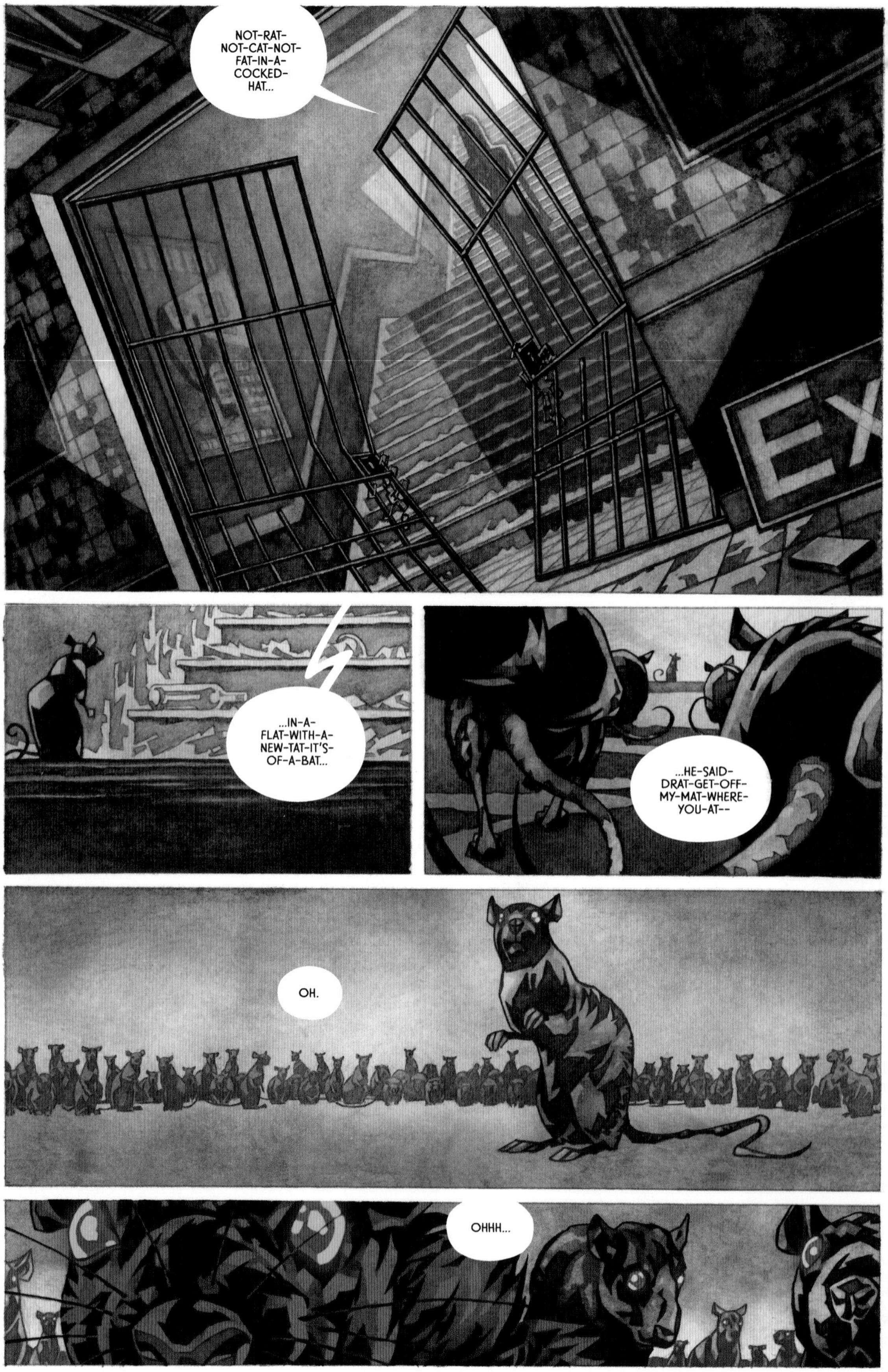
NOT-RAT-NOT-CAT-NOT-FAT-IN-A-COCKED-HAT...
EX
...IN-A-FLAT-WITH-A-NEW-TAT-IT'S-OF-A-BAT...
...HE-SAID-DRAT-GET-OFF-MY-MAT-WHERE-YOU-AT--
OH.
OHHH...

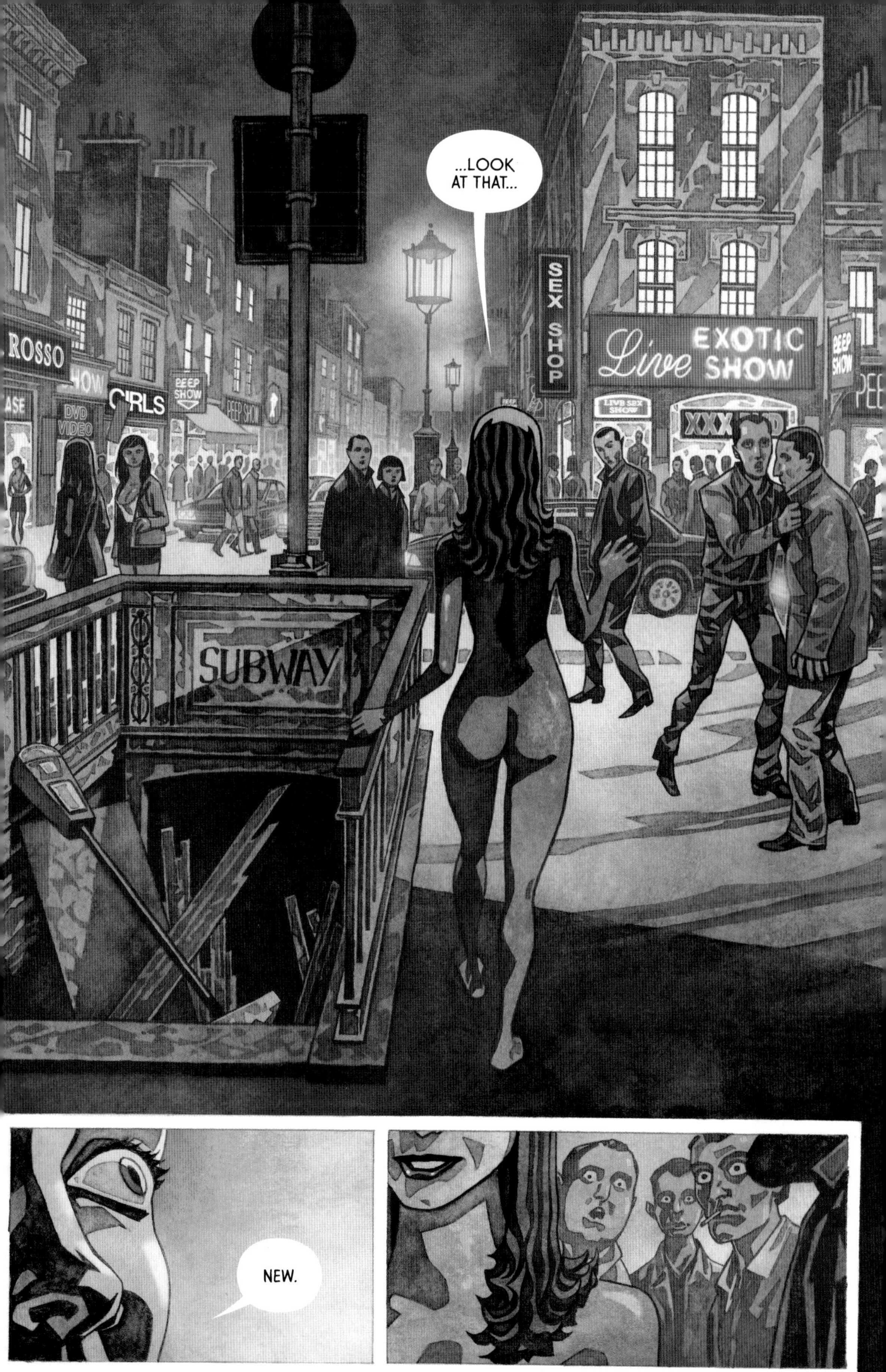

...LOOK AT THAT...
SEX SHOP
Live EXOTIC SHOW
ROSSO
GIRLS
DVD VIDEO
PEEP SHOW
LIVE SEX SHOW
SUBWAY
NEW.

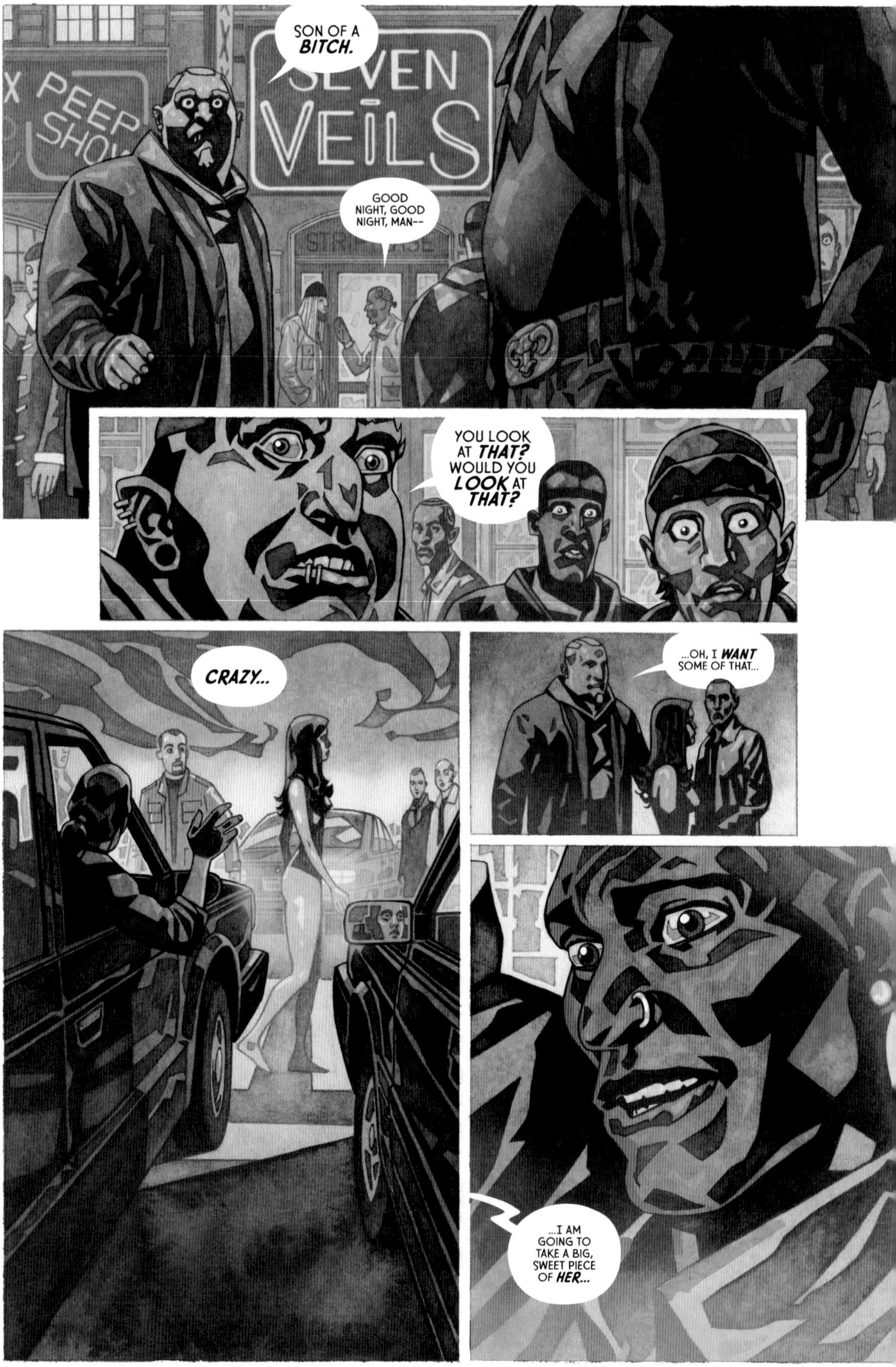
SON OF A BITCH.
X PEEP SHOW
SEVEN VEILS
GOOD NIGHT, GOOD NIGHT, MAN--
YOU LOOK AT THAT? WOULD YOU LOOK AT THAT?
CRAZY...
...OH, I WANT SOME OF THAT...
...I AM GOING TO TAKE A BIG, SWEET PIECE OF HER...

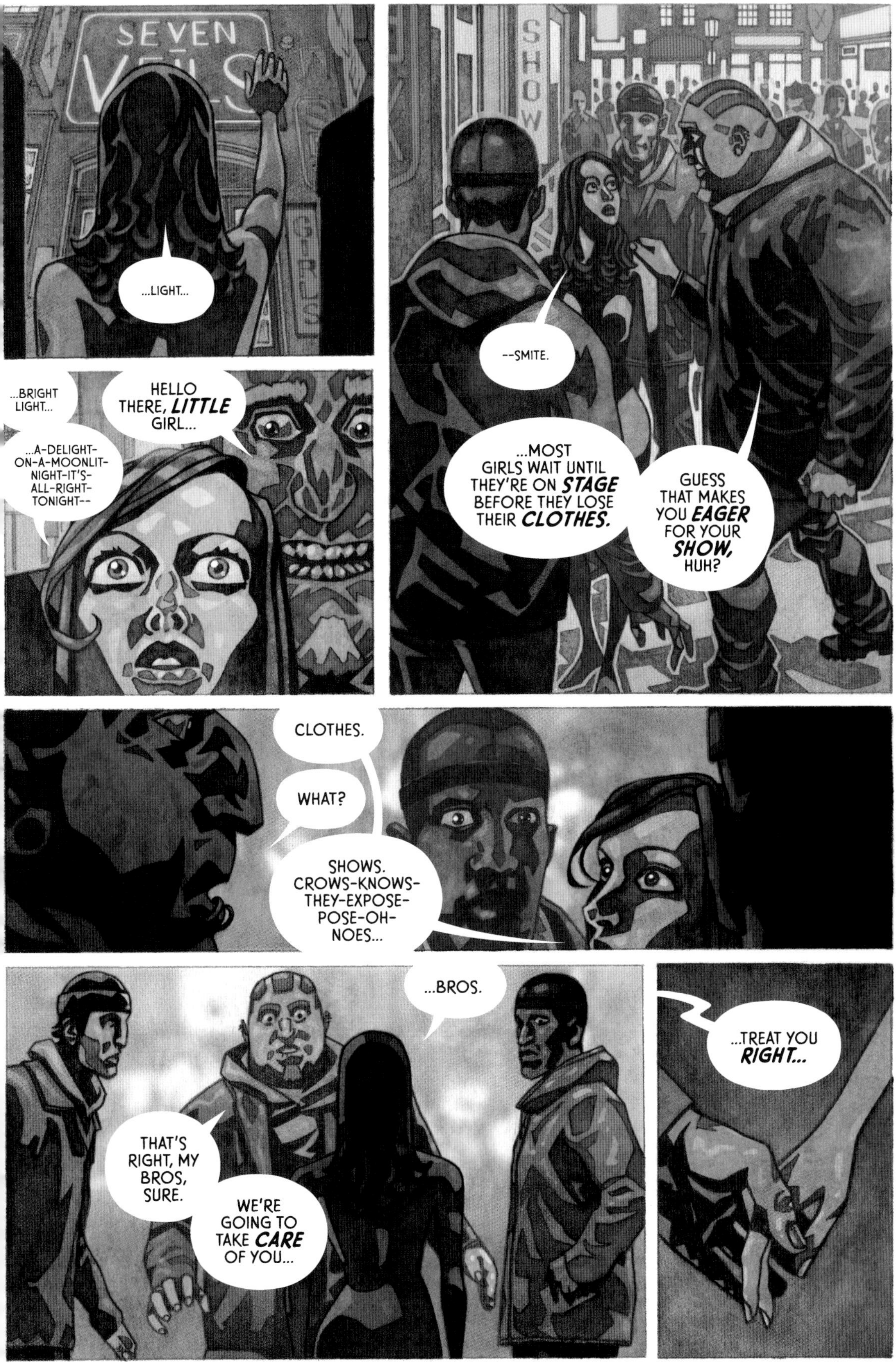
SEVEN VEILS
...LIGHT...
SHOW
GIRLS
...BRIGHT LIGHT...
...A-DELIGHT-ON-A-MOONLIT-NIGHT-IT'S-ALL-RIGHT-TONIGHT--
HELLO THERE, *LITTLE* GIRL...
--SMITE.
...MOST GIRLS WAIT UNTIL THEY'RE ON *STAGE* BEFORE THEY LOSE THEIR *CLOTHES.*
GUESS THAT MAKES YOU *EAGER* FOR YOUR *SHOW,* HUH?
CLOTHES.
WHAT?
SHOWS. CROWS-KNOWS-THEY-EXPOSE-POSE-OH-NOES...
...BROS.
THAT'S RIGHT, MY BROS, SURE.
WE'RE GOING TO TAKE *CARE* OF YOU...
...TREAT YOU *RIGHT...*

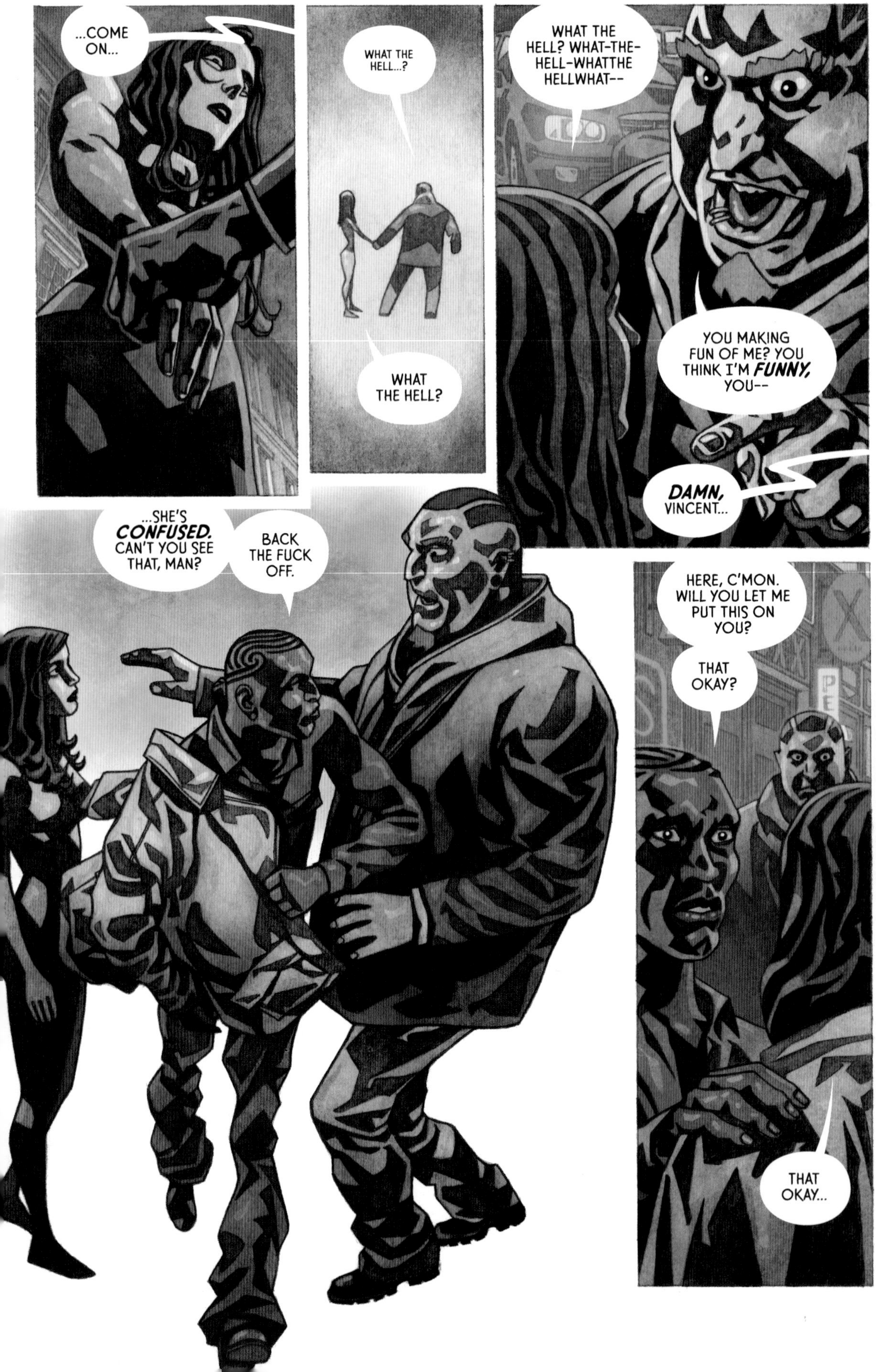
...COME ON...
WHAT THE HELL...?
WHAT THE HELL?
WHAT THE HELL? WHAT-THE-HELL-WHATTHE HELLWHAT--
YOU MAKING FUN OF ME? YOU THINK I'M *FUNNY,* YOU--
DAMN, VINCENT...
...SHE'S *CONFUSED.* CAN'T YOU SEE THAT, MAN?
BACK THE FUCK OFF.
HERE, C'MON. WILL YOU LET ME PUT THIS ON YOU?
THAT OKAY?
THAT OKAY...

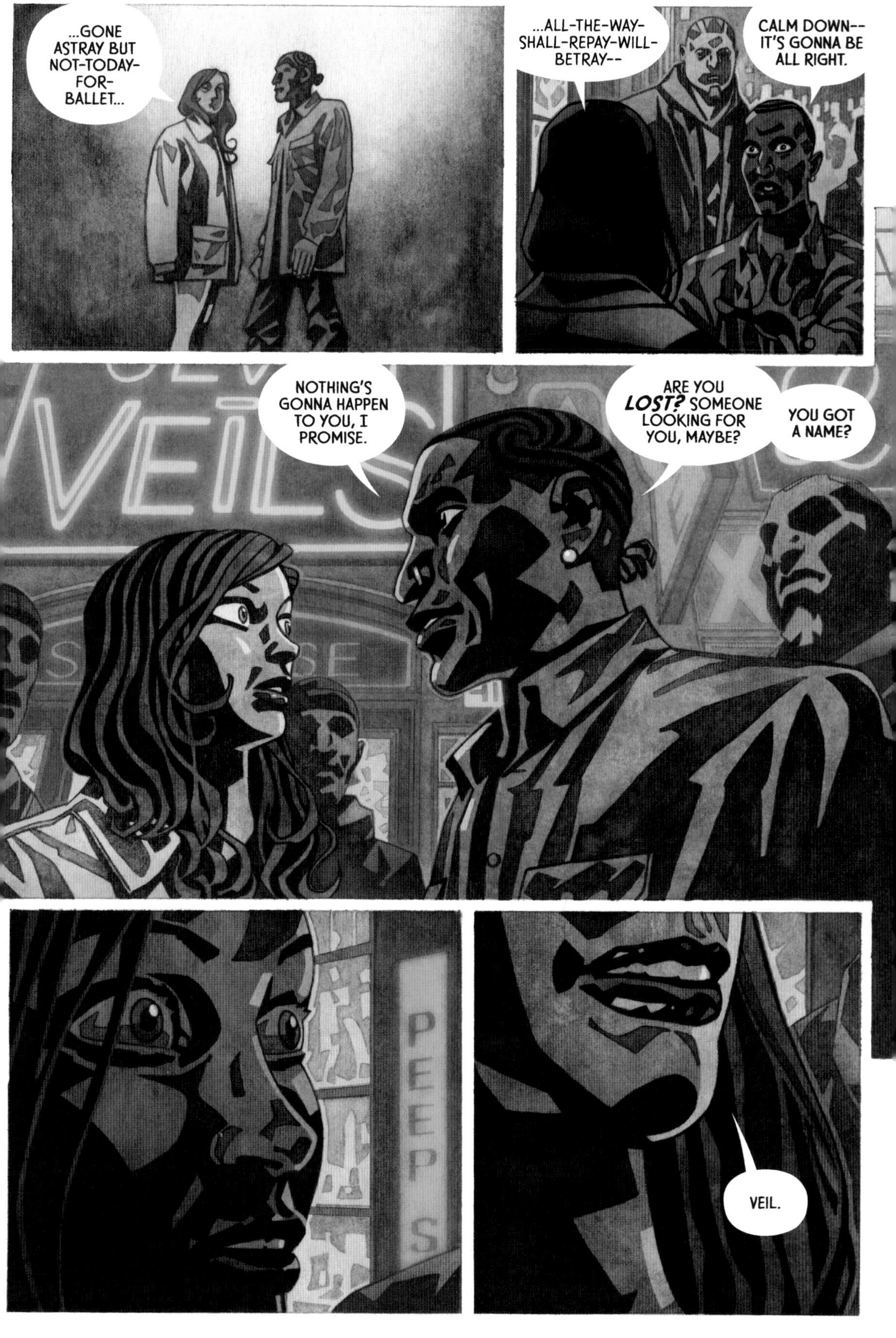

...GONE ASTRAY BUT NOT-TODAY-FOR-BALLET...
...ALL-THE-WAY-SHALL-REPAY-WILL-BETRAY--
CALM DOWN-- IT'S GONNA BE ALL RIGHT.
NOTHING'S GONNA HAPPEN TO YOU, I PROMISE.
ARE YOU *LOST?* SOMEONE LOOKING FOR YOU, MAYBE?
YOU GOT A NAME?
VEILS
PEEP S
VEIL.

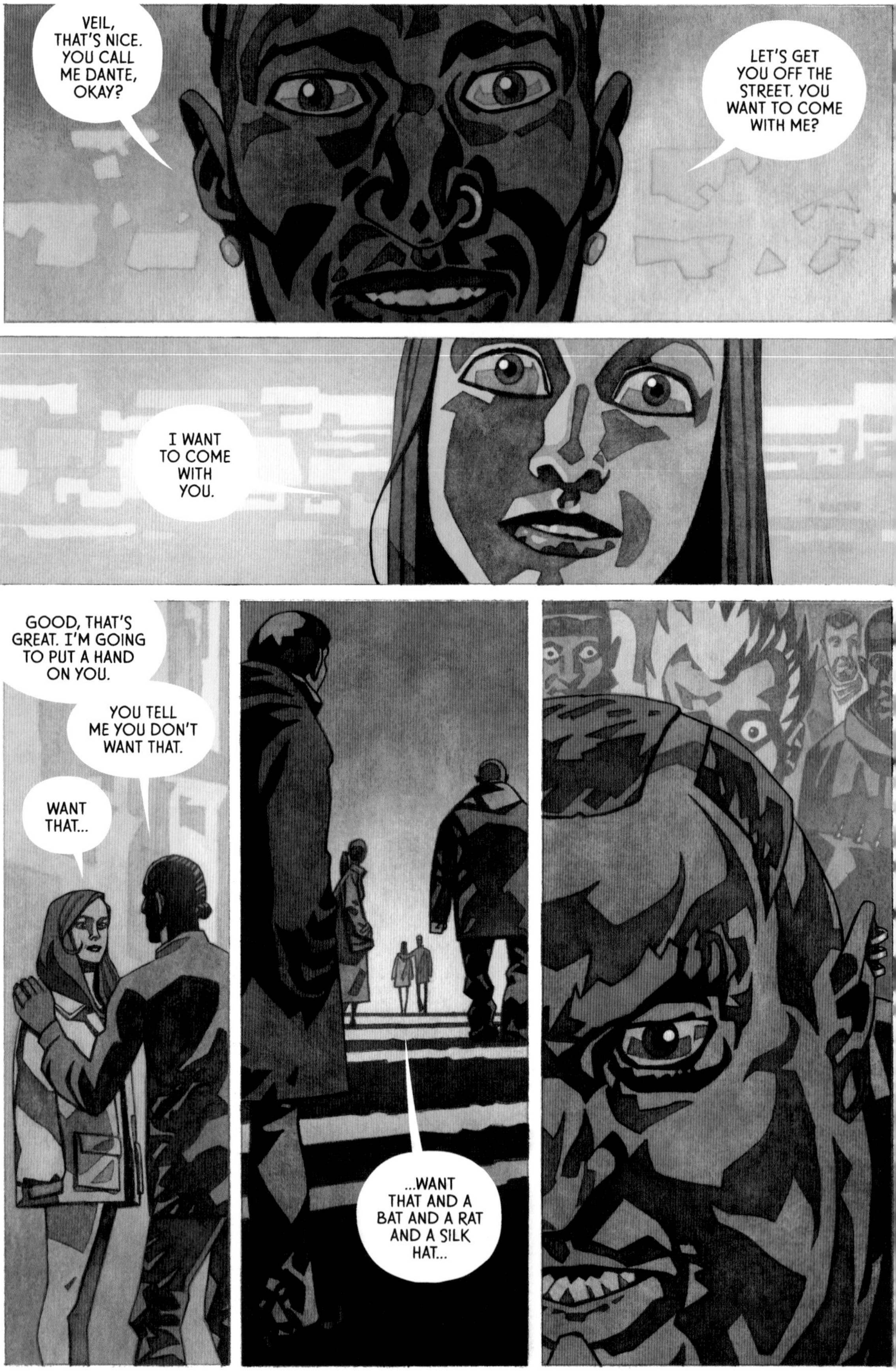
VEIL, THAT'S NICE. YOU CALL ME DANTE, OKAY?
LET'S GET YOU OFF THE STREET. YOU WANT TO COME WITH ME?
I WANT TO COME WITH YOU.
GOOD, THAT'S GREAT. I'M GOING TO PUT A HAND ON YOU.
YOU TELL ME YOU DON'T WANT THAT.
WANT THAT...
...WANT THAT AND A BAT AND A RAT AND A SILK HAT...

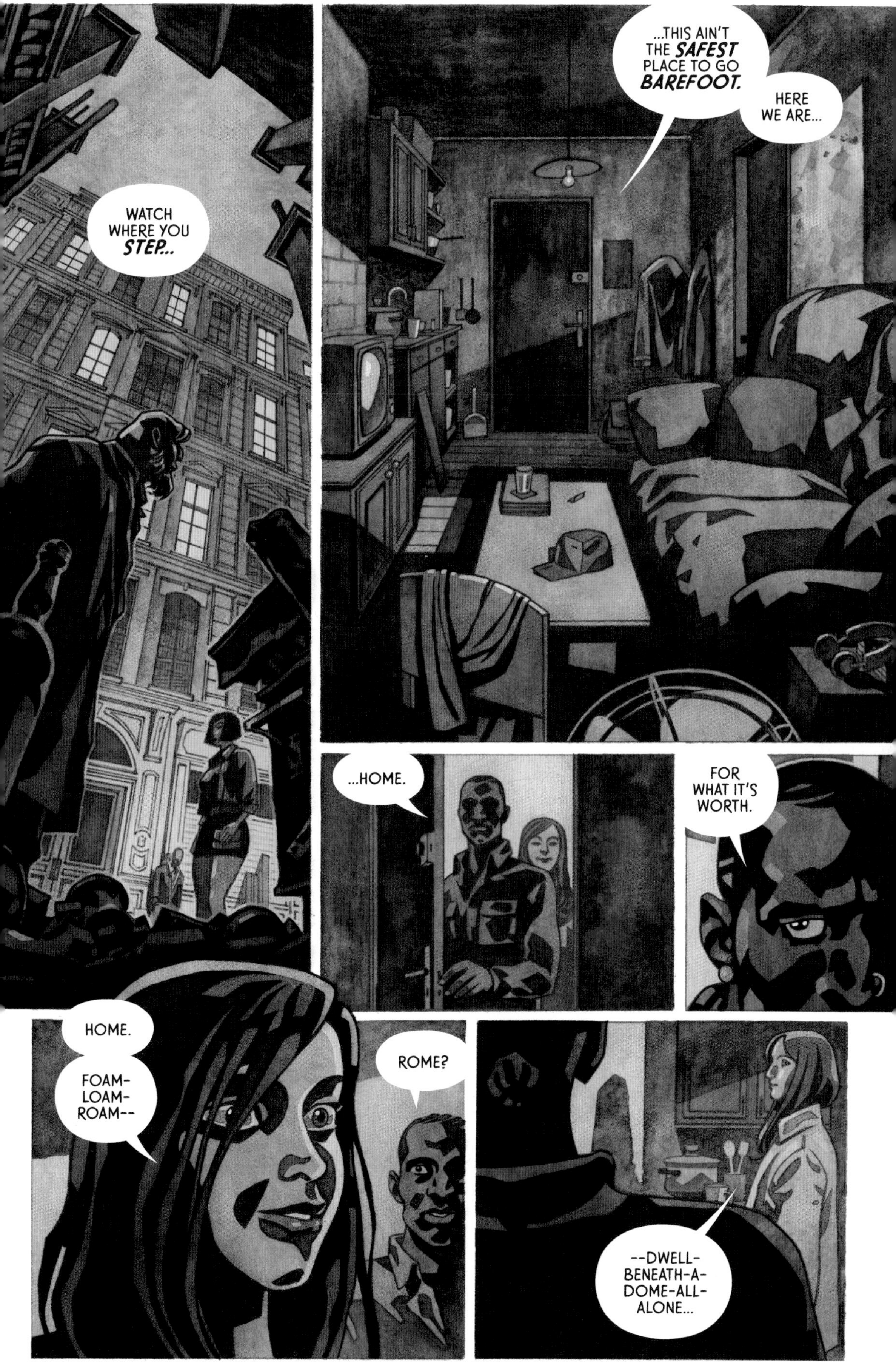
WATCH WHERE YOU STEP...
...THIS AIN'T THE SAFEST PLACE TO GO BAREFOOT.
HERE WE ARE...
...HOME.
FOR WHAT IT'S WORTH.
HOME.
FOAM-LOAM-ROAM--
ROME?
--DWELL-BENEATH-A-DOME-ALL-ALONE...

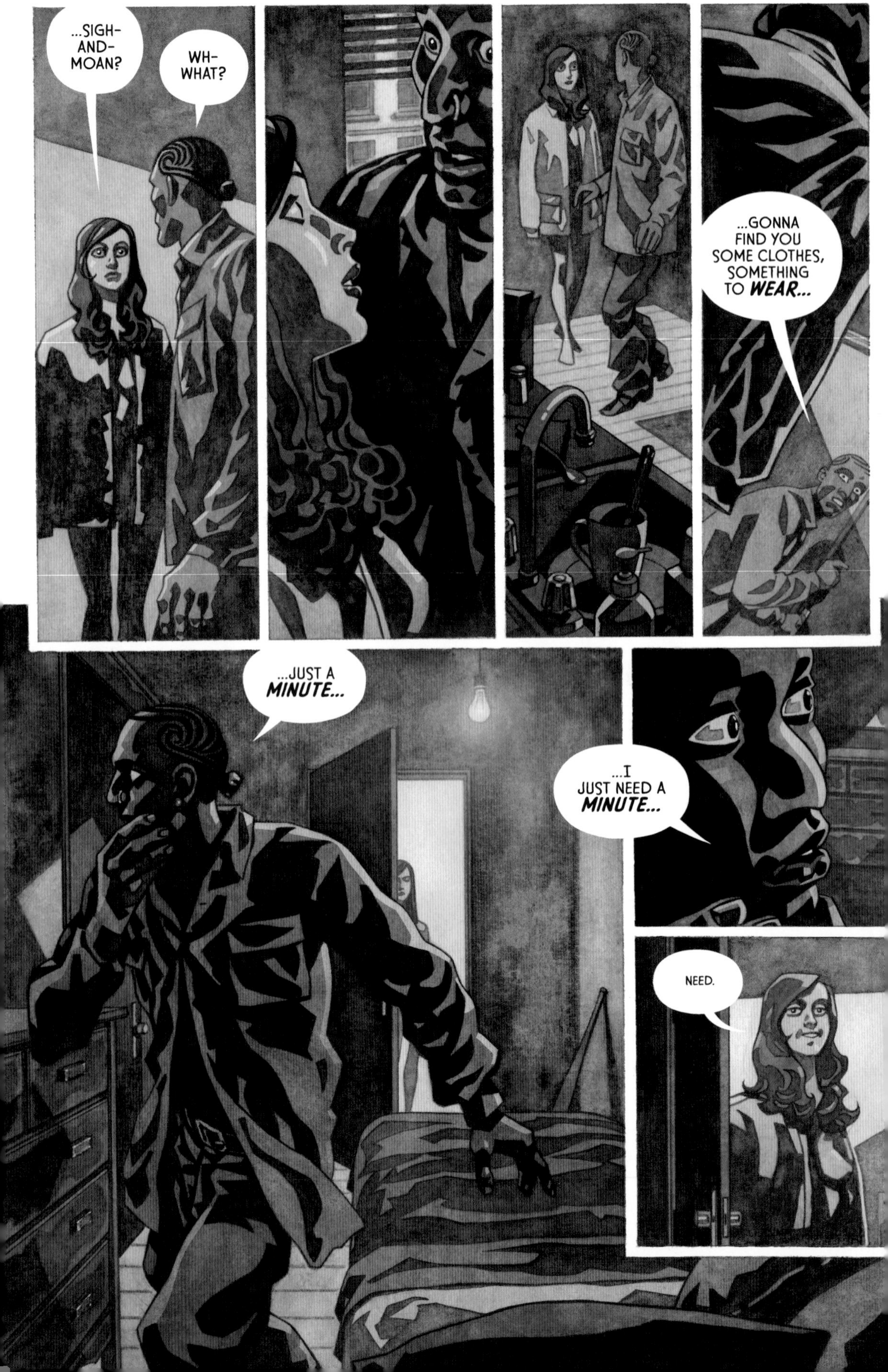
...SIGH-AND-MOAN?
WH-WHAT?
...GONNA FIND YOU SOME CLOTHES, SOMETHING TO *WEAR...*
...JUST A *MINUTE...*
...I JUST NEED A *MINUTE...*
NEED.

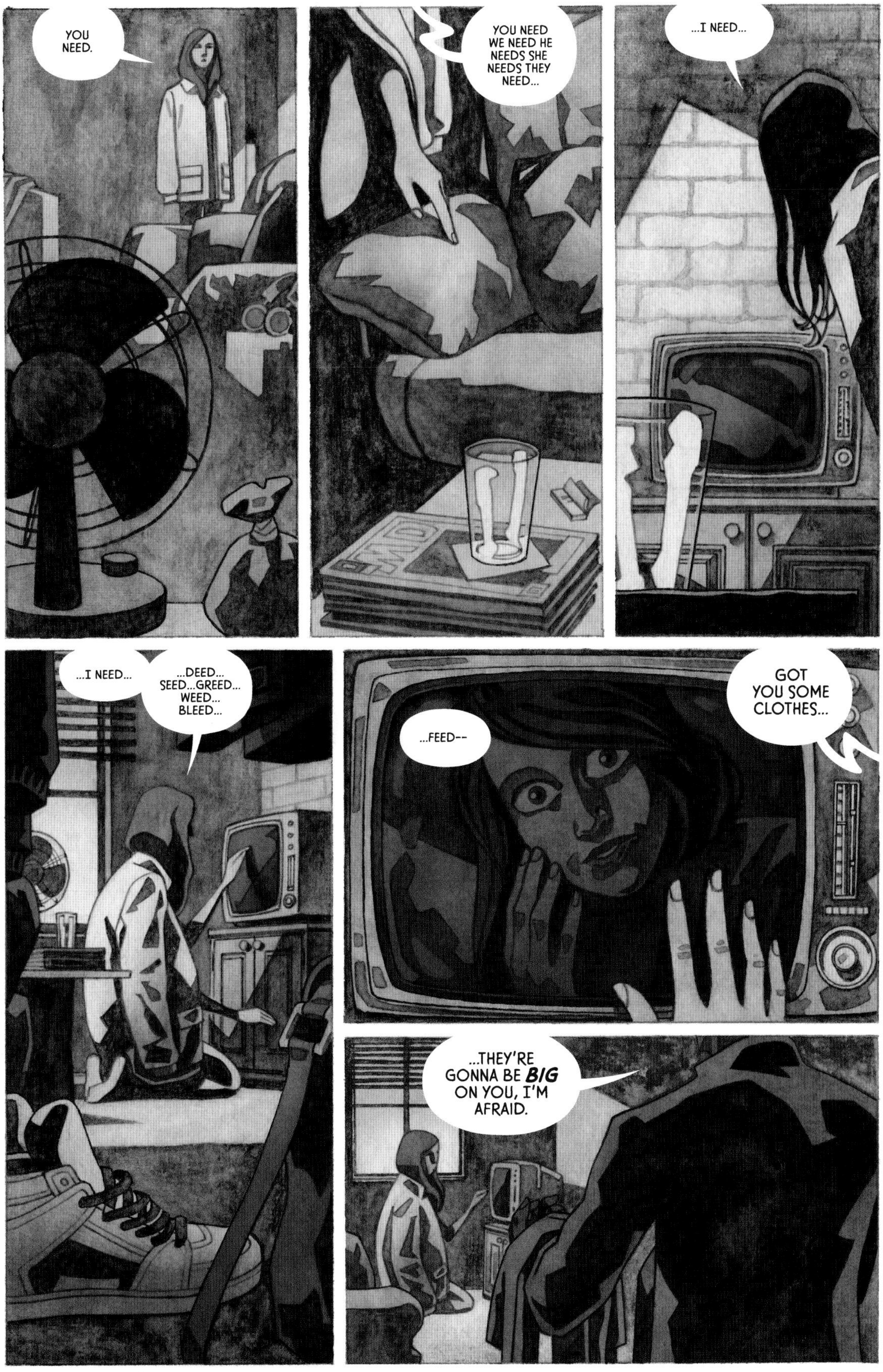
YOU NEED.
YOU NEED WE NEED HE NEEDS SHE NEEDS THEY NEED...
...I NEED...
...I NEED...
...DEED... SEED...GREED... WEED... BLEED...
...FEED--
GOT YOU SOME CLOTHES...
...THEY'RE GONNA BE ***BIG*** ON YOU, I'M AFRAID.

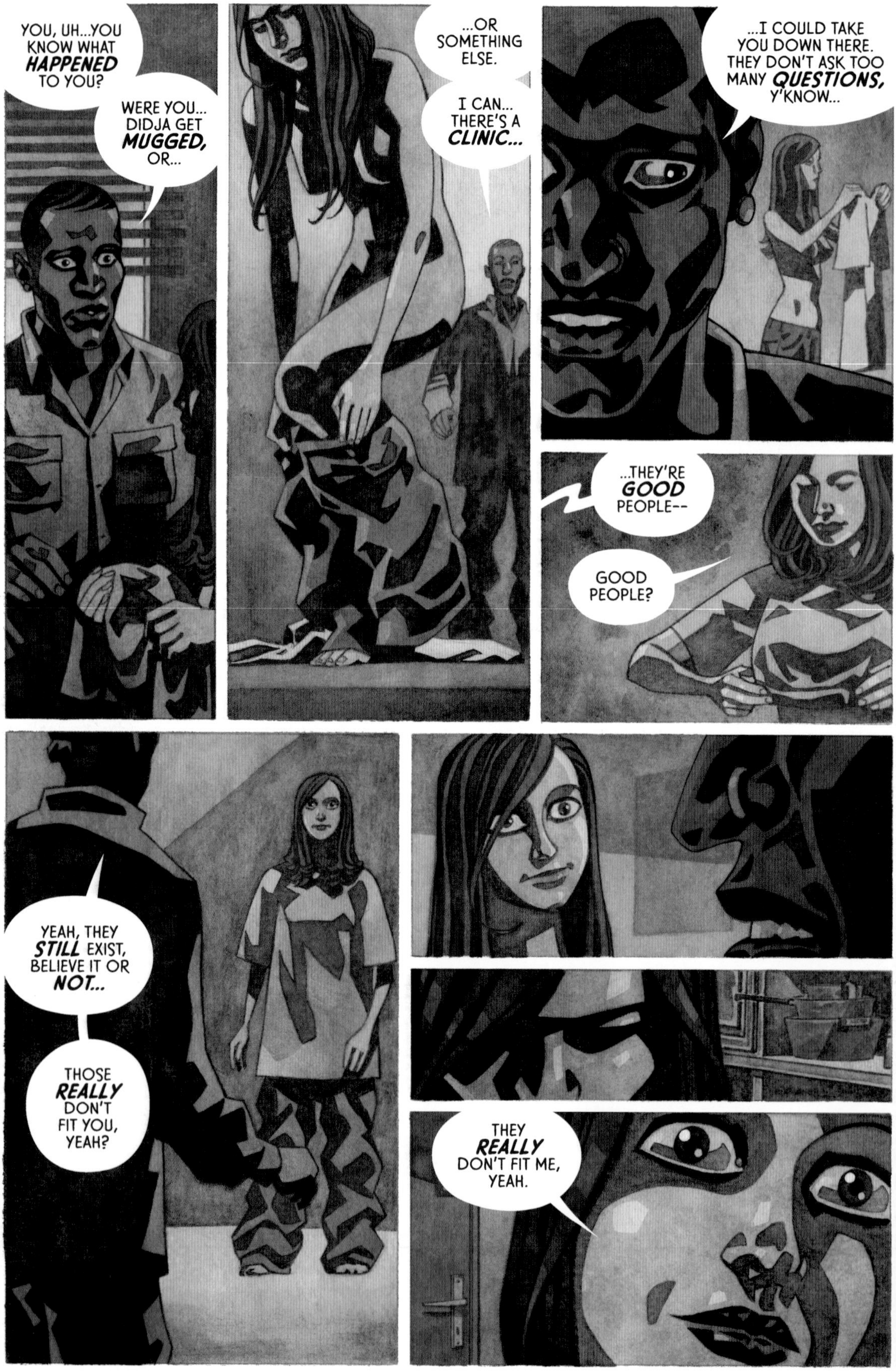
YOU, UH...YOU KNOW WHAT HAPPENED TO YOU?
WERE YOU... DIDJA GET MUGGED, OR...
...OR SOMETHING ELSE.
I CAN... THERE'S A CLINIC...
...I COULD TAKE YOU DOWN THERE. THEY DON'T ASK TOO MANY QUESTIONS, Y'KNOW...
...THEY'RE GOOD PEOPLE--
GOOD PEOPLE?
YEAH, THEY STILL EXIST, BELIEVE IT OR NOT...
THOSE REALLY DON'T FIT YOU, YEAH?
THEY REALLY DON'T FIT ME, YEAH.

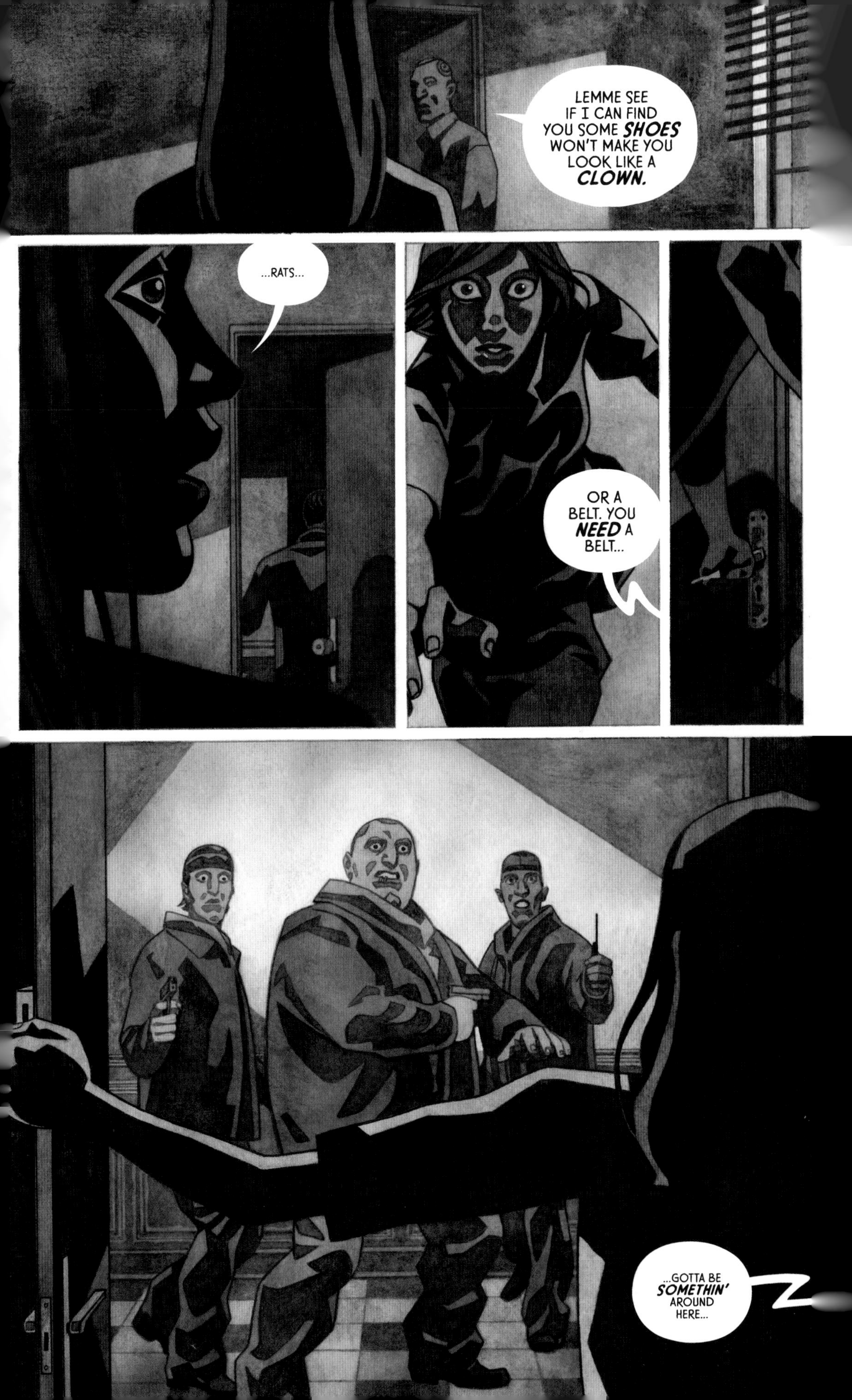
LEMME SEE IF I CAN FIND YOU SOME SHOES WON'T MAKE YOU LOOK LIKE A CLOWN.
...RATS...
OR A BELT. YOU NEED A BELT...
...GOTTA BE SOMETHIN' AROUND HERE...

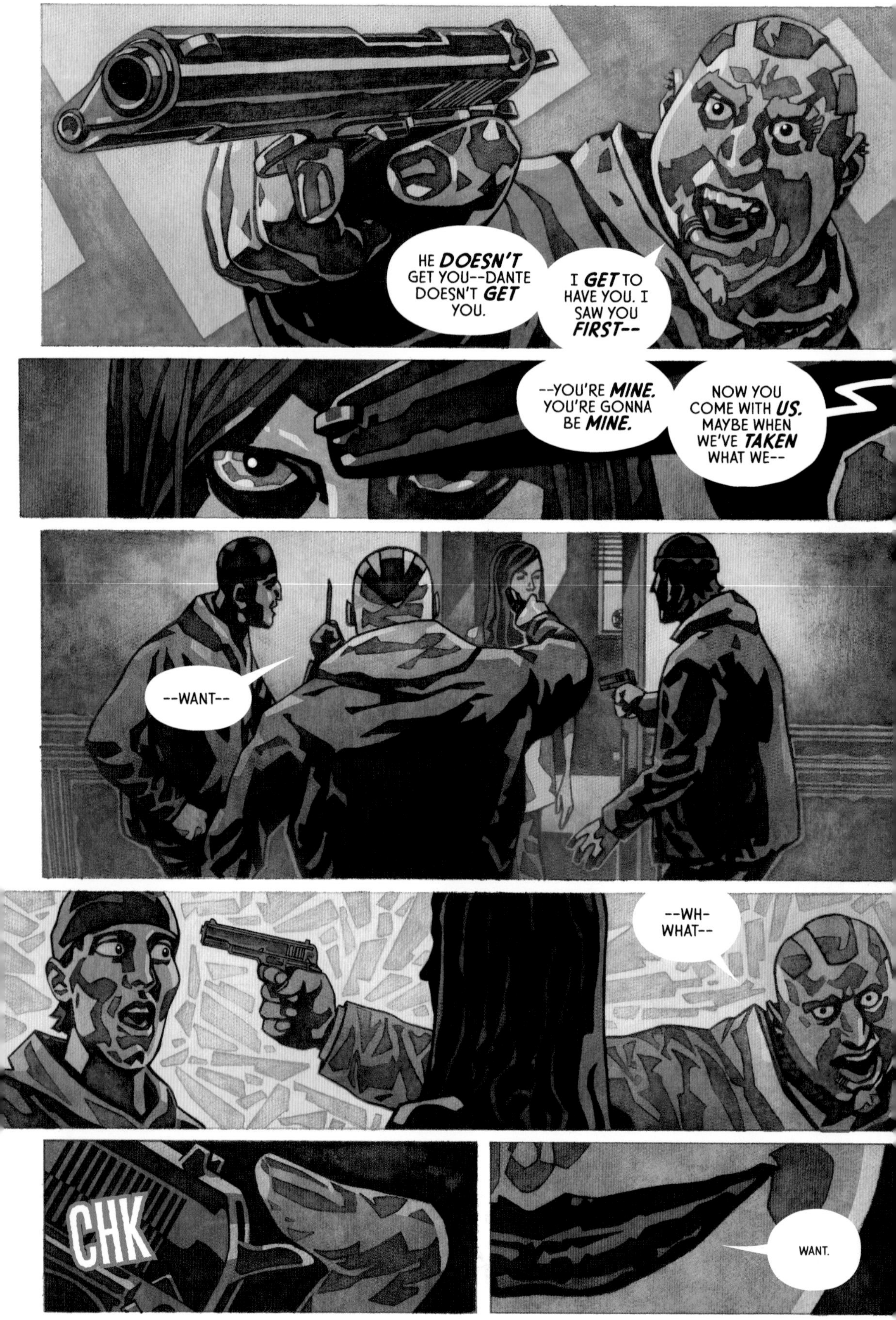
HE DOESN'T GET YOU--DANTE DOESN'T GET YOU.
I GET TO HAVE YOU. I SAW YOU FIRST--
--YOU'RE MINE. YOU'RE GONNA BE MINE.
NOW YOU COME WITH US. MAYBE WHEN WE'VE TAKEN WHAT WE--
--WANT--
--WH- WHAT--
CHK
WANT.

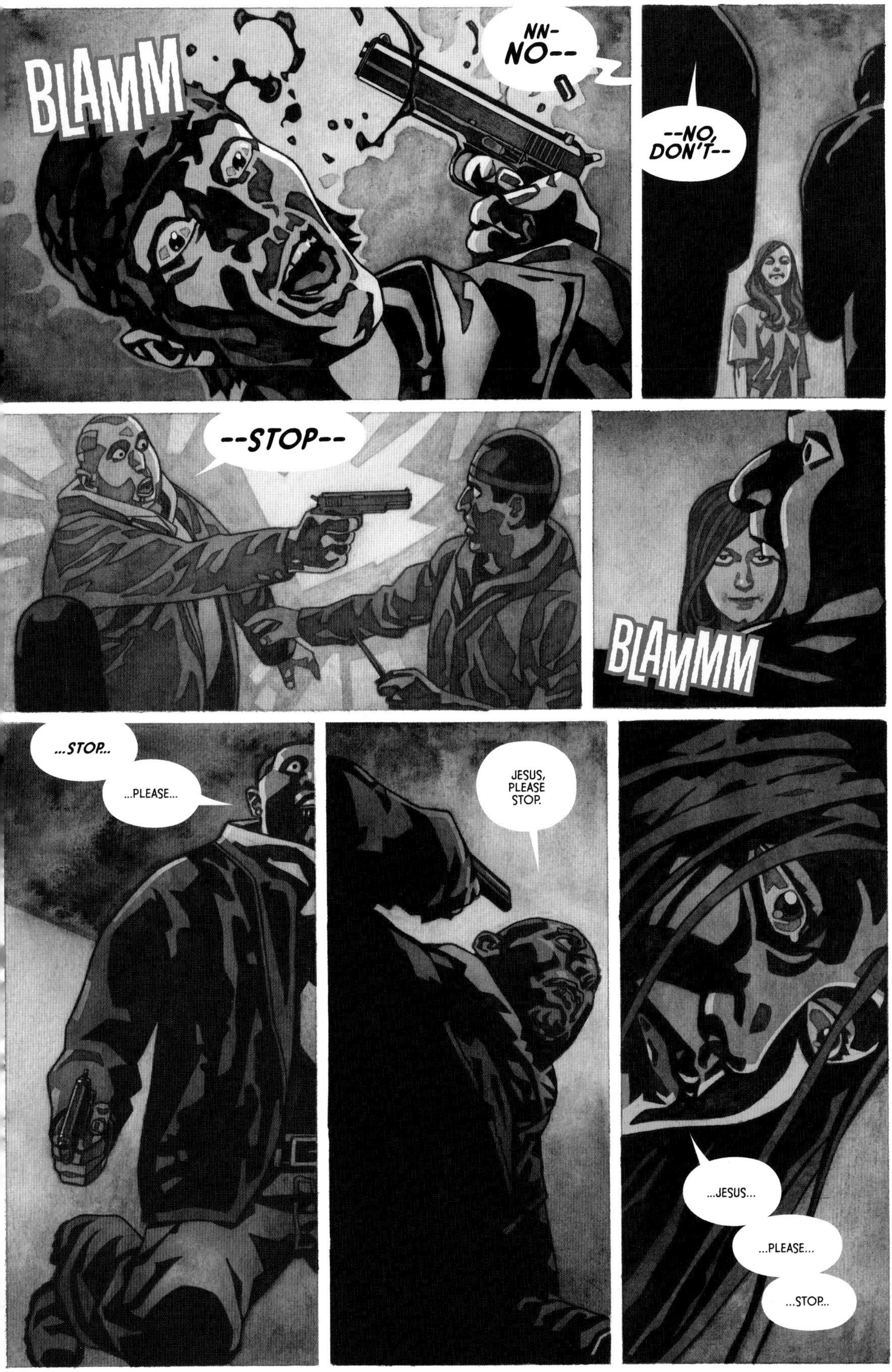
BLAMM
NN-
NO--
--NO,
DON'T--
--STOP--
BLAMMM
...STOP...
...PLEASE...
JESUS,
PLEASE
STOP.
...JESUS...
...PLEASE...
...STOP...

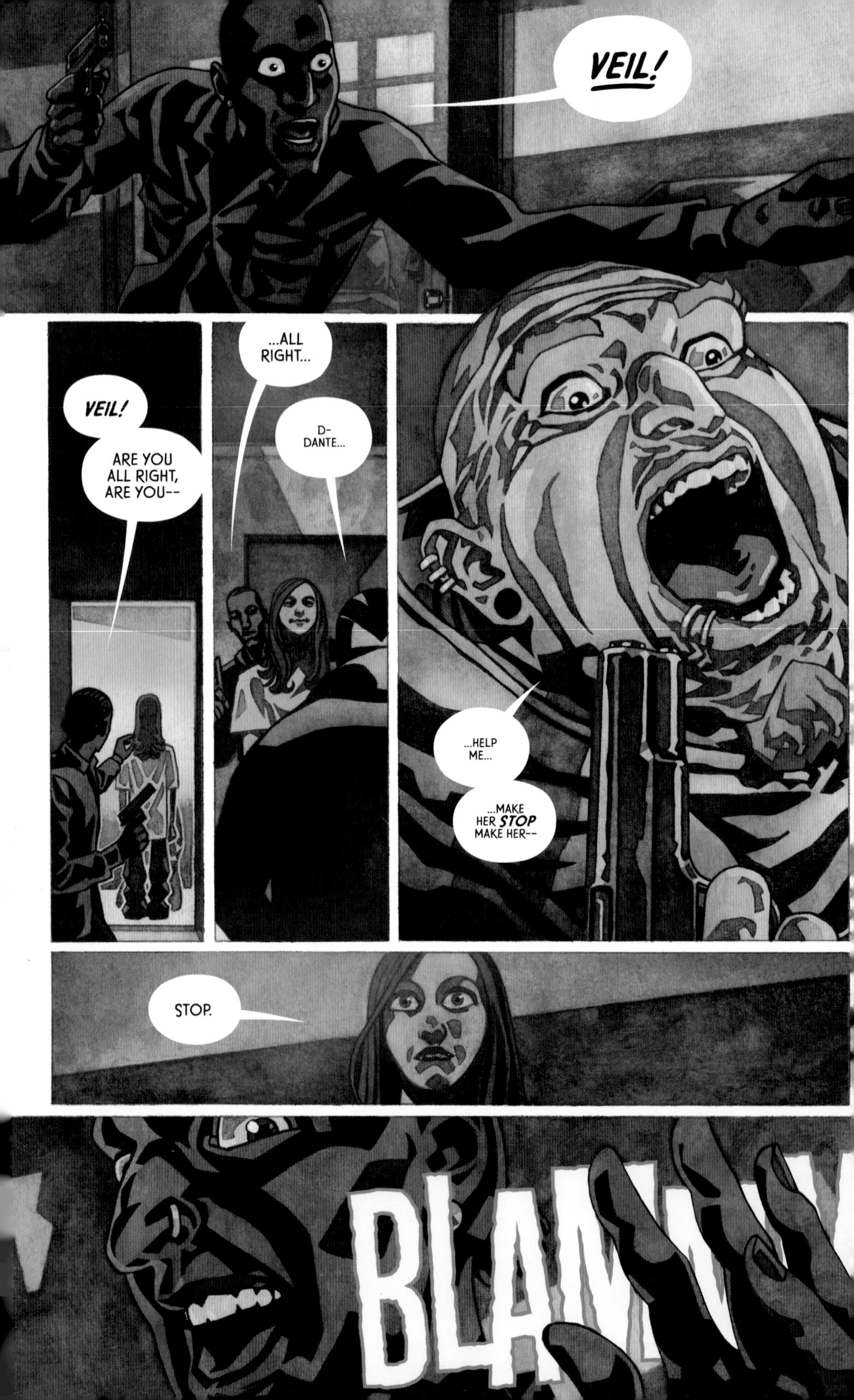

VEIL!
VEIL!
ARE YOU ALL RIGHT, ARE YOU--
...ALL RIGHT...
D- DANTE...
...HELP ME...
...MAKE HER STOP MAKE HER--
STOP.
BLAM

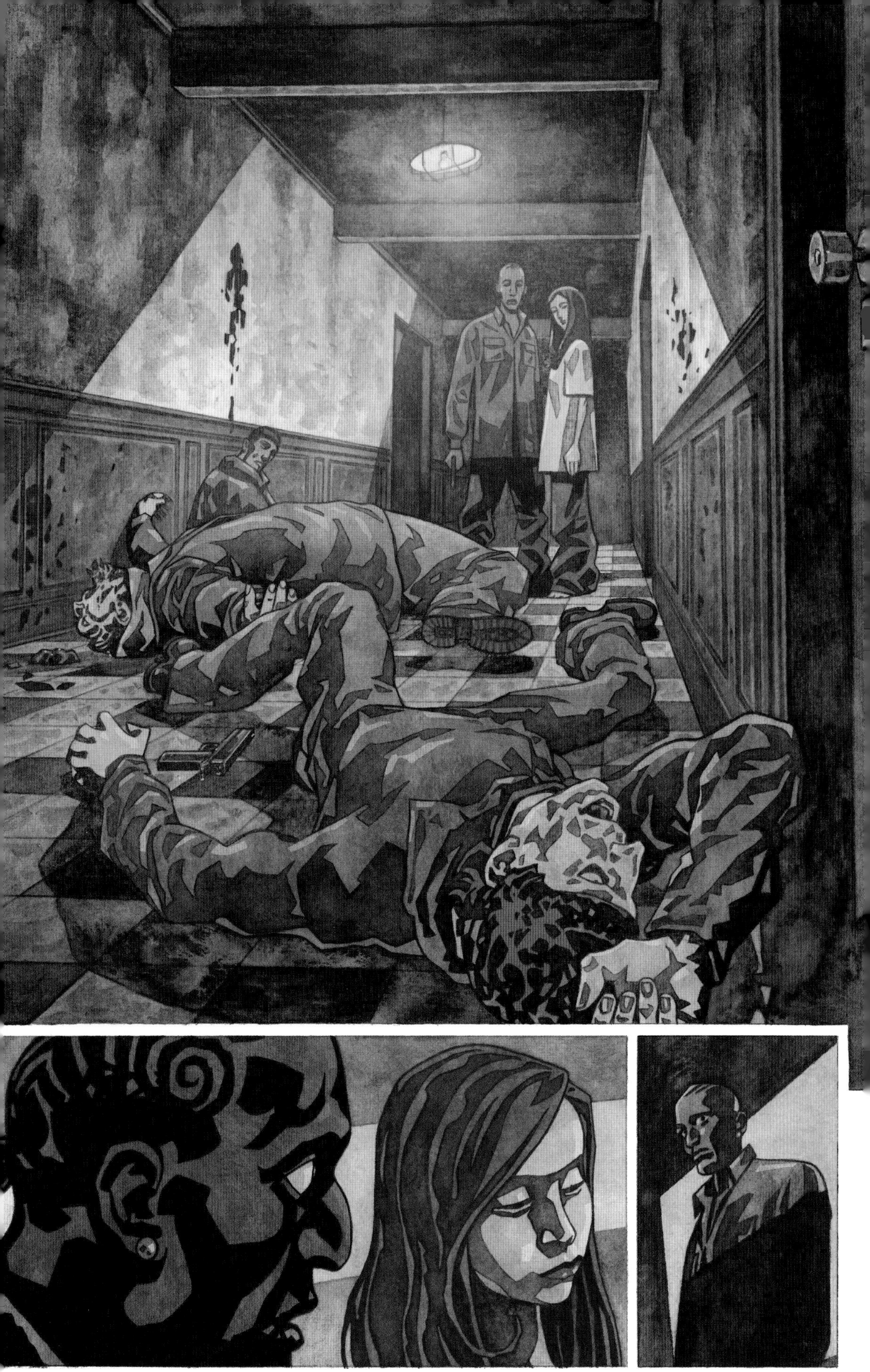

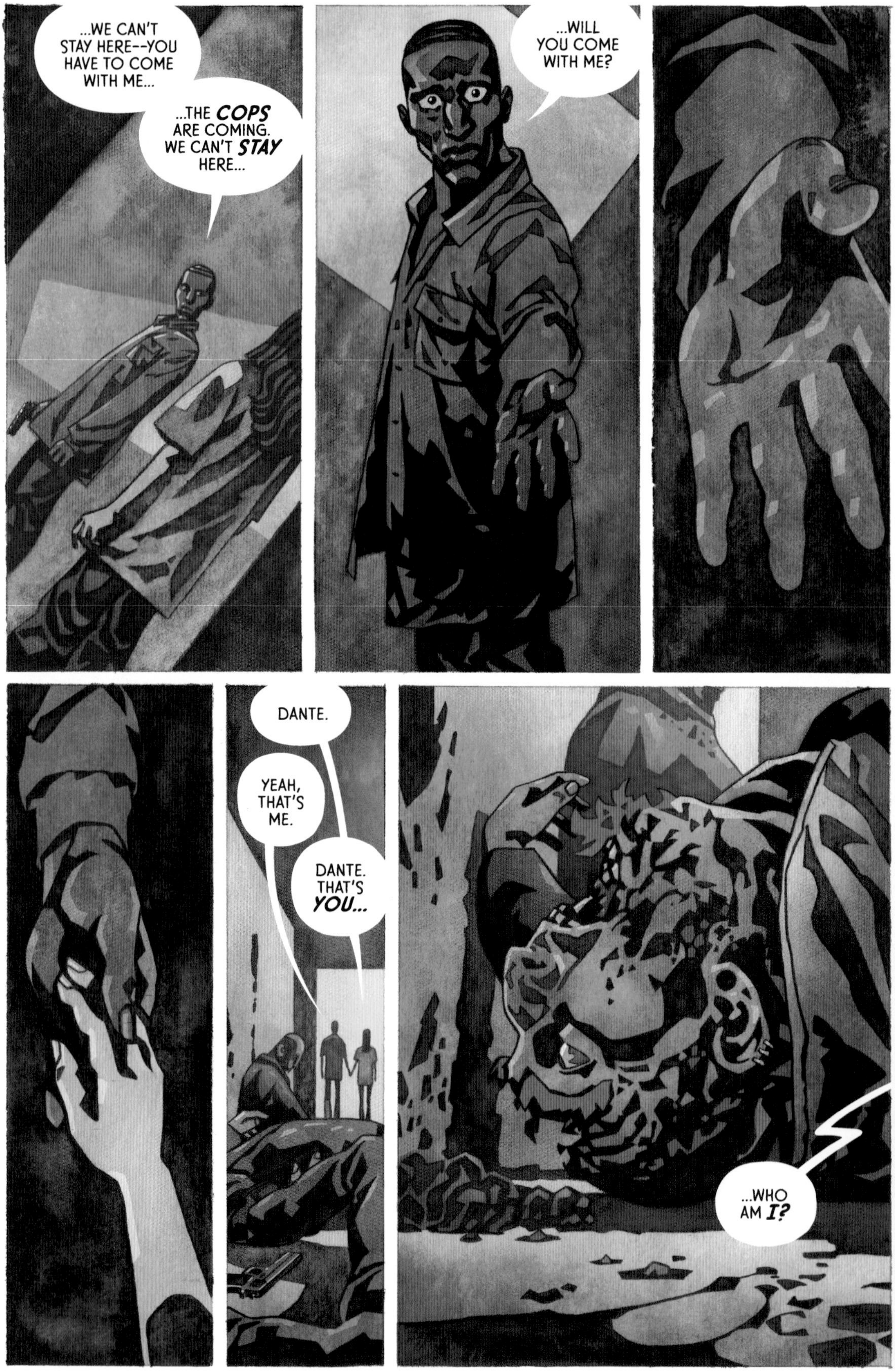
...WE CAN'T STAY HERE--YOU HAVE TO COME WITH ME...
...THE COPS ARE COMING. WE CAN'T STAY HERE...
...WILL YOU COME WITH ME?
DANTE.
YEAH, THAT'S ME.
DANTE. THAT'S YOU...
...WHO AM I?

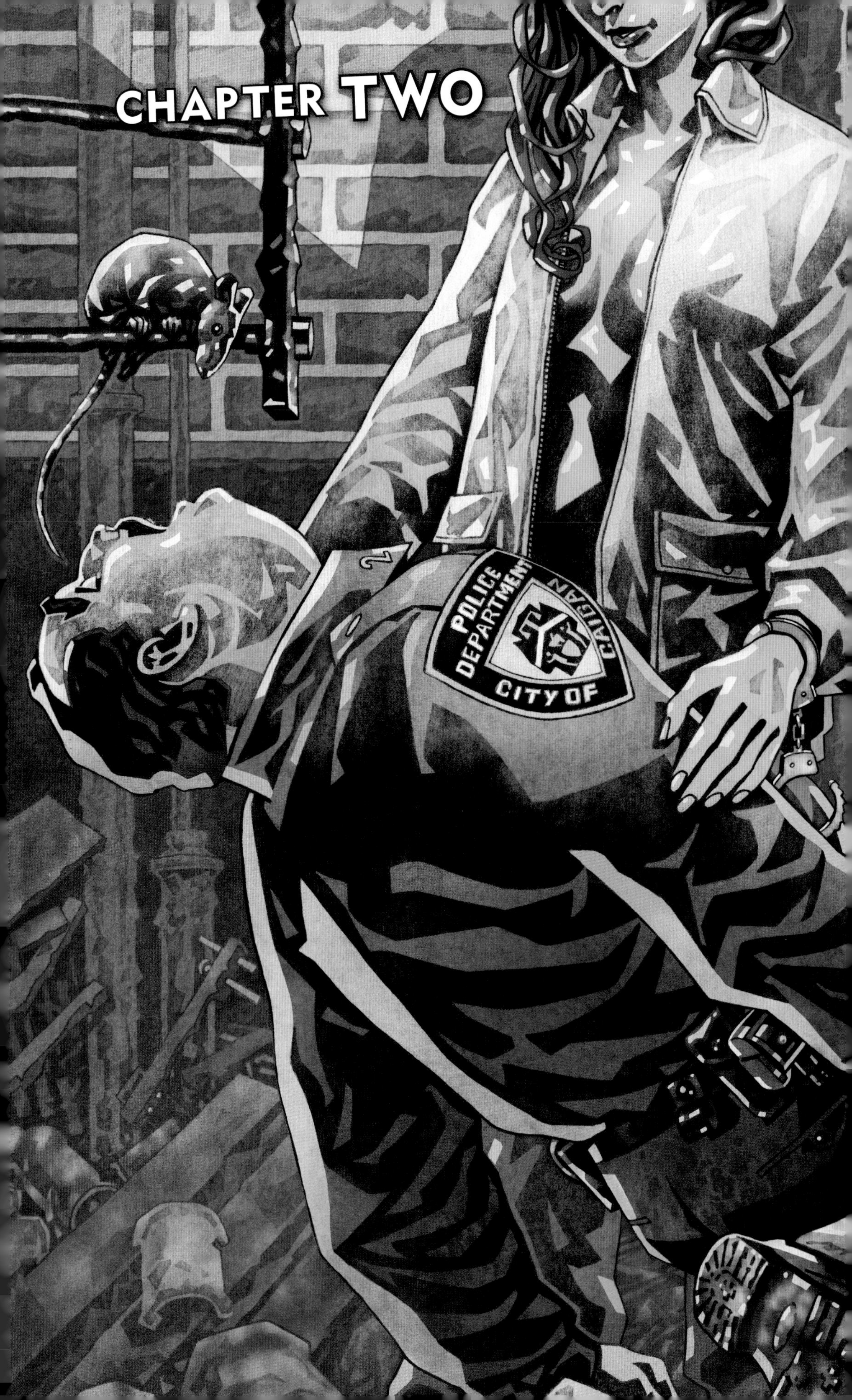
CHAPTER TWO
POLICE DEPARTMENT
CITY OF

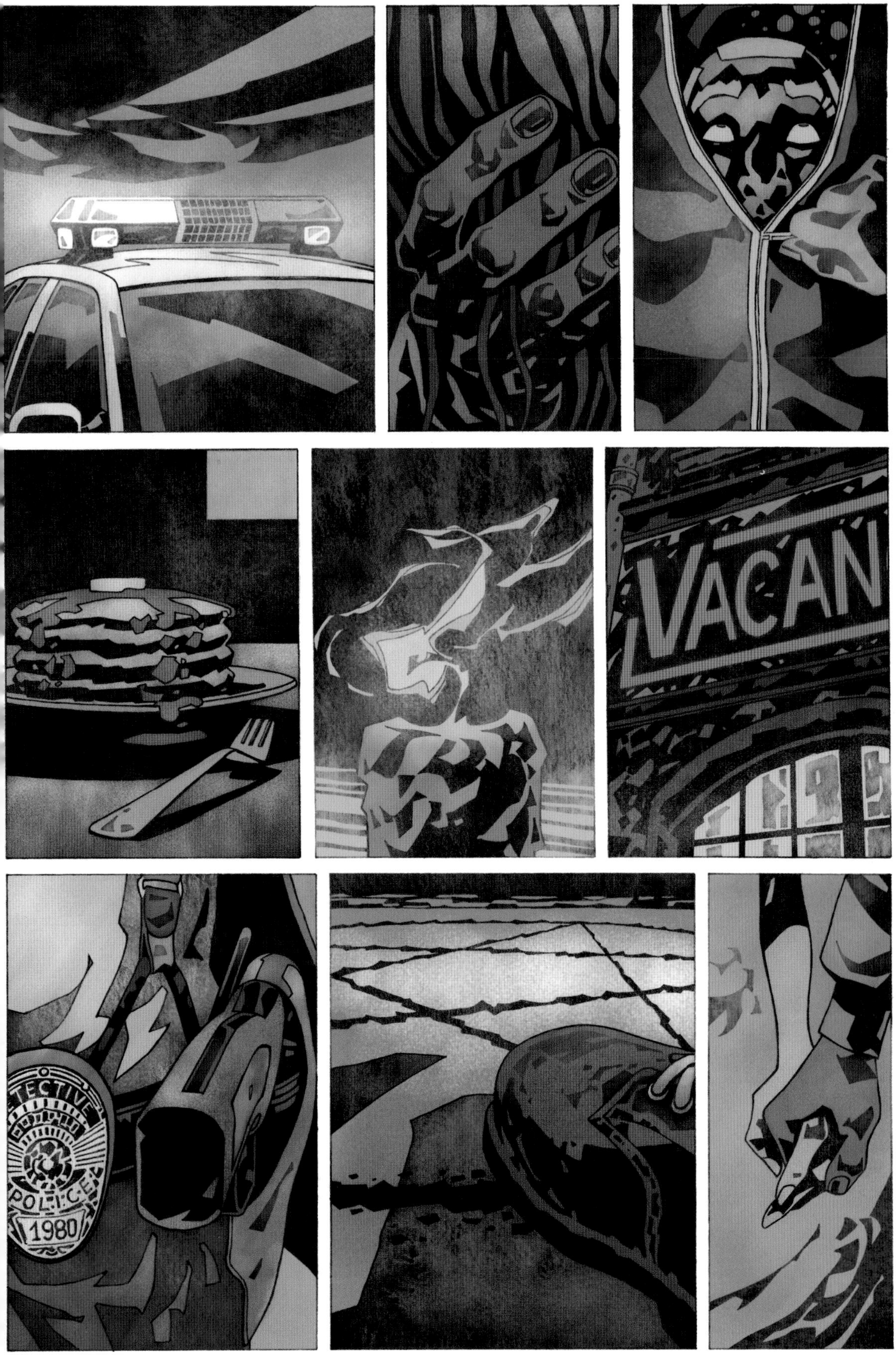
VACAN
TECTIVE
POLICE
1980

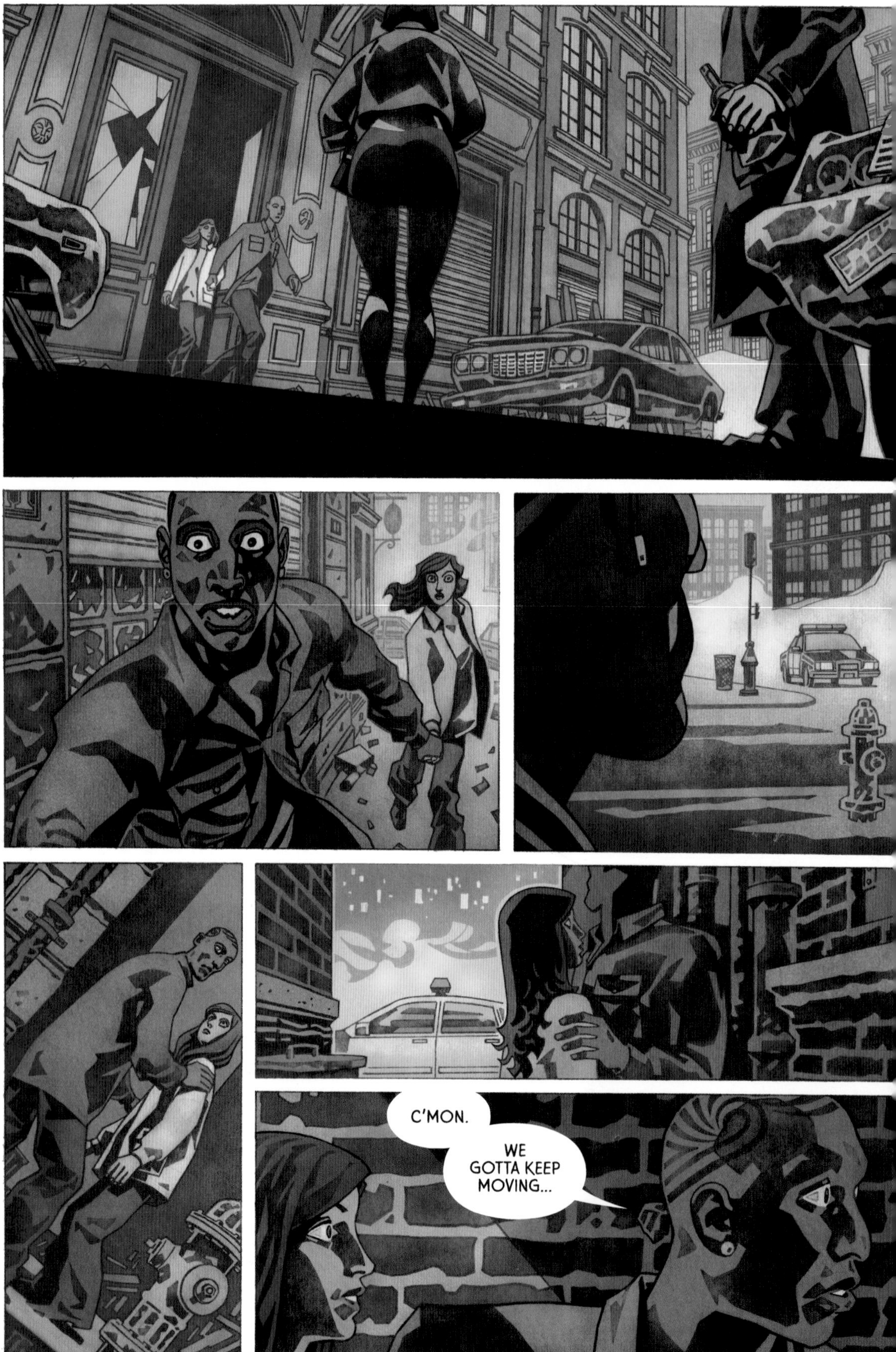
C'MON.
WE GOTTA KEEP MOVING...

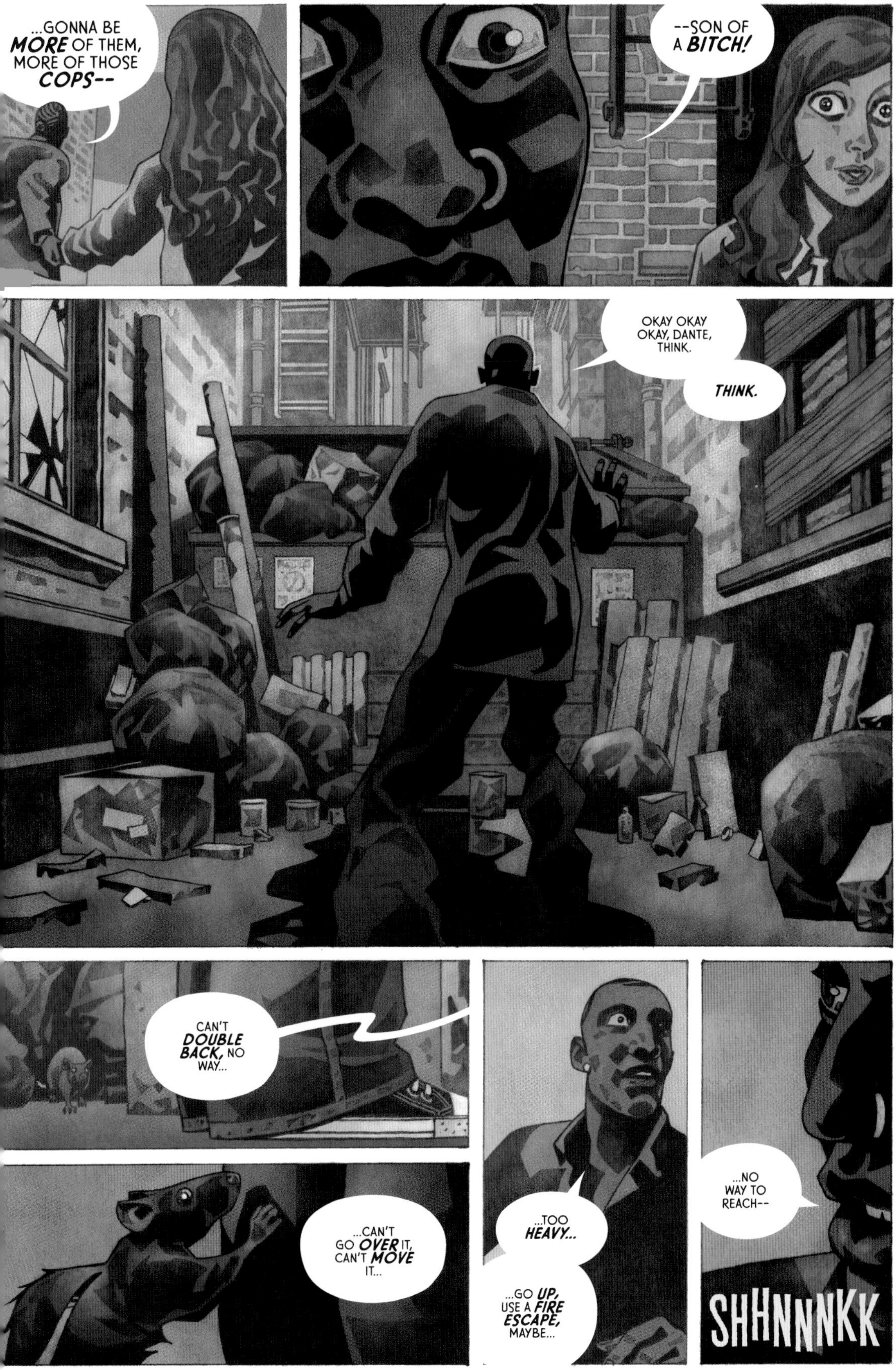
...GONNA BE MORE OF THEM, MORE OF THOSE COPS--
--SON OF A BITCH!
OKAY OKAY OKAY, DANTE, THINK.
THINK.
CAN'T DOUBLE BACK, NO WAY...
...CAN'T GO OVER IT, CAN'T MOVE IT...
...TOO HEAVY...
...GO UP, USE A FIRE ESCAPE, MAYBE...
...NO WAY TO REACH--
SHHNNNKK

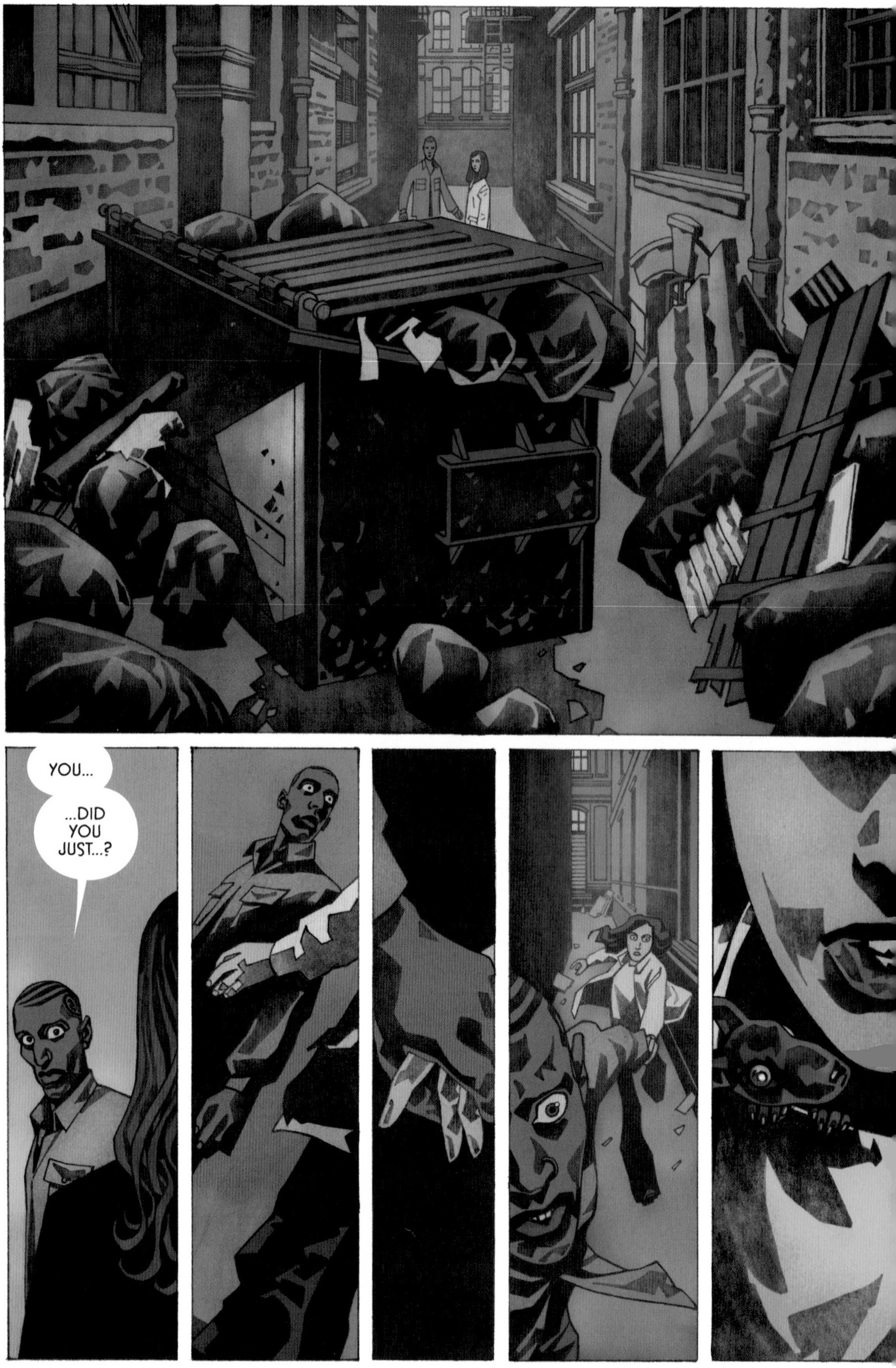
YOU...
...DID YOU JUST...?

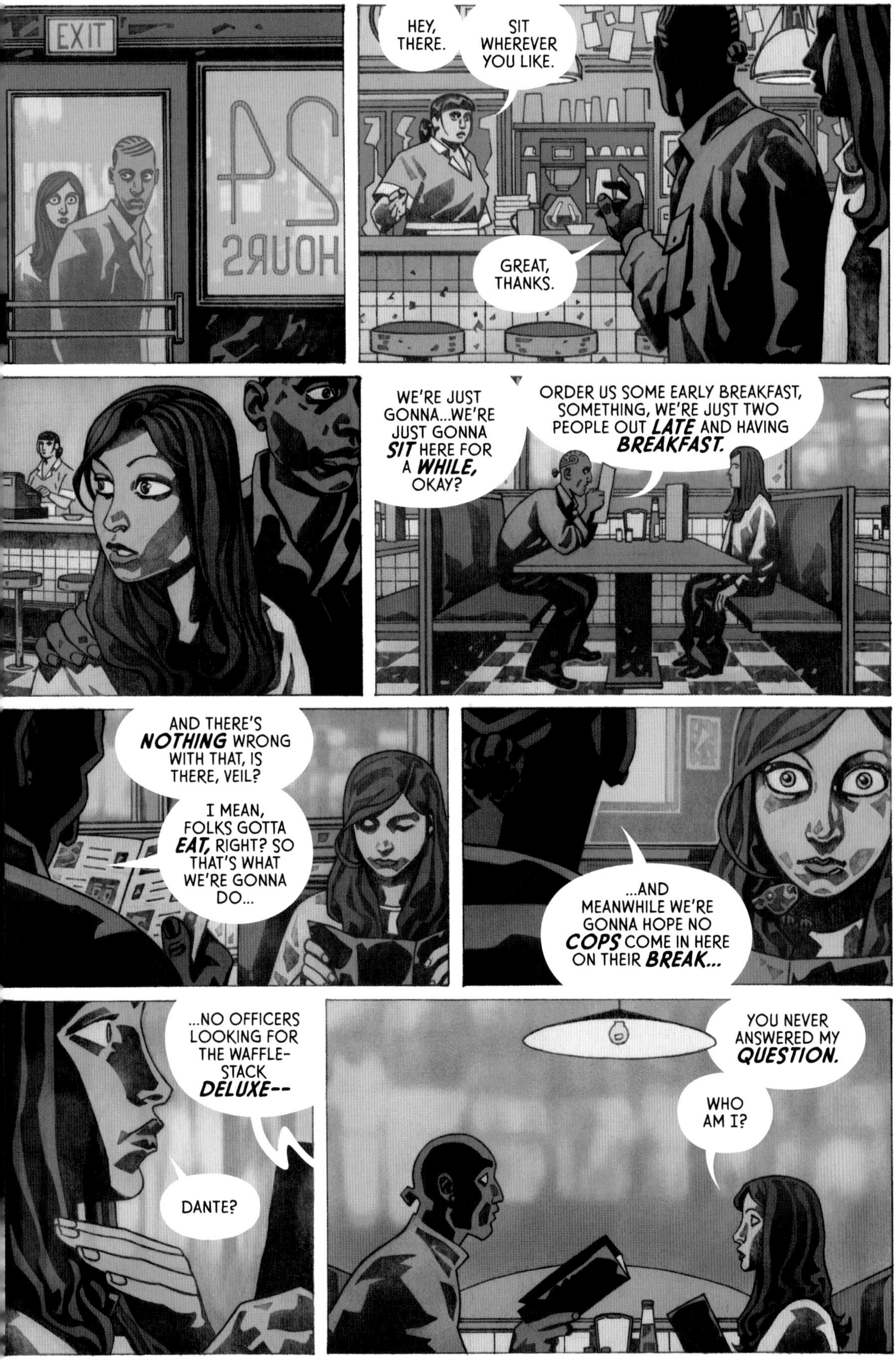
EXIT
24 HOURS
HEY, THERE.
SIT WHEREVER YOU LIKE.
GREAT, THANKS.
WE'RE JUST GONNA...WE'RE JUST GONNA SIT HERE FOR A WHILE, OKAY?
ORDER US SOME EARLY BREAKFAST, SOMETHING, WE'RE JUST TWO PEOPLE OUT LATE AND HAVING BREAKFAST.
AND THERE'S NOTHING WRONG WITH THAT, IS THERE, VEIL?
I MEAN, FOLKS GOTTA EAT, RIGHT? SO THAT'S WHAT WE'RE GONNA DO...
...AND MEANWHILE WE'RE GONNA HOPE NO COPS COME IN HERE ON THEIR BREAK...
...NO OFFICERS LOOKING FOR THE WAFFLE-STACK DELUXE--
DANTE?
YOU NEVER ANSWERED MY QUESTION.
WHO AM I?

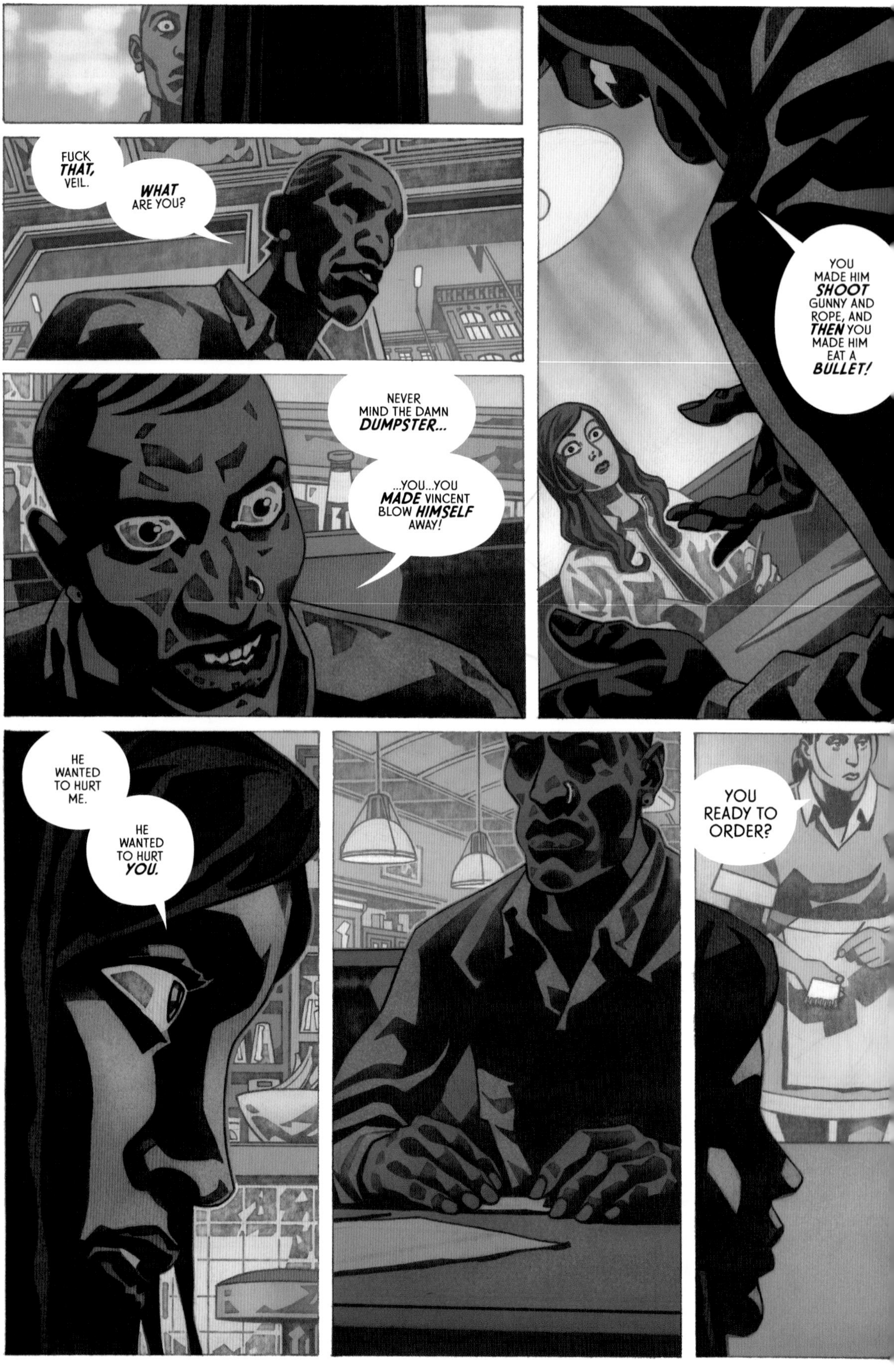
FUCK THAT, VEIL.
WHAT ARE YOU?
NEVER MIND THE DAMN DUMPSTER...
...YOU...YOU MADE VINCENT BLOW HIMSELF AWAY!
YOU MADE HIM SHOOT GUNNY AND ROPE, AND THEN YOU MADE HIM EAT A BULLET!
HE WANTED TO HURT ME.
HE WANTED TO HURT YOU.
YOU READY TO ORDER?

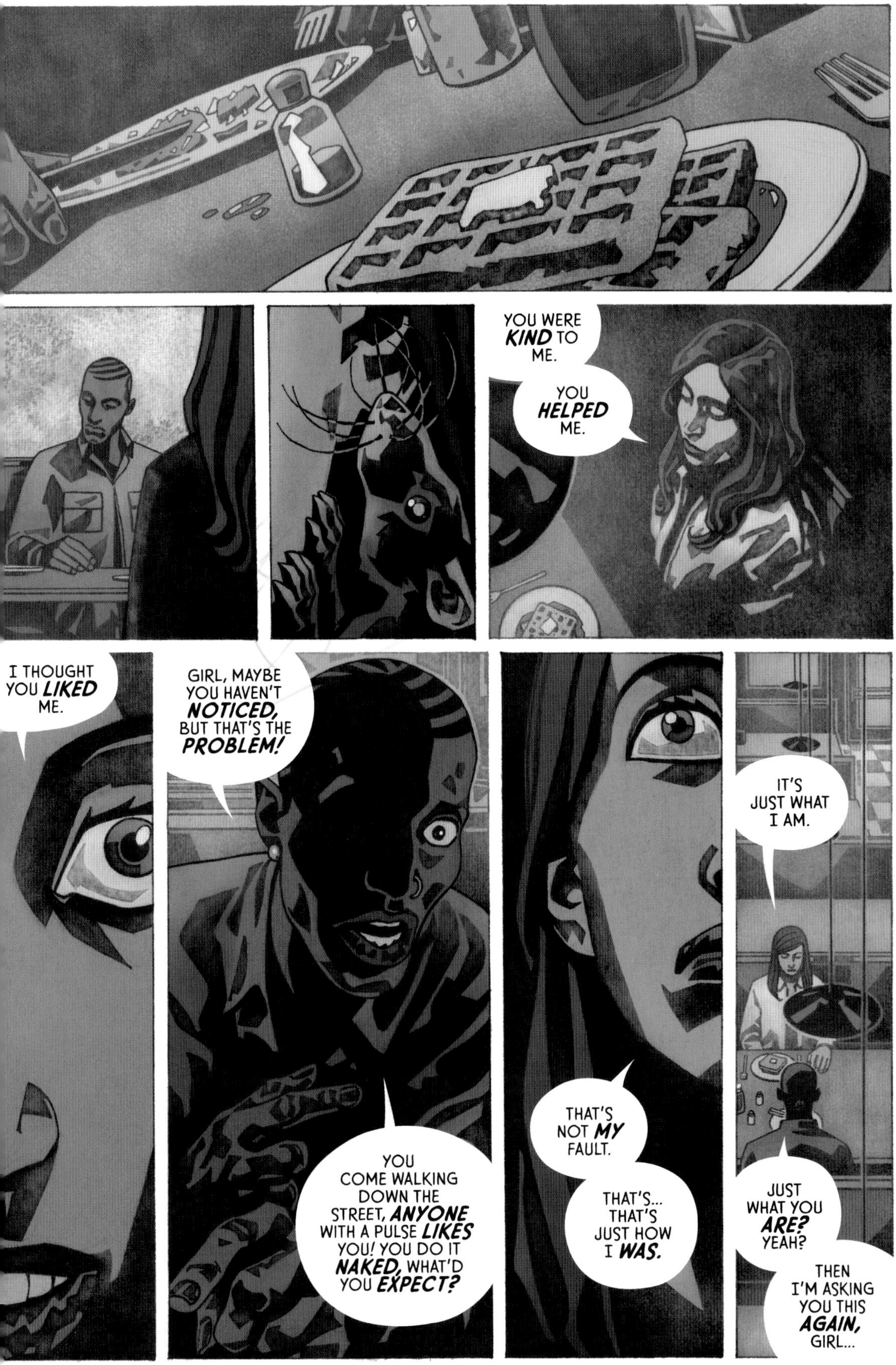
YOU WERE KIND TO ME.
YOU HELPED ME.
I THOUGHT YOU LIKED ME.
GIRL, MAYBE YOU HAVEN'T NOTICED, BUT THAT'S THE PROBLEM!
YOU COME WALKING DOWN THE STREET, ANYONE WITH A PULSE LIKES YOU! YOU DO IT NAKED, WHAT'D YOU EXPECT?
THAT'S NOT MY FAULT.
THAT'S... THAT'S JUST HOW I WAS.
IT'S JUST WHAT I AM.
JUST WHAT YOU ARE? YEAH?
THEN I'M ASKING YOU THIS AGAIN, GIRL...

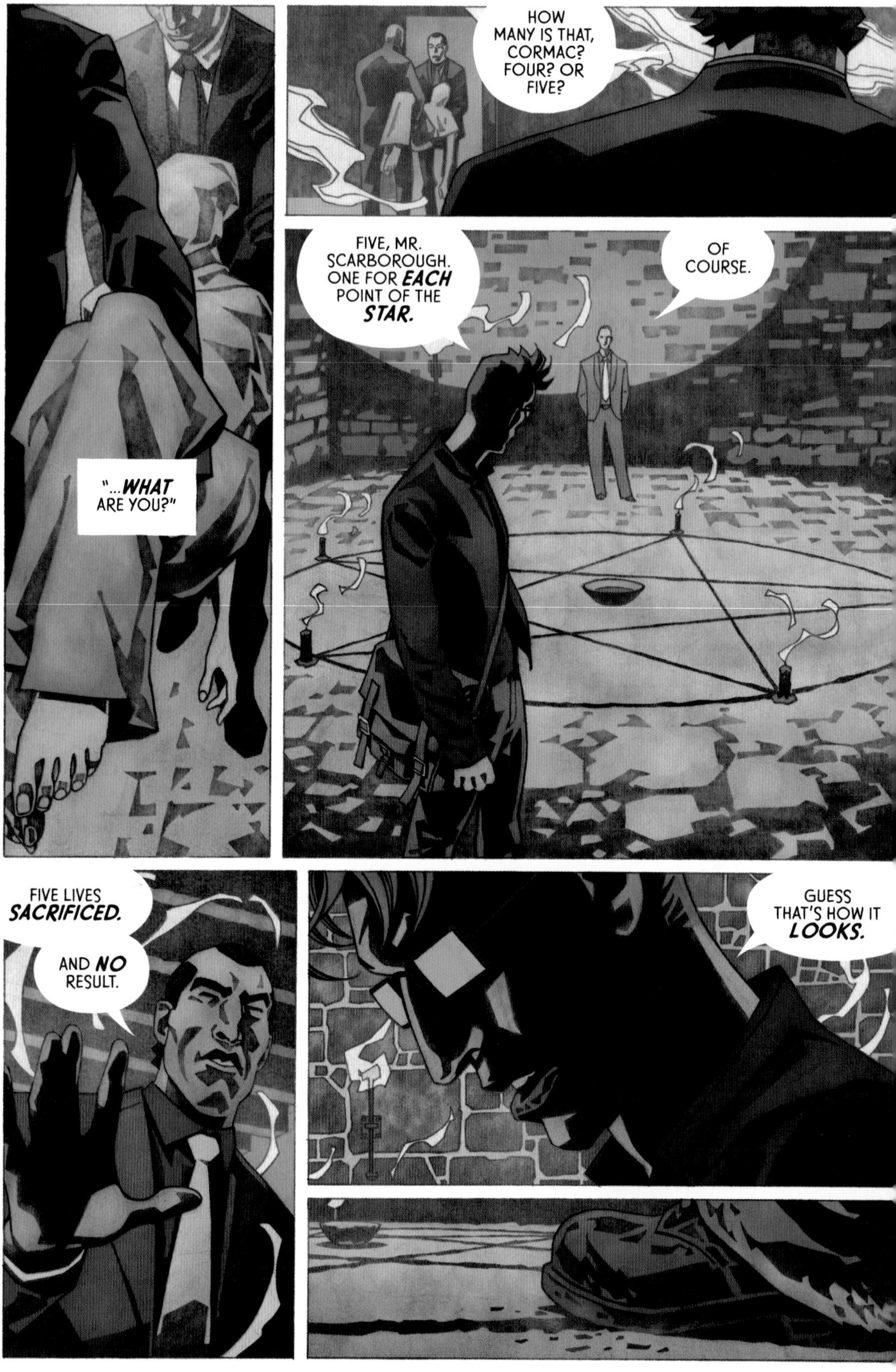
"...WHAT ARE YOU?"
HOW MANY IS THAT, CORMAC? FOUR? OR FIVE?
FIVE, MR. SCARBOROUGH. ONE FOR EACH POINT OF THE STAR.
OF COURSE.
FIVE LIVES SACRIFICED.
AND NO RESULT.
GUESS THAT'S HOW IT LOOKS.

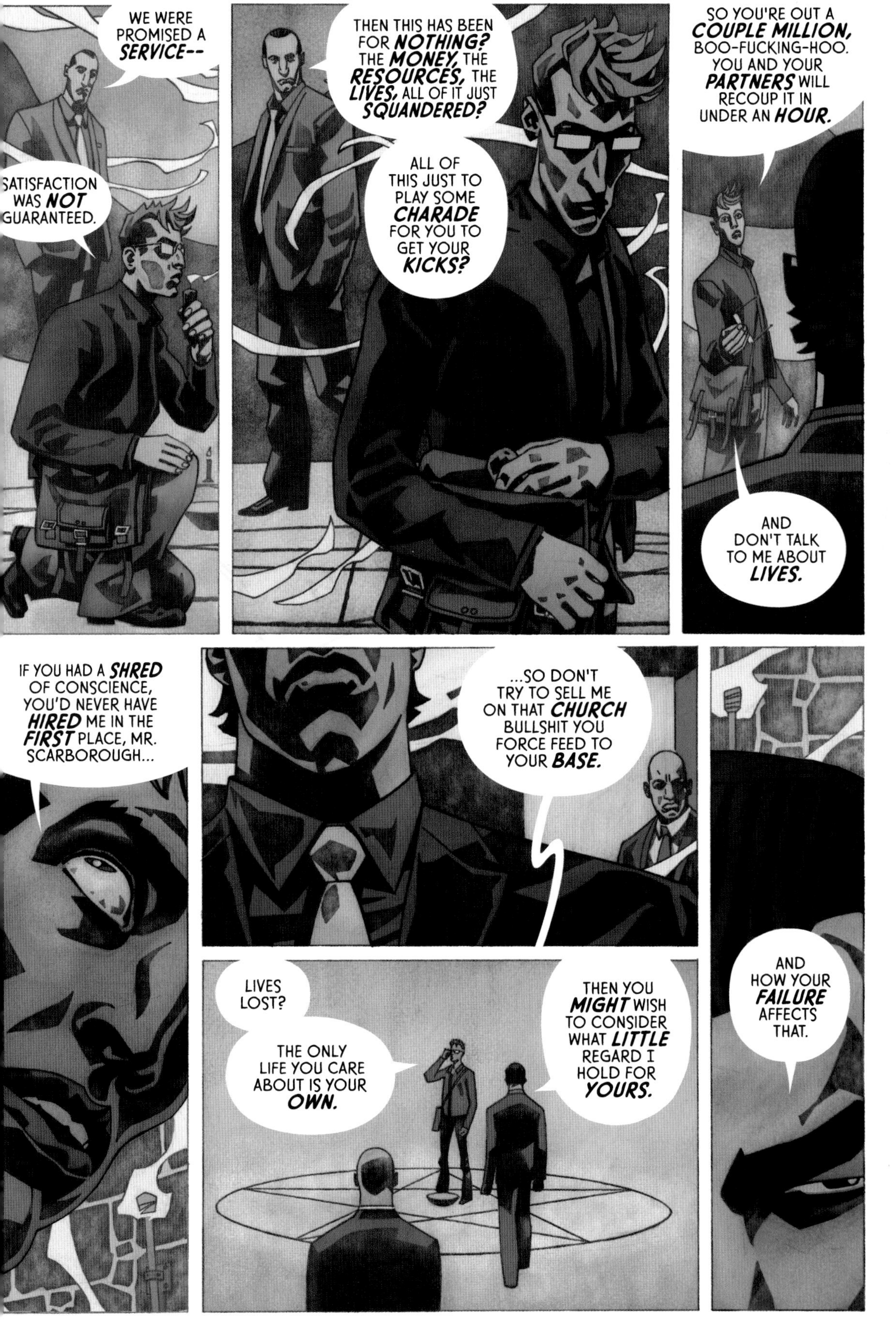
WE WERE PROMISED A SERVICE--
SATISFACTION WAS NOT GUARANTEED.
THEN THIS HAS BEEN FOR NOTHING? THE MONEY, THE RESOURCES, THE LIVES, ALL OF IT JUST SQUANDERED?
ALL OF THIS JUST TO PLAY SOME CHARADE FOR YOU TO GET YOUR KICKS?
SO YOU'RE OUT A COUPLE MILLION, BOO-FUCKING-HOO. YOU AND YOUR PARTNERS WILL RECOUP IT IN UNDER AN HOUR.
AND DON'T TALK TO ME ABOUT LIVES.
IF YOU HAD A SHRED OF CONSCIENCE, YOU'D NEVER HAVE HIRED ME IN THE FIRST PLACE, MR. SCARBOROUGH...
...SO DON'T TRY TO SELL ME ON THAT CHURCH BULLSHIT YOU FORCE FEED TO YOUR BASE.
LIVES LOST?
THE ONLY LIFE YOU CARE ABOUT IS YOUR OWN.
THEN YOU MIGHT WISH TO CONSIDER WHAT LITTLE REGARD I HOLD FOR YOURS.
AND HOW YOUR FAILURE AFFECTS THAT.

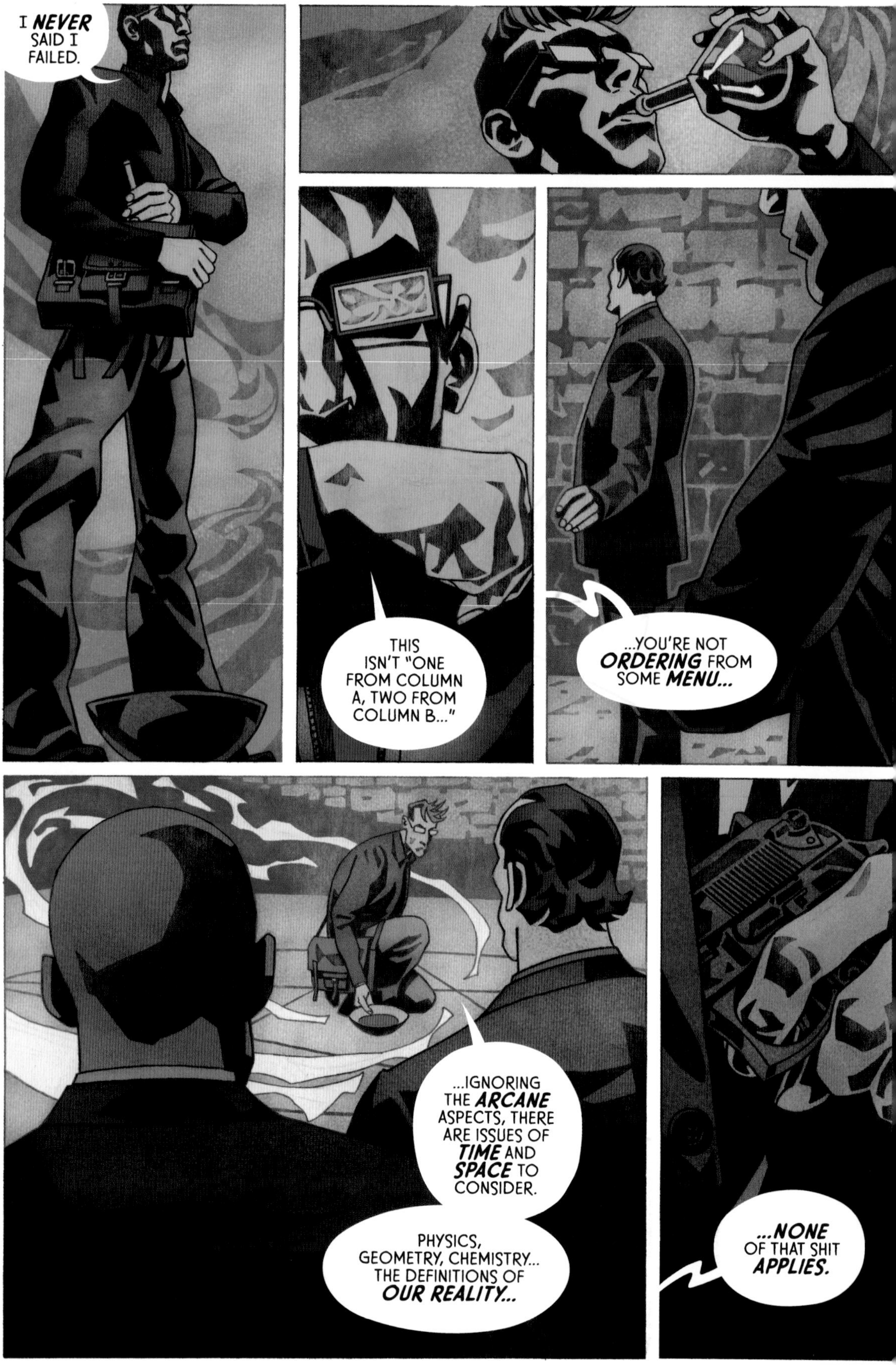
I NEVER SAID I FAILED.
THIS ISN'T "ONE FROM COLUMN A, TWO FROM COLUMN B..."
...YOU'RE NOT ORDERING FROM SOME MENU...
...IGNORING THE ARCANE ASPECTS, THERE ARE ISSUES OF TIME AND SPACE TO CONSIDER.
PHYSICS, GEOMETRY, CHEMISTRY... THE DEFINITIONS OF OUR REALITY...
...NONE OF THAT SHIT APPLIES.

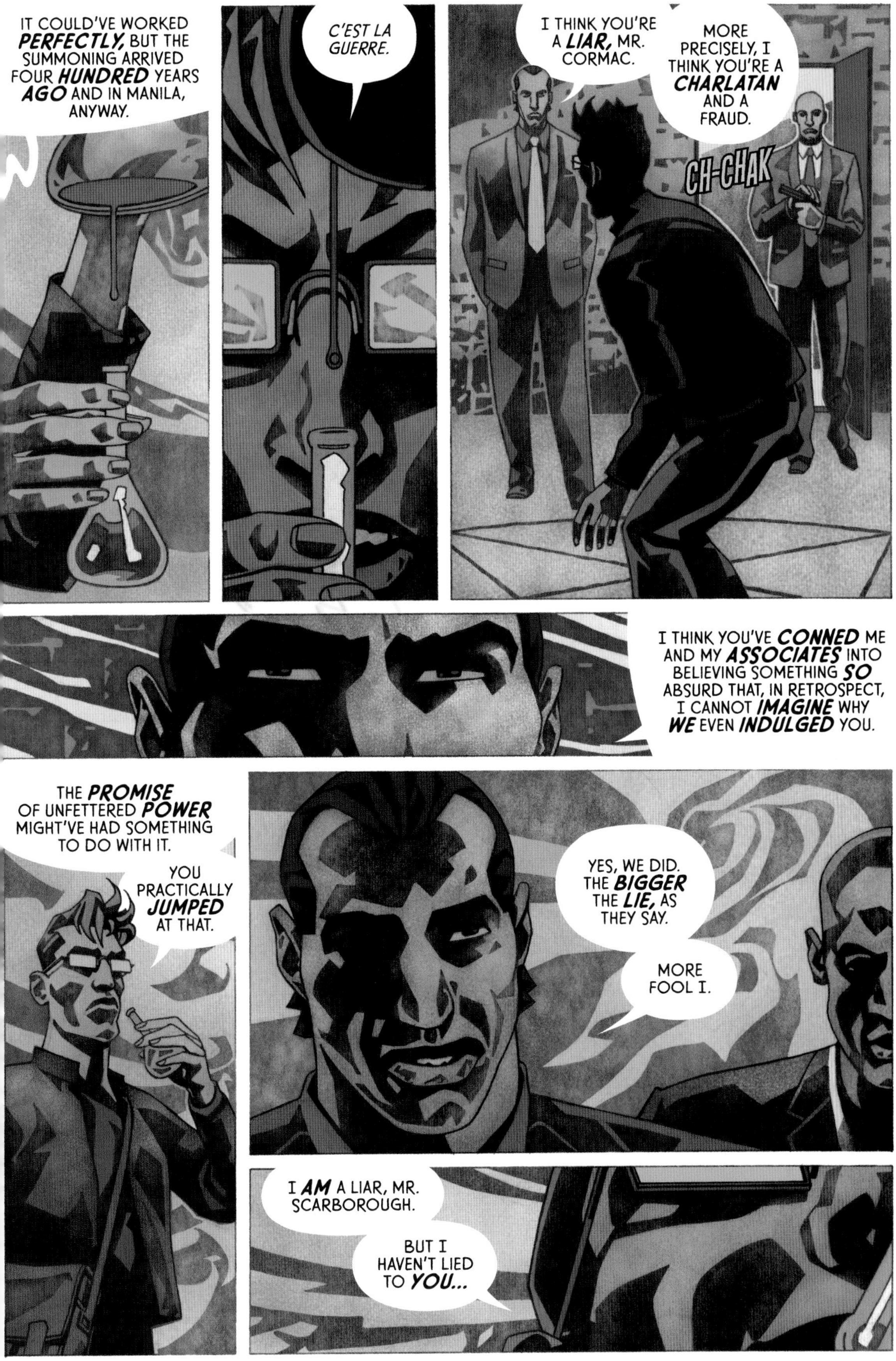
IT COULD'VE WORKED PERFECTLY, BUT THE SUMMONING ARRIVED FOUR HUNDRED YEARS AGO AND IN MANILA, ANYWAY.
C'EST LA GUERRE.
I THINK YOU'RE A LIAR, MR. CORMAC.
MORE PRECISELY, I THINK YOU'RE A CHARLATAN AND A FRAUD.
CH-CHAK
I THINK YOU'VE CONNED ME AND MY ASSOCIATES INTO BELIEVING SOMETHING SO ABSURD THAT, IN RETROSPECT, I CANNOT IMAGINE WHY WE EVEN INDULGED YOU.
THE PROMISE OF UNFETTERED POWER MIGHT'VE HAD SOMETHING TO DO WITH IT.
YOU PRACTICALLY JUMPED AT THAT.
YES, WE DID. THE BIGGER THE LIE, AS THEY SAY.
MORE FOOL I.
I AM A LIAR, MR. SCARBOROUGH.
BUT I HAVEN'T LIED TO YOU...

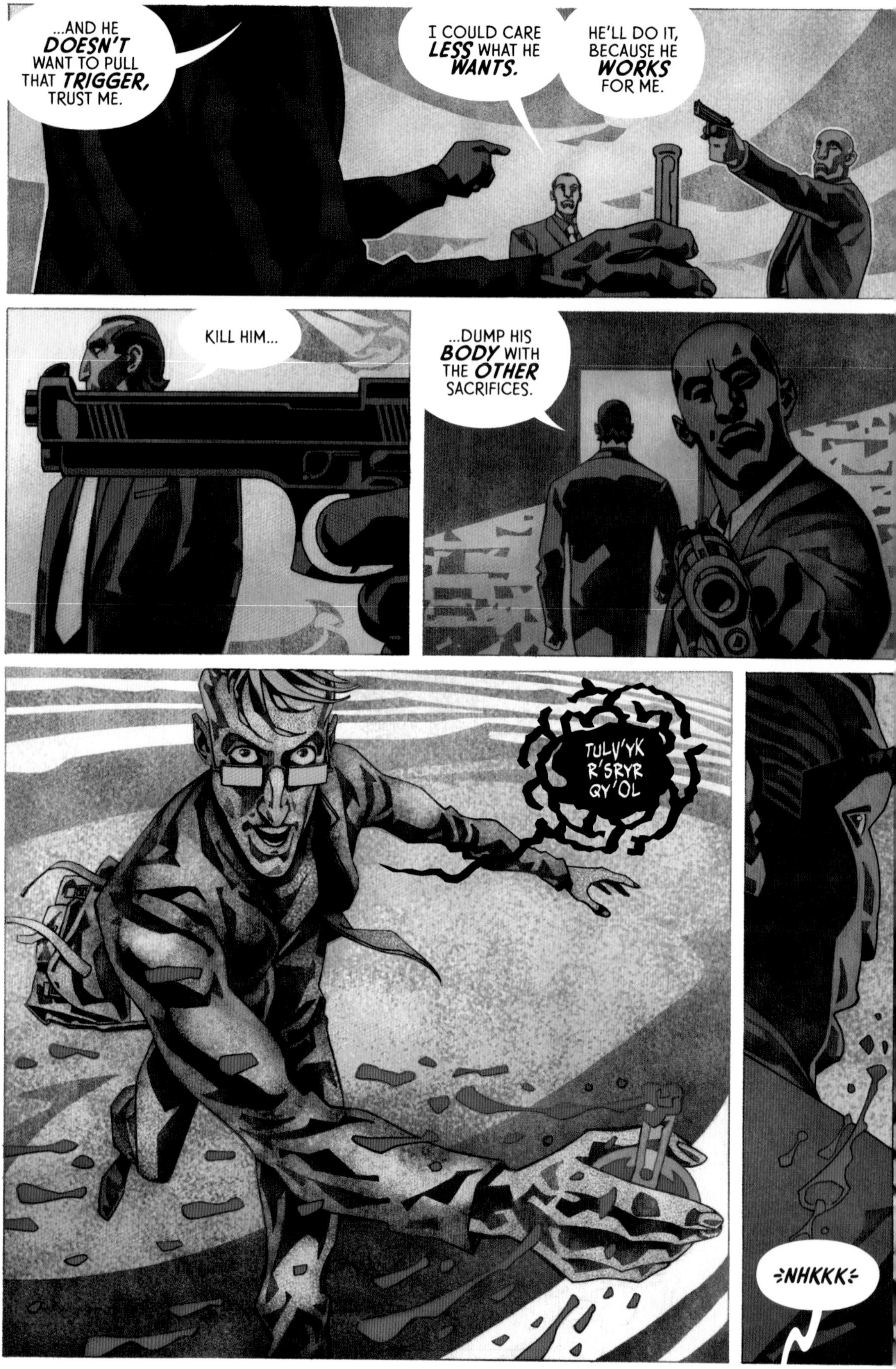

...AND HE DOESN'T WANT TO PULL THAT TRIGGER, TRUST ME.
I COULD CARE LESS WHAT HE WANTS.
HE'LL DO IT, BECAUSE HE WORKS FOR ME.
KILL HIM...
...DUMP HIS BODY WITH THE OTHER SACRIFICES.
TULV'YK R'SRYR QY'OL
NHKKK

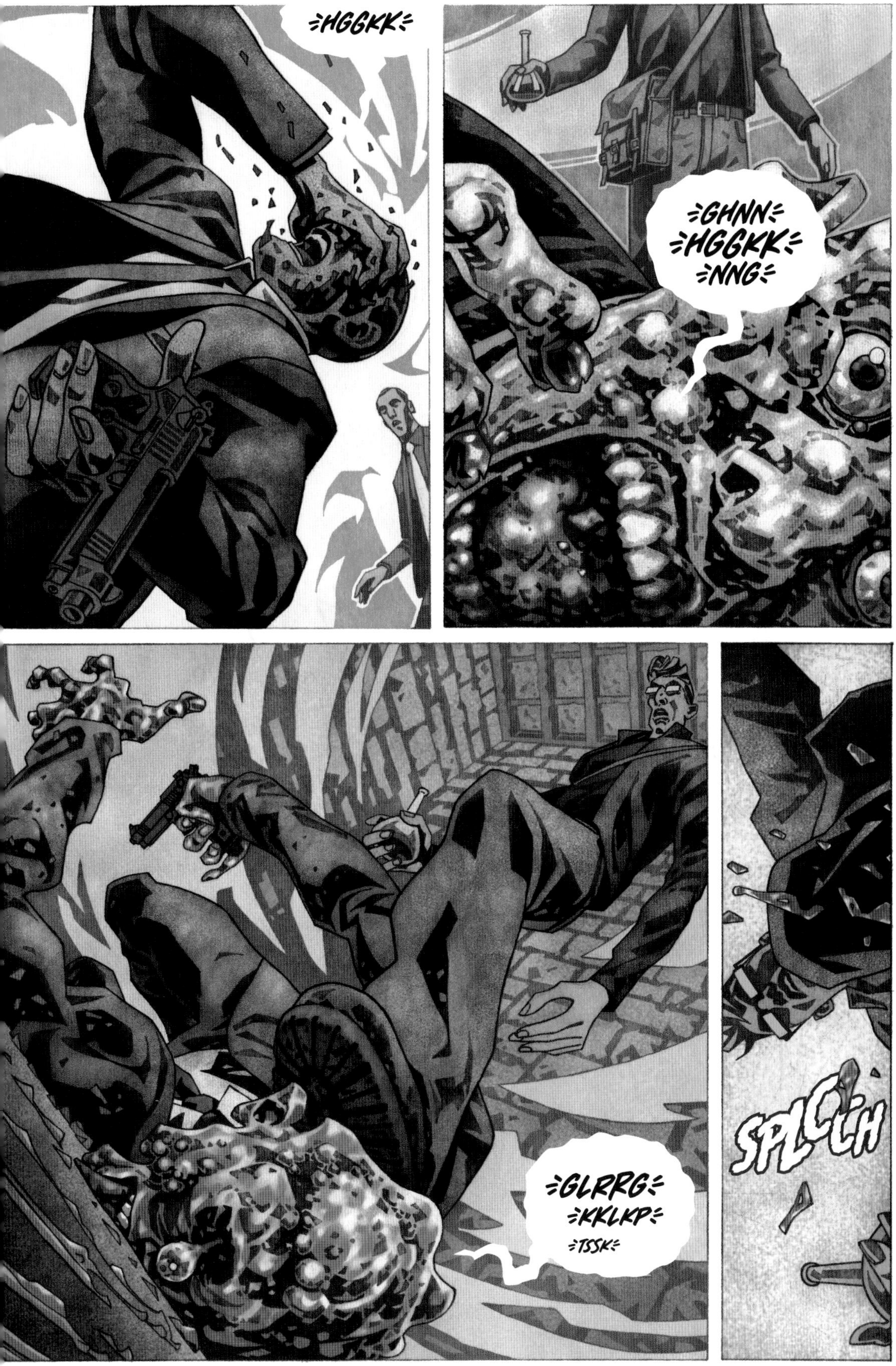
HGGKK
GHNN
HGGKK
NNG
GLRRG
KKLKP
TSSK
SPLCCH

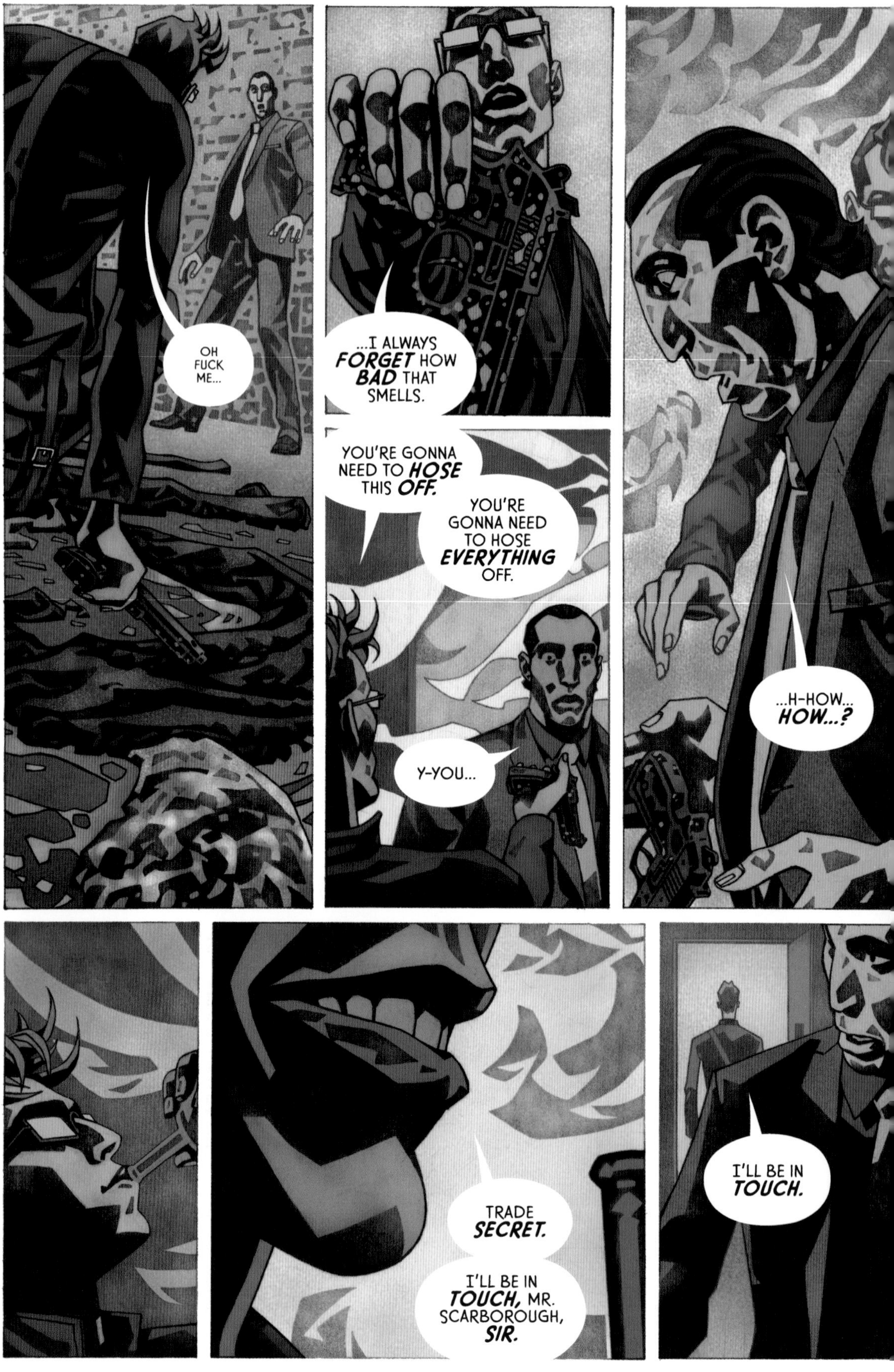
OH FUCK ME...
...I ALWAYS FORGET HOW BAD THAT SMELLS.
YOU'RE GONNA NEED TO HOSE THIS OFF.
YOU'RE GONNA NEED TO HOSE EVERYTHING OFF.
Y-YOU...
...H-HOW... HOW...?
TRADE SECRET.
I'LL BE IN TOUCH, MR. SCARBOROUGH, SIR.
I'LL BE IN TOUCH.

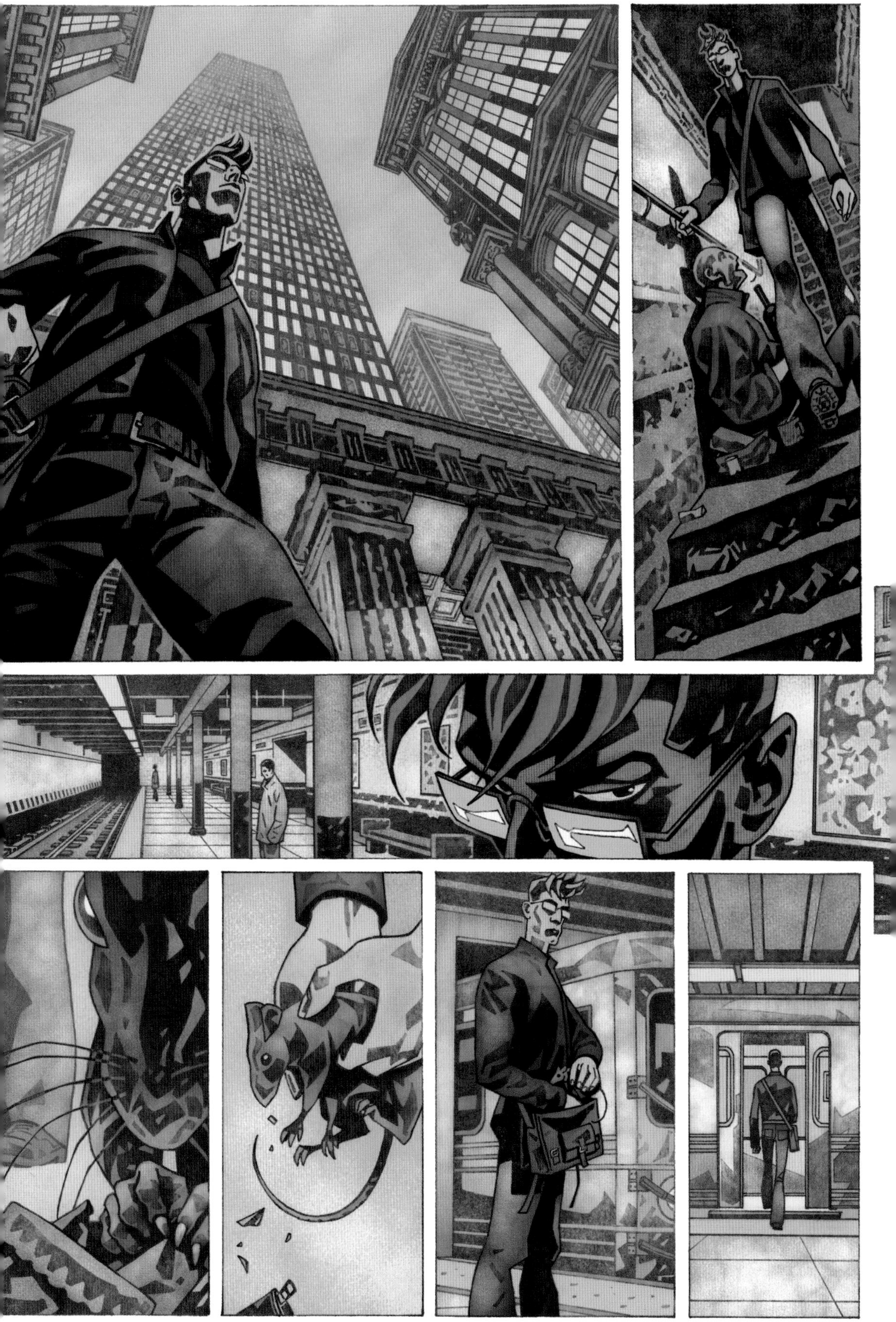

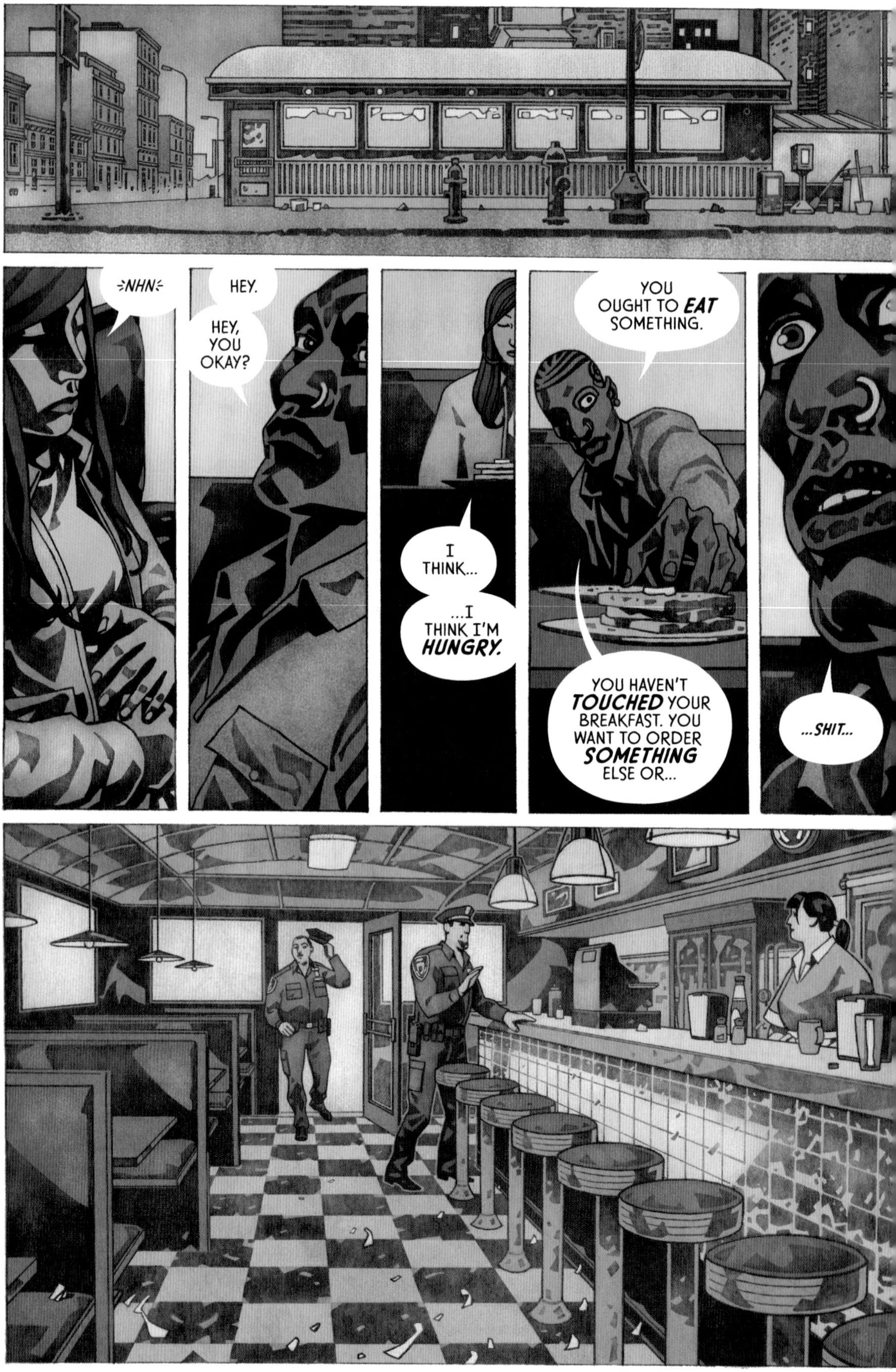

NHN
HEY.
HEY, YOU OKAY?
I THINK...
...I THINK I'M HUNGRY.
YOU OUGHT TO EAT SOMETHING.
YOU HAVEN'T TOUCHED YOUR BREAKFAST. YOU WANT TO ORDER SOMETHING ELSE OR...
...SHIT...

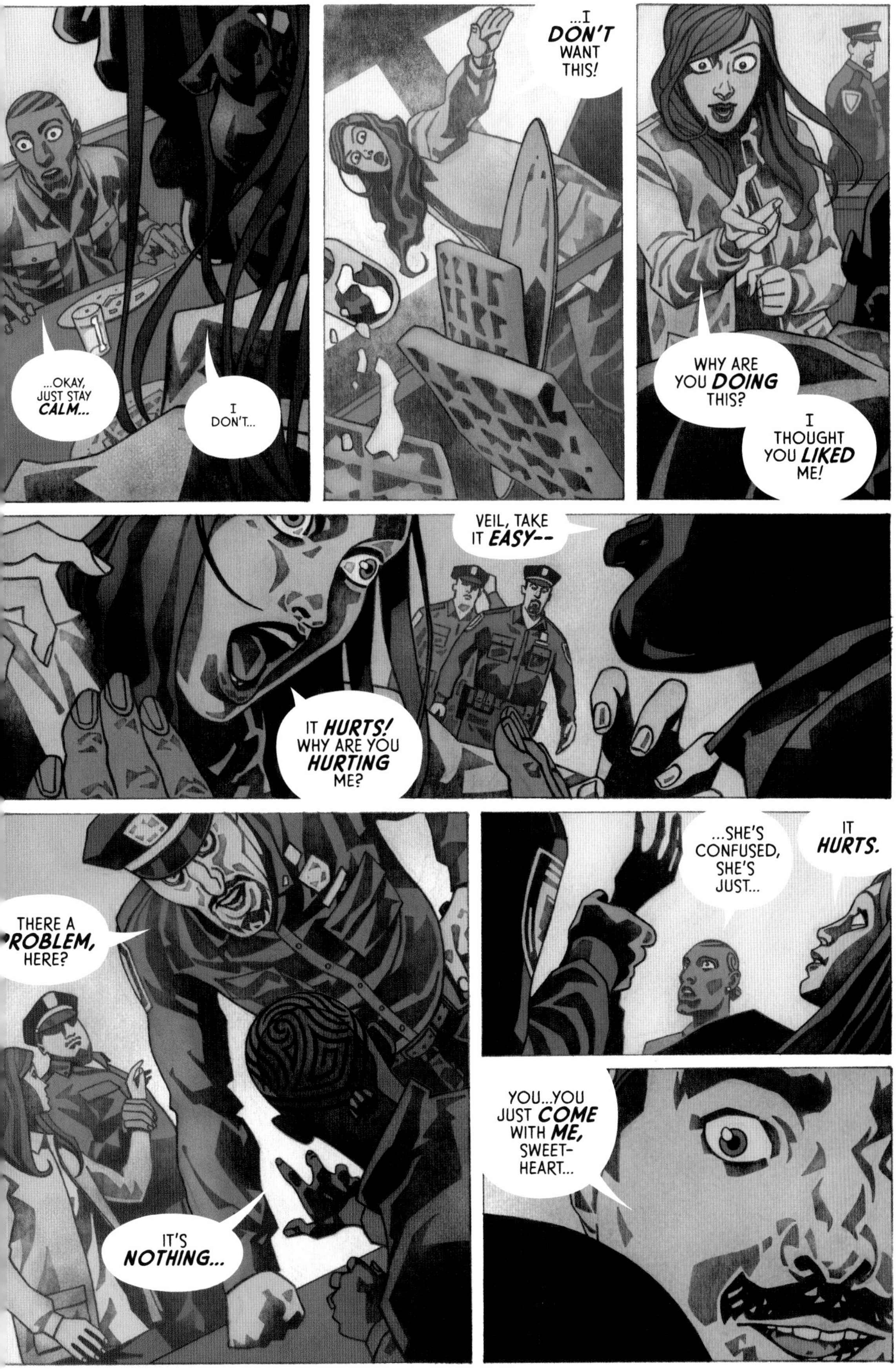
...OKAY, JUST STAY CALM...
I DON'T...
...I DON'T WANT THIS!
WHY ARE YOU DOING THIS?
I THOUGHT YOU LIKED ME!
VEIL, TAKE IT EASY--
IT HURTS! WHY ARE YOU HURTING ME?
THERE A PROBLEM, HERE?
IT'S NOTHING...
...SHE'S CONFUSED, SHE'S JUST...
IT HURTS.
YOU...YOU JUST COME WITH ME, SWEET-HEART...

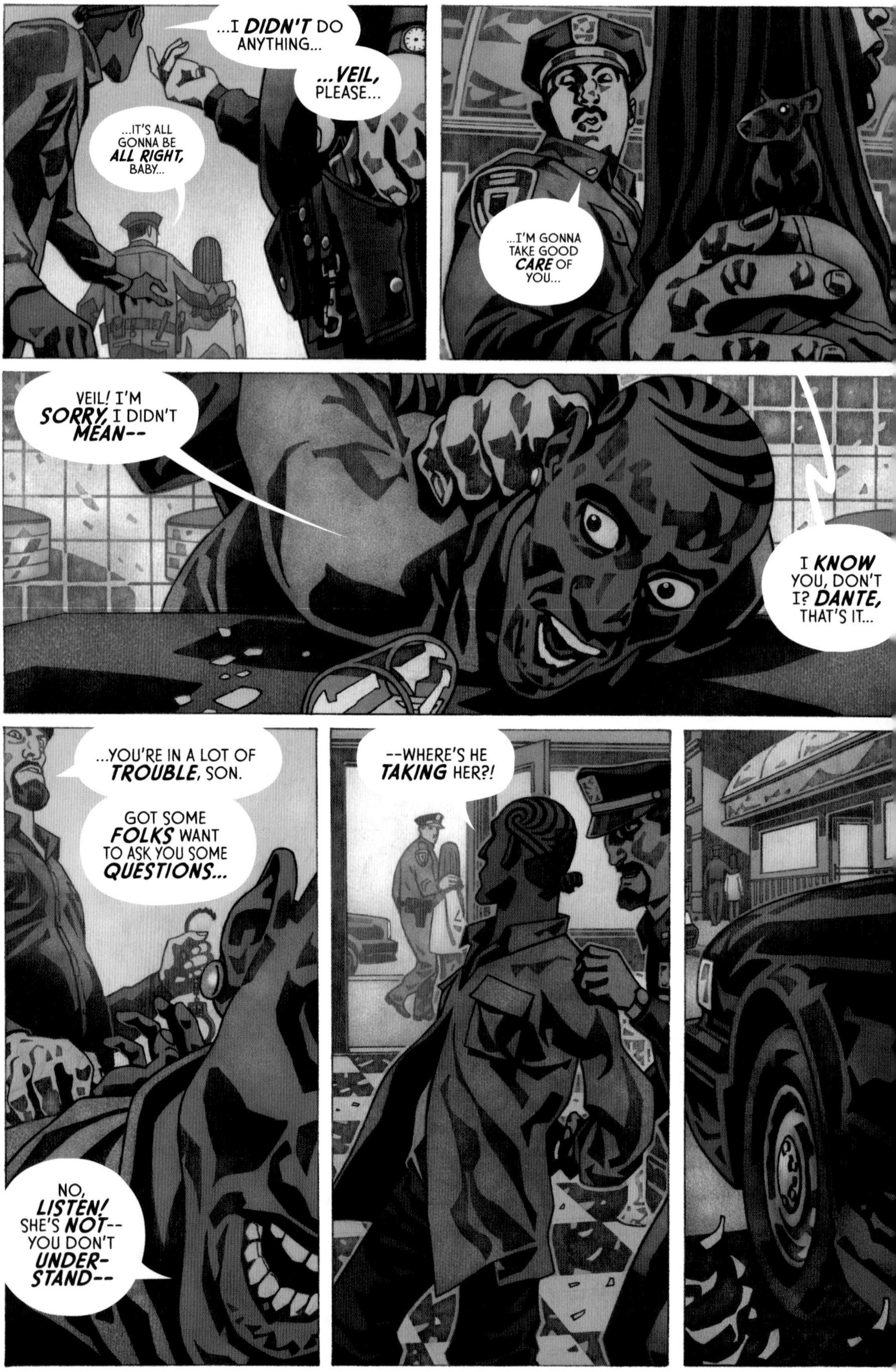
...I DIDN'T DO ANYTHING...
...VEIL, PLEASE...
...IT'S ALL GONNA BE ALL RIGHT, BABY...
...I'M GONNA TAKE GOOD CARE OF YOU...
VEIL! I'M SORRY, I DIDN'T MEAN--
I KNOW YOU, DON'T I? DANTE, THAT'S IT...
...YOU'RE IN A LOT OF TROUBLE, SON.
GOT SOME FOLKS WANT TO ASK YOU SOME QUESTIONS...
NO, LISTEN! SHE'S NOT-- YOU DON'T UNDER-STAND--
--WHERE'S HE TAKING HER?!

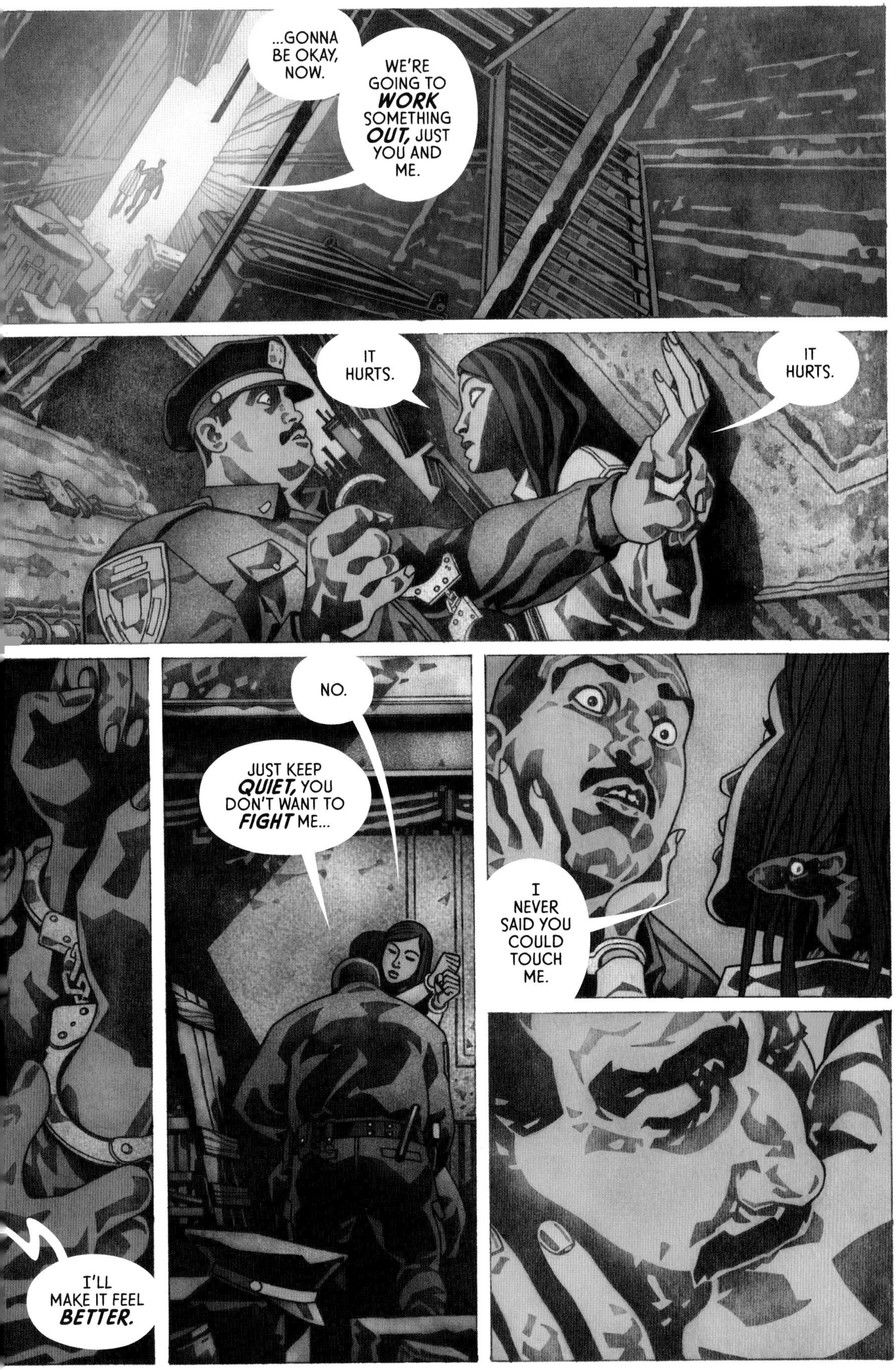
...GONNA BE OKAY, NOW.
WE'RE GOING TO WORK SOMETHING OUT, JUST YOU AND ME.
IT HURTS.
IT HURTS.
NO.
JUST KEEP QUIET, YOU DON'T WANT TO FIGHT ME...
I'LL MAKE IT FEEL BETTER.
I NEVER SAID YOU COULD TOUCH ME.

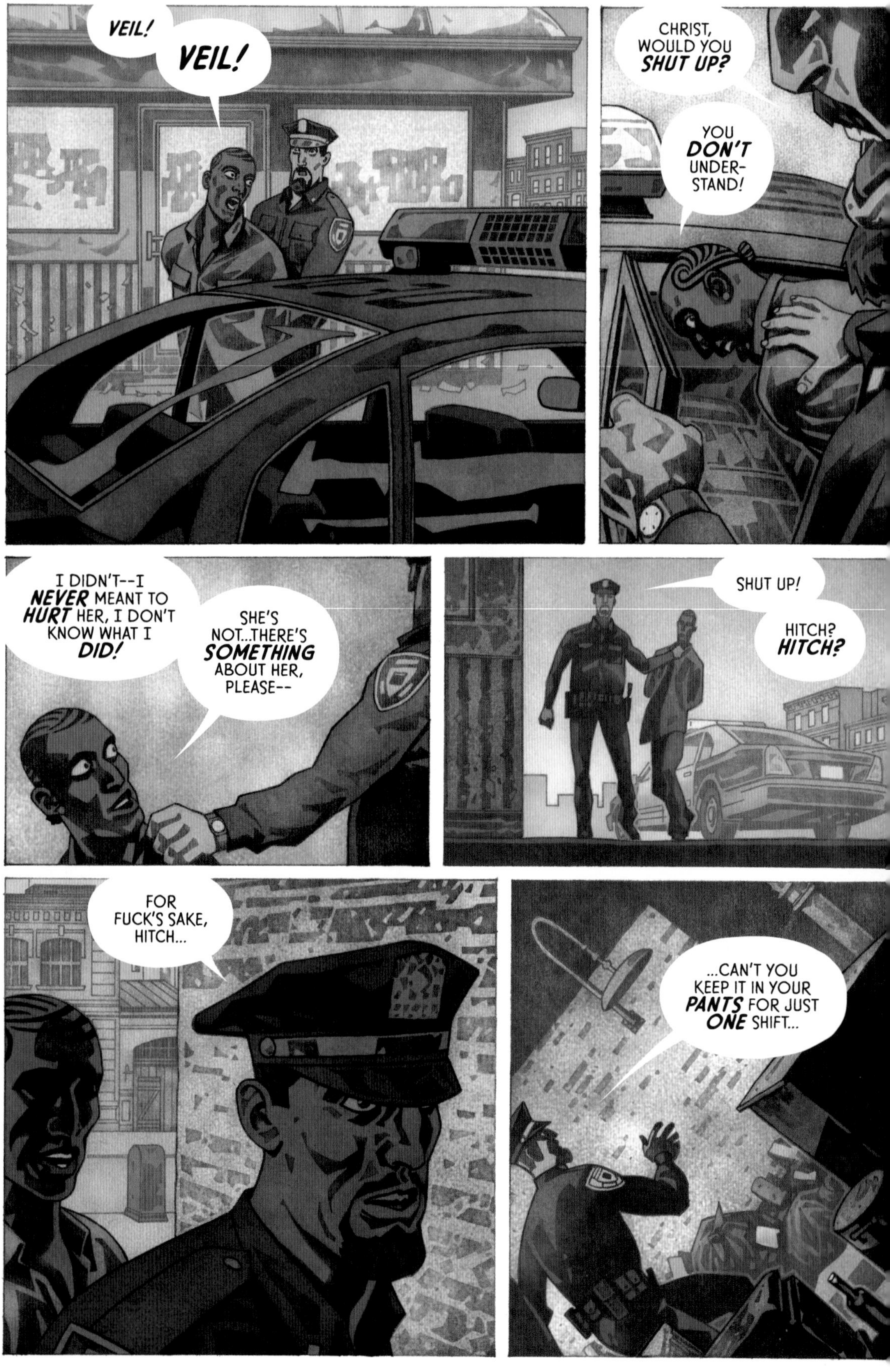
VEIL!
VEIL!
CHRIST, WOULD YOU SHUT UP?
YOU DON'T UNDER-STAND!
I DIDN'T--I NEVER MEANT TO HURT HER, I DON'T KNOW WHAT I DID!
SHE'S NOT...THERE'S SOMETHING ABOUT HER, PLEASE--
SHUT UP!
HITCH? HITCH?
FOR FUCK'S SAKE, HITCH...
...CAN'T YOU KEEP IT IN YOUR PANTS FOR JUST ONE SHIFT...

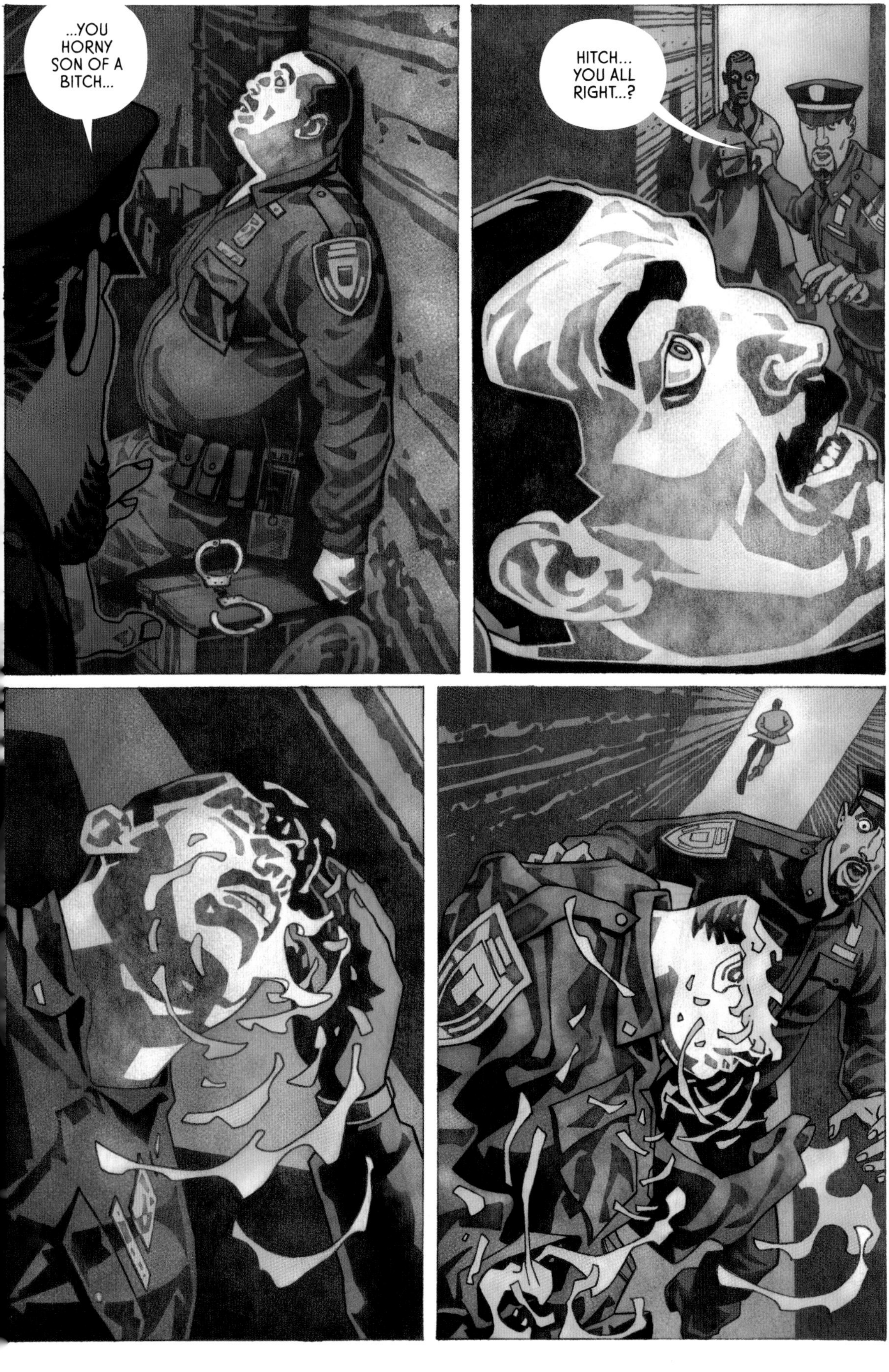
...YOU HORNY SON OF A BITCH...
HITCH... YOU ALL RIGHT...?

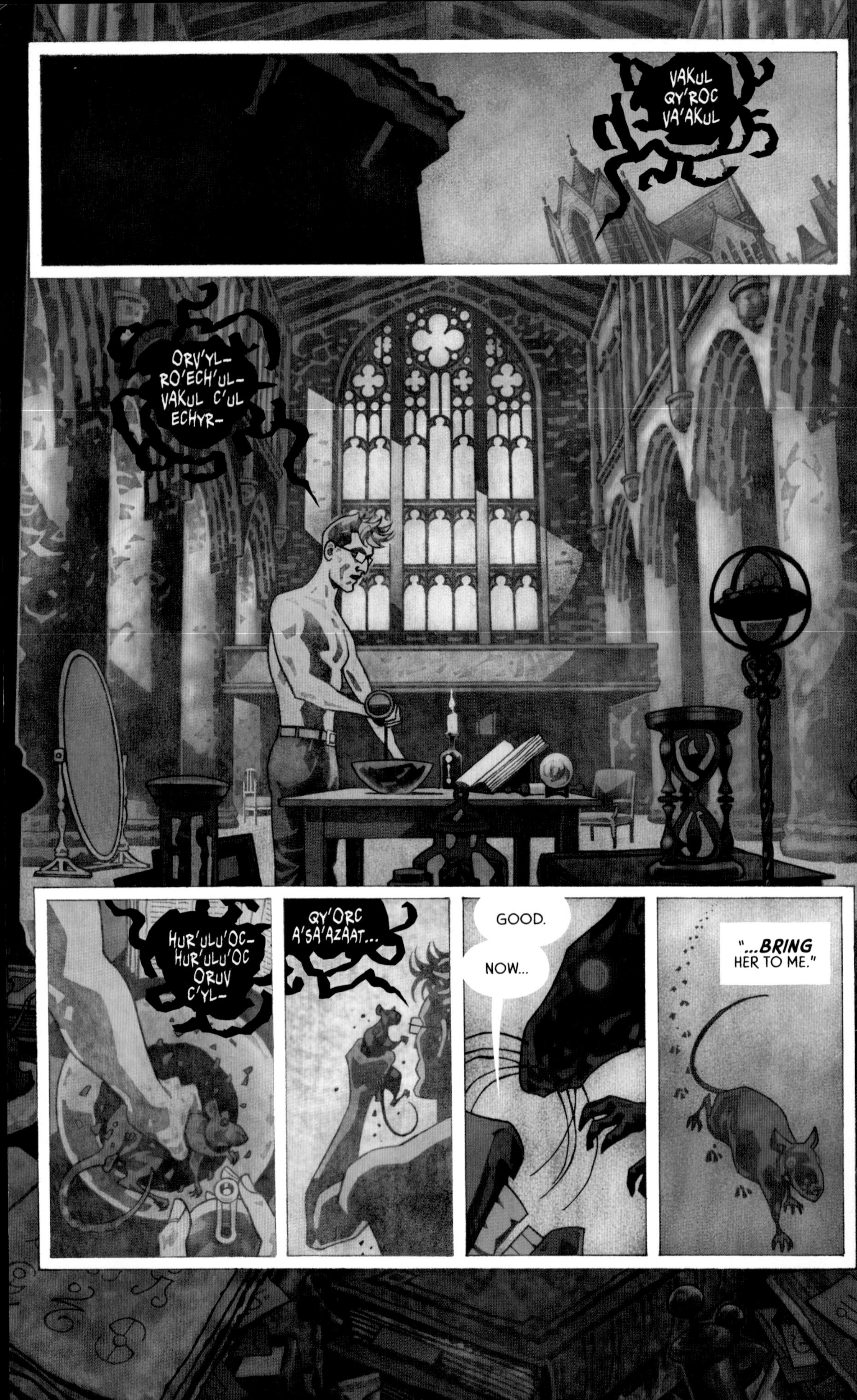
VAKUL QY'ROC VA'AKUL
ORV'YL- RO'ECH'UL- VAKUL C'UL ECHYR-
HUR'ULU'OC- HUR'ULU'OC ORUV C'YL-
QY'ORC A'SA'AZAAT...
GOOD.
NOW...
"...BRING HER TO ME."

CHAPTER THREE

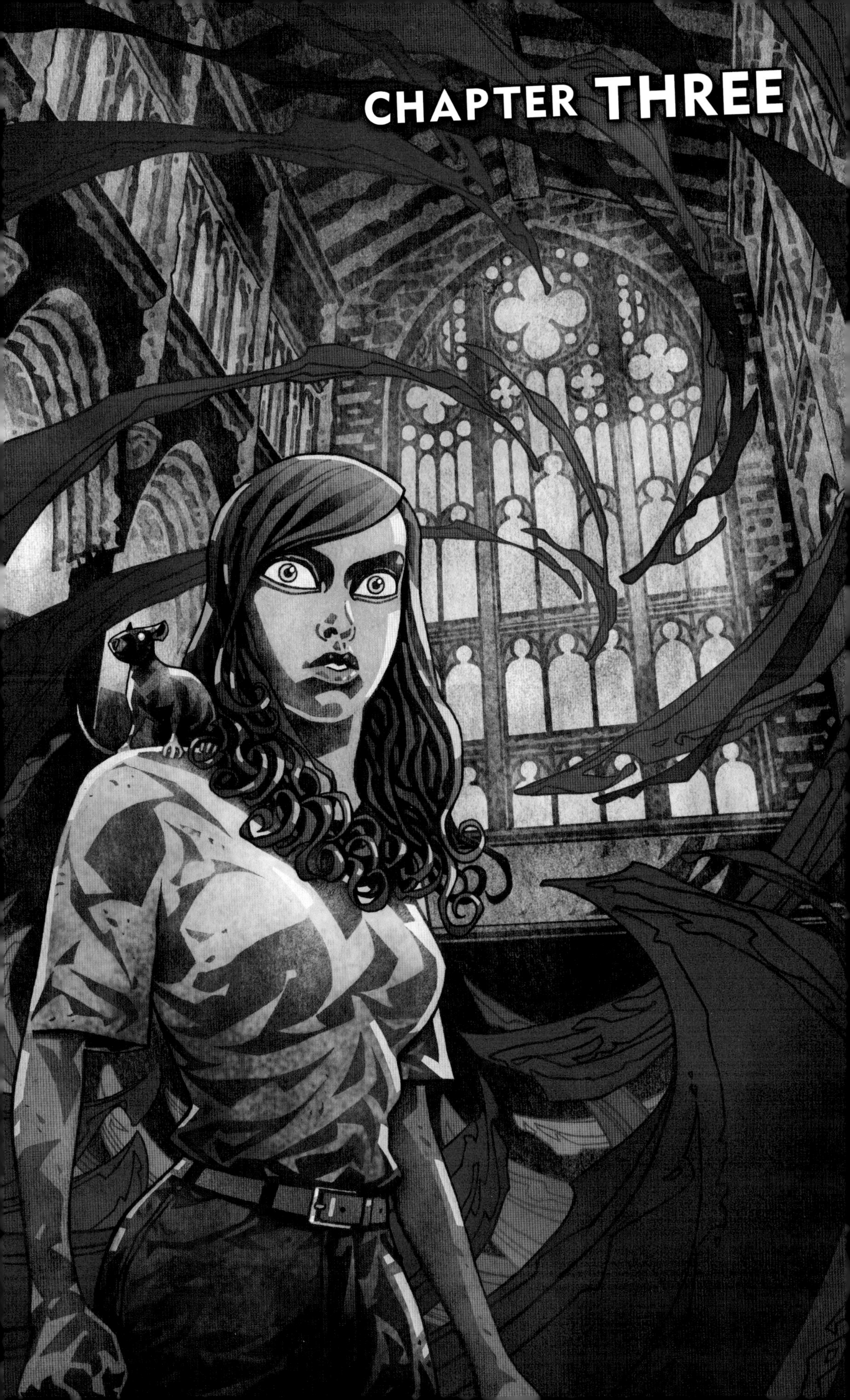

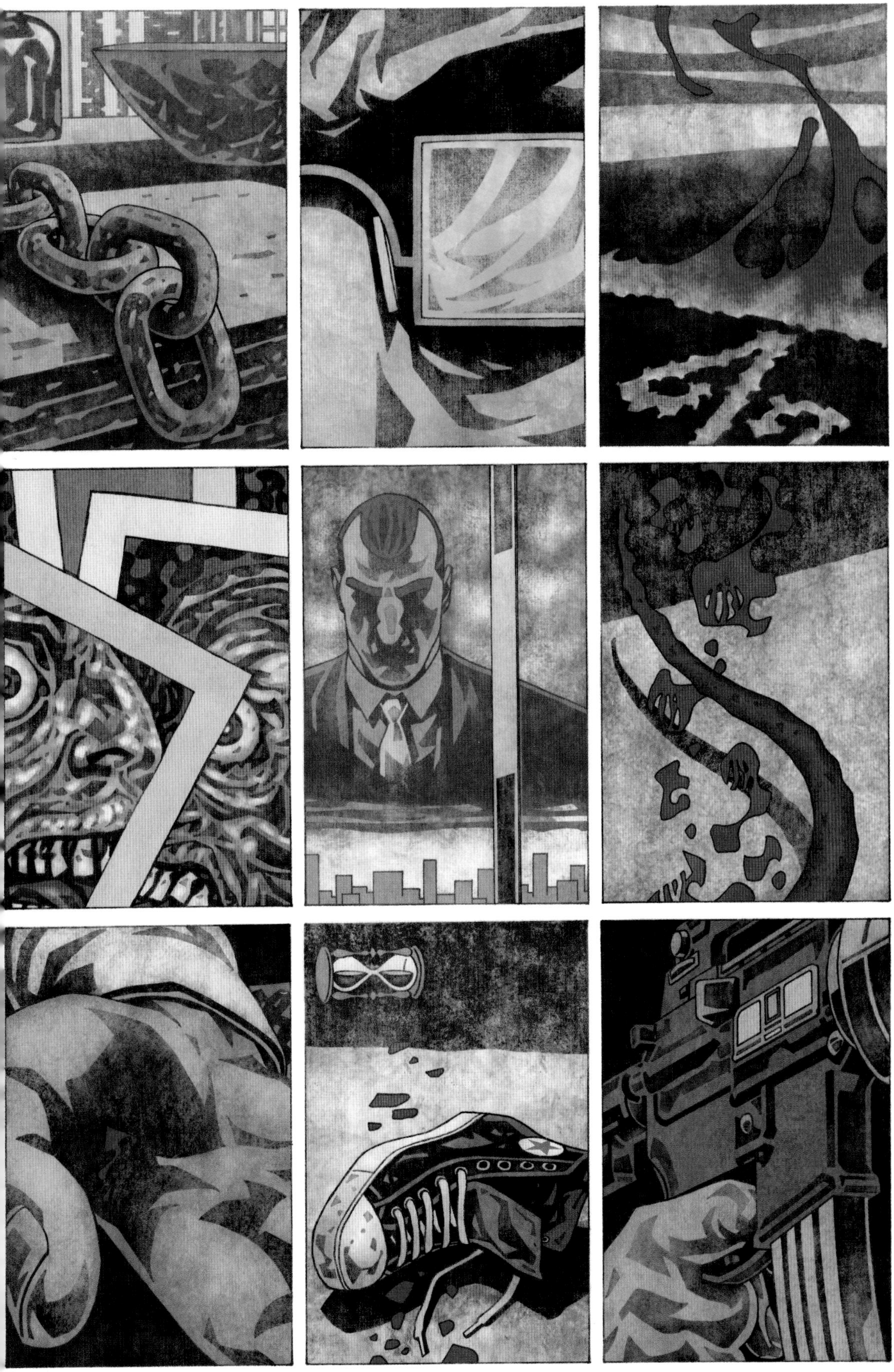

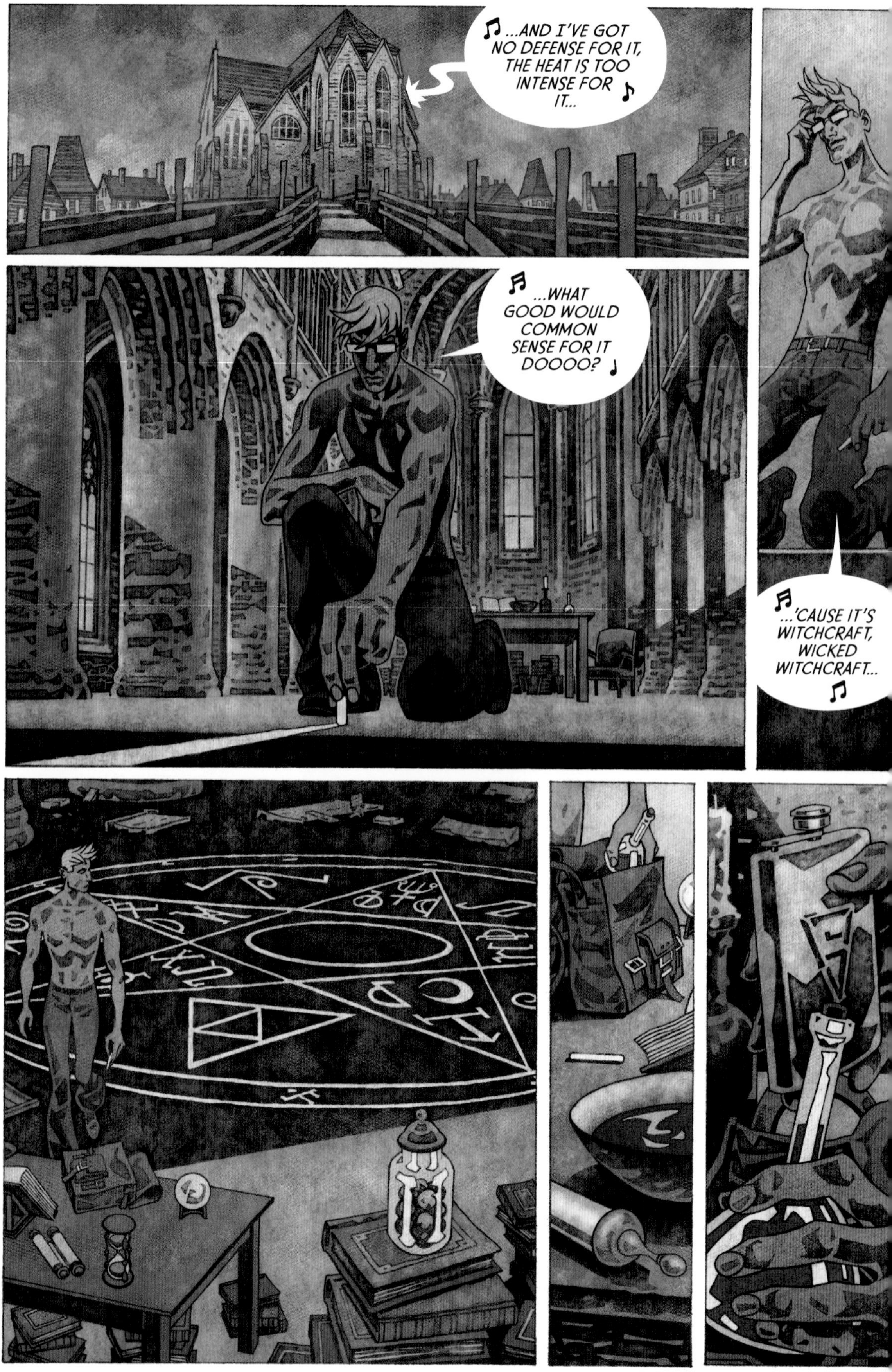
♫ ...AND I'VE GOT NO DEFENSE FOR IT, THE HEAT IS TOO INTENSE FOR IT... ♪
♬ ...WHAT GOOD WOULD COMMON SENSE FOR IT DOOOO? ♩
♬ ...'CAUSE IT'S WITCHCRAFT, WICKED WITCHCRAFT... ♫

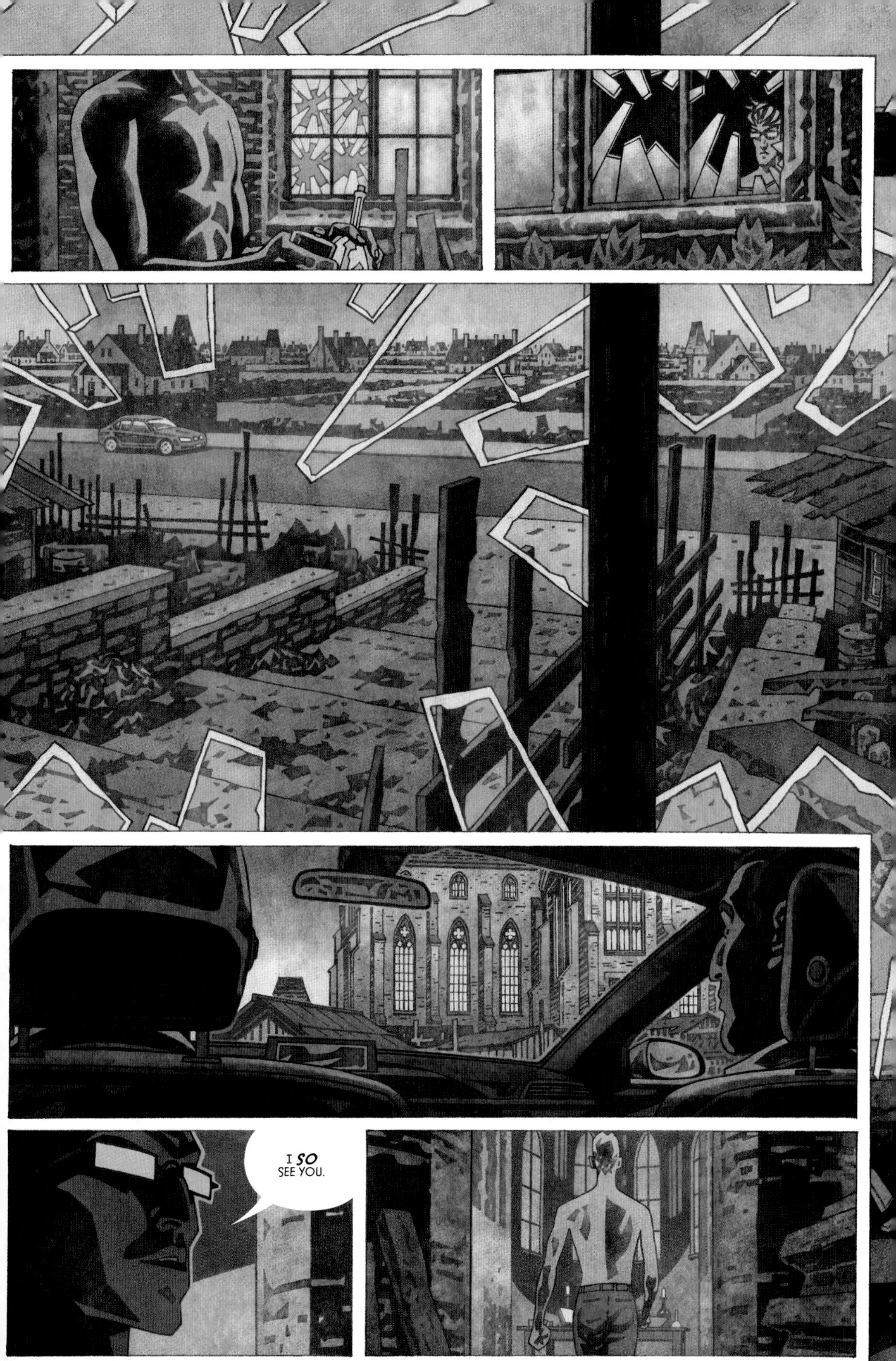
I SO SEE YOU.

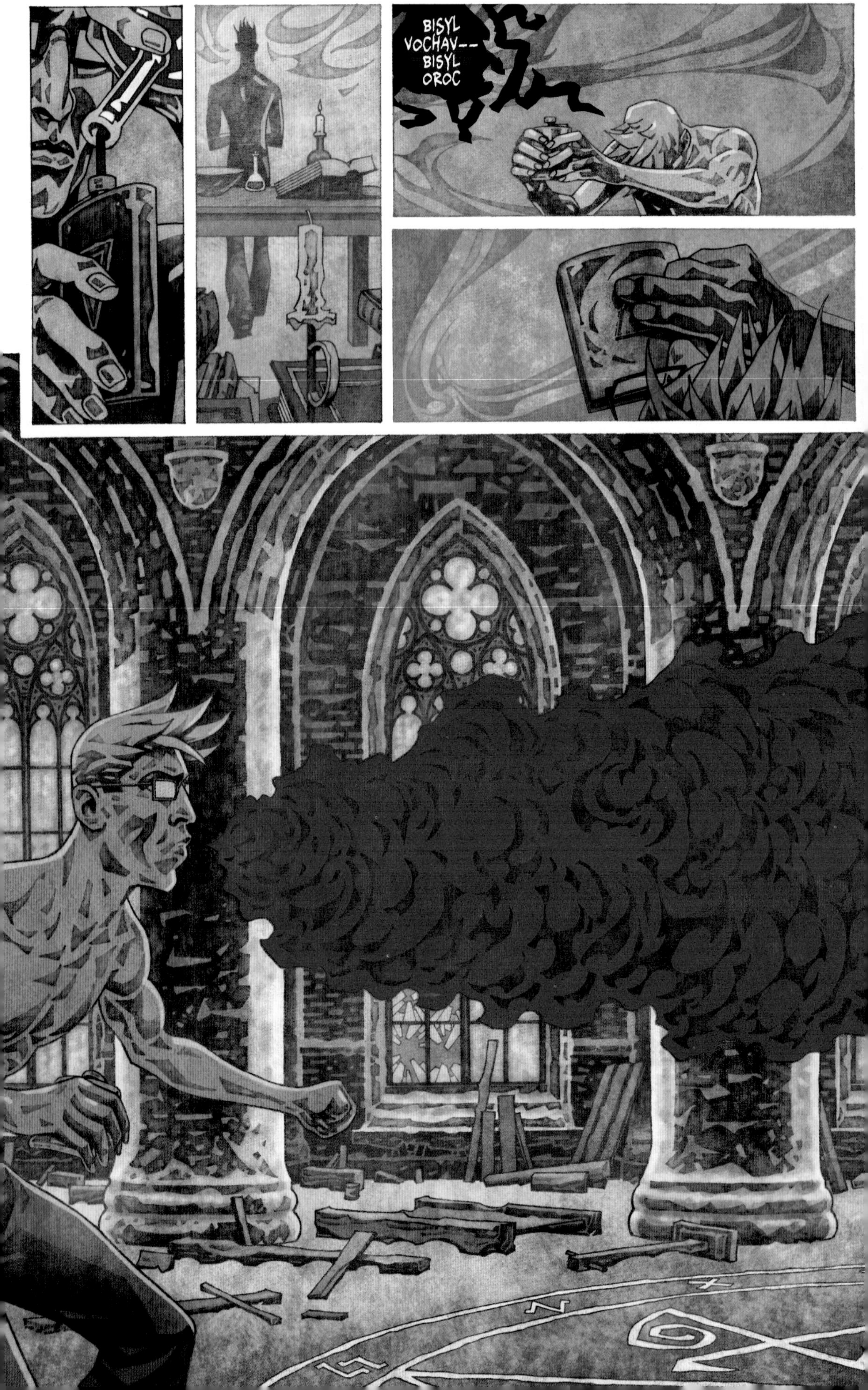
BISYL VOCHAV-- BISYL OROC

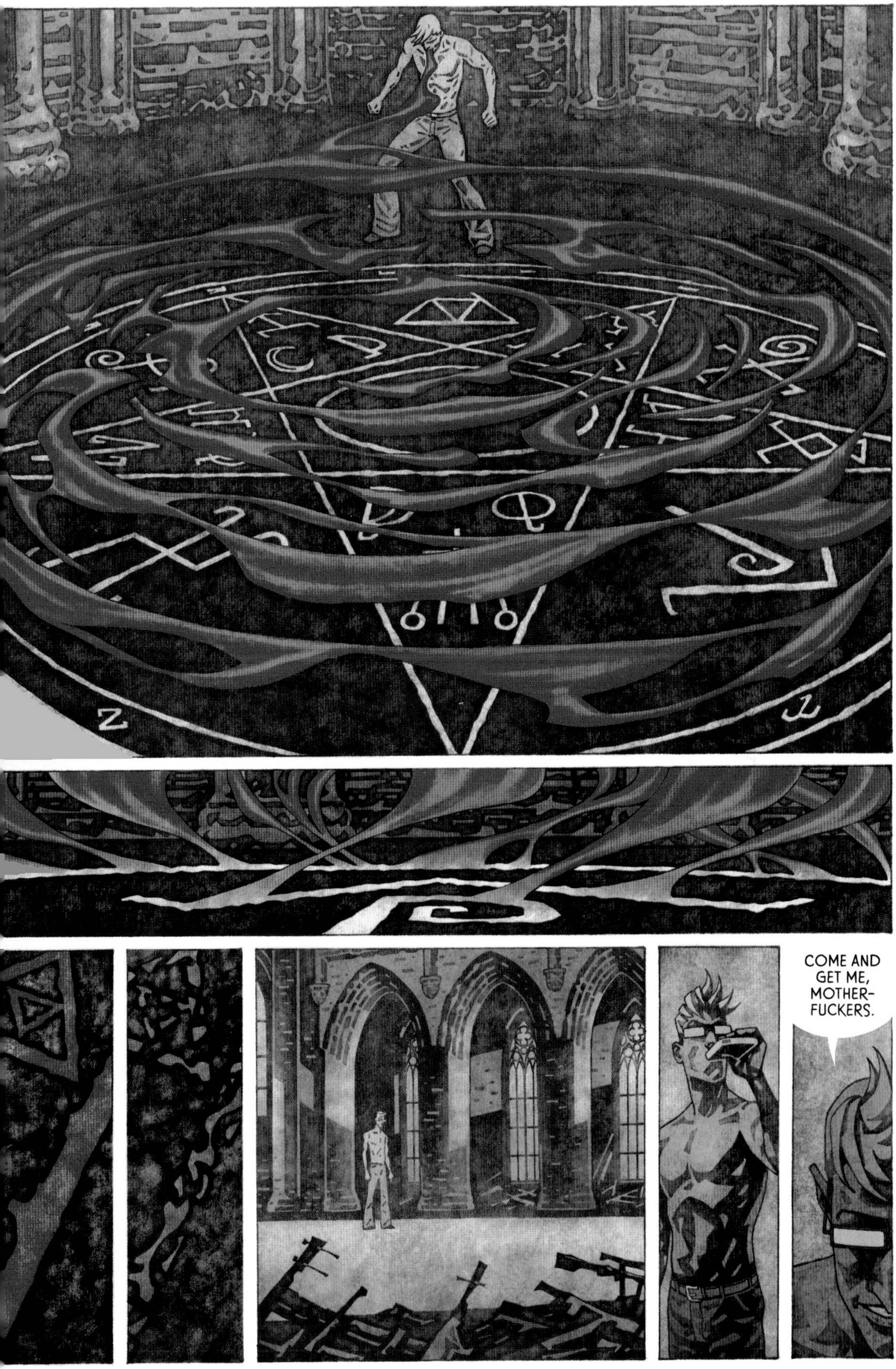
COME AND
GET ME,
MOTHER-
FUCKERS.

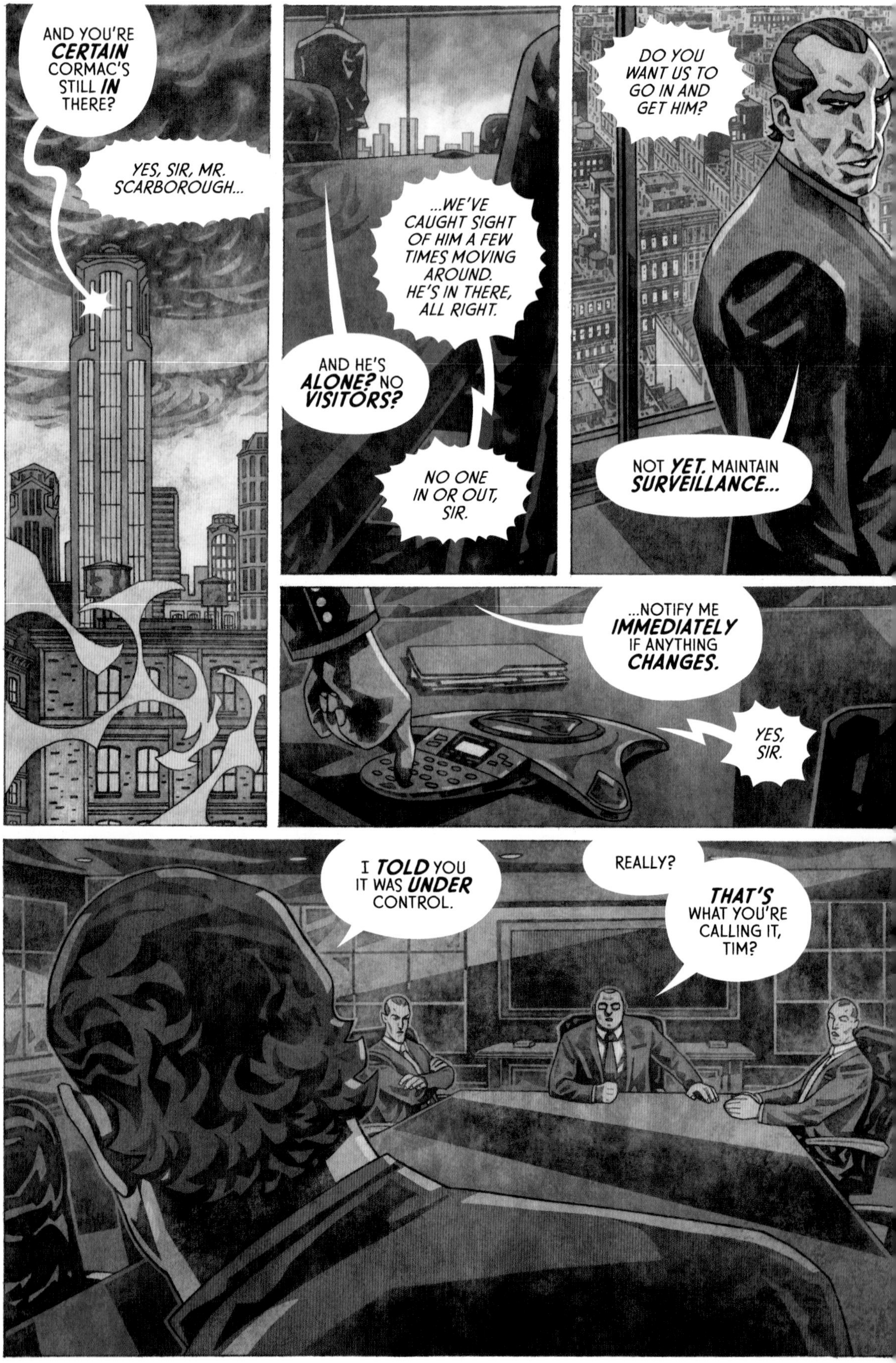
AND YOU'RE CERTAIN CORMAC'S STILL IN THERE?
YES, SIR, MR. SCARBOROUGH...
...WE'VE CAUGHT SIGHT OF HIM A FEW TIMES MOVING AROUND. HE'S IN THERE, ALL RIGHT.
AND HE'S ALONE? NO VISITORS?
NO ONE IN OR OUT, SIR.
DO YOU WANT US TO GO IN AND GET HIM?
NOT YET. MAINTAIN SURVEILLANCE...
...NOTIFY ME IMMEDIATELY IF ANYTHING CHANGES.
YES, SIR.
I TOLD YOU IT WAS UNDER CONTROL.
REALLY?
THAT'S WHAT YOU'RE CALLING IT, TIM?

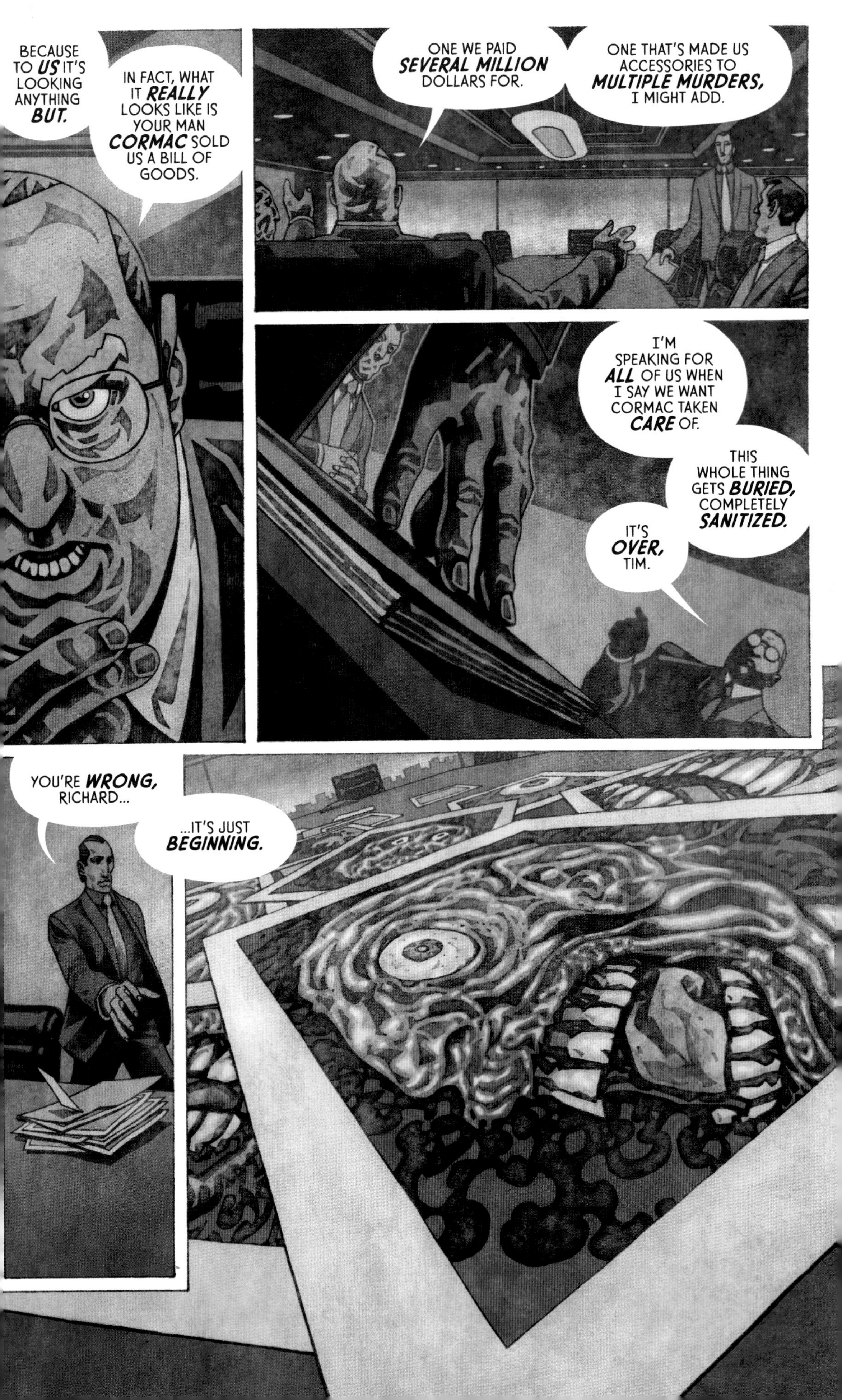
BECAUSE TO *US* IT'S LOOKING ANYTHING *BUT.*
IN FACT, WHAT IT *REALLY* LOOKS LIKE IS YOUR MAN *CORMAC* SOLD US A BILL OF GOODS.
ONE WE PAID *SEVERAL MILLION* DOLLARS FOR.
ONE THAT'S MADE US ACCESSORIES TO *MULTIPLE MURDERS,* I MIGHT ADD.
I'M SPEAKING FOR *ALL* OF US WHEN I SAY WE WANT CORMAC TAKEN *CARE* OF.
THIS WHOLE THING GETS *BURIED,* COMPLETELY *SANITIZED.*
IT'S *OVER,* TIM.
YOU'RE *WRONG,* RICHARD...
...IT'S JUST *BEGINNING.*

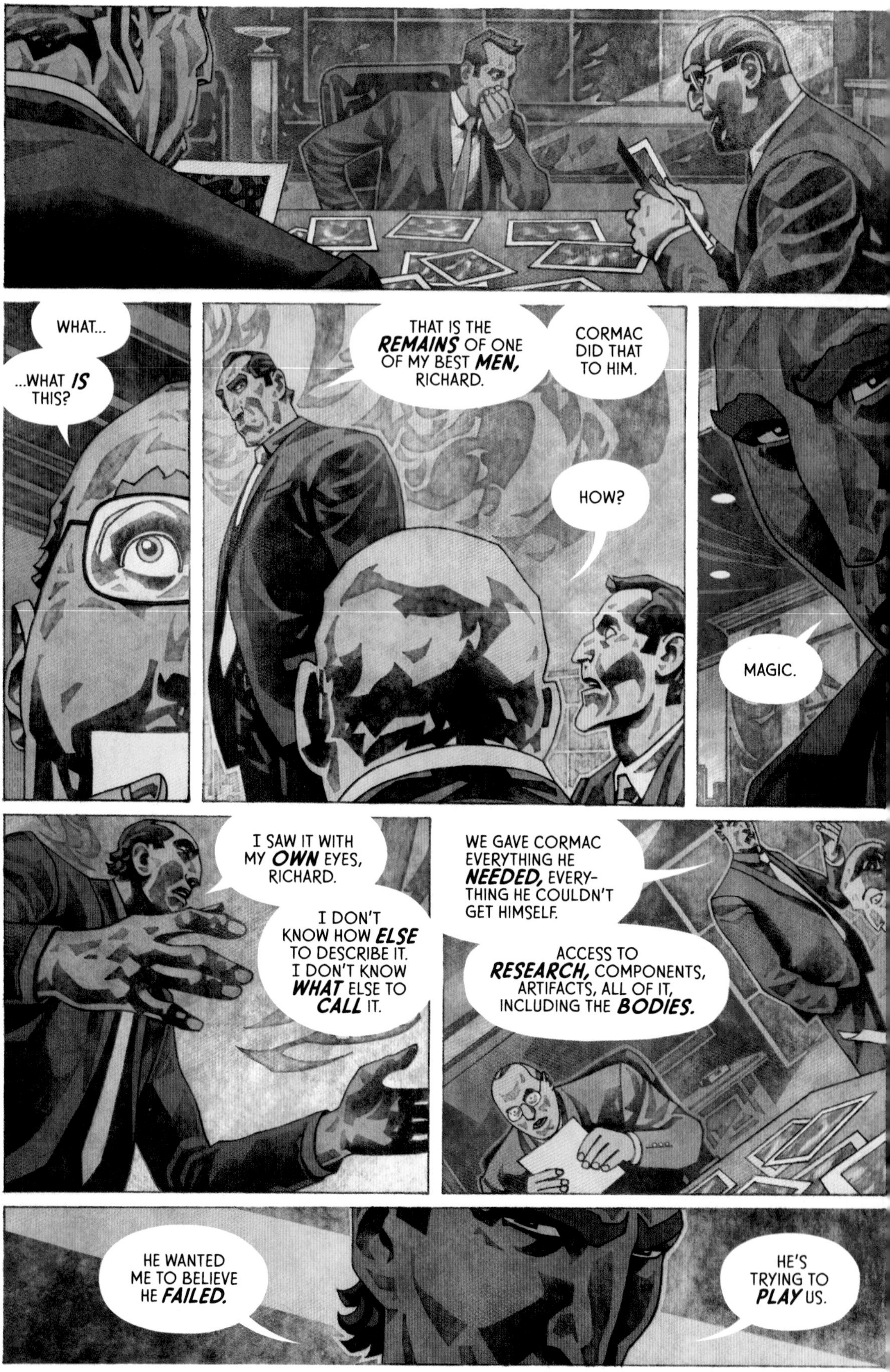
WHAT...
...WHAT IS THIS?
THAT IS THE REMAINS OF ONE OF MY BEST MEN, RICHARD.
CORMAC DID THAT TO HIM.
HOW?
MAGIC.
I SAW IT WITH MY OWN EYES, RICHARD.
I DON'T KNOW HOW ELSE TO DESCRIBE IT. I DON'T KNOW WHAT ELSE TO CALL IT.
WE GAVE CORMAC EVERYTHING HE NEEDED, EVERY-THING HE COULDN'T GET HIMSELF.
ACCESS TO RESEARCH, COMPONENTS, ARTIFACTS, ALL OF IT, INCLUDING THE BODIES.
HE WANTED ME TO BELIEVE HE FAILED.
HE'S TRYING TO PLAY US.

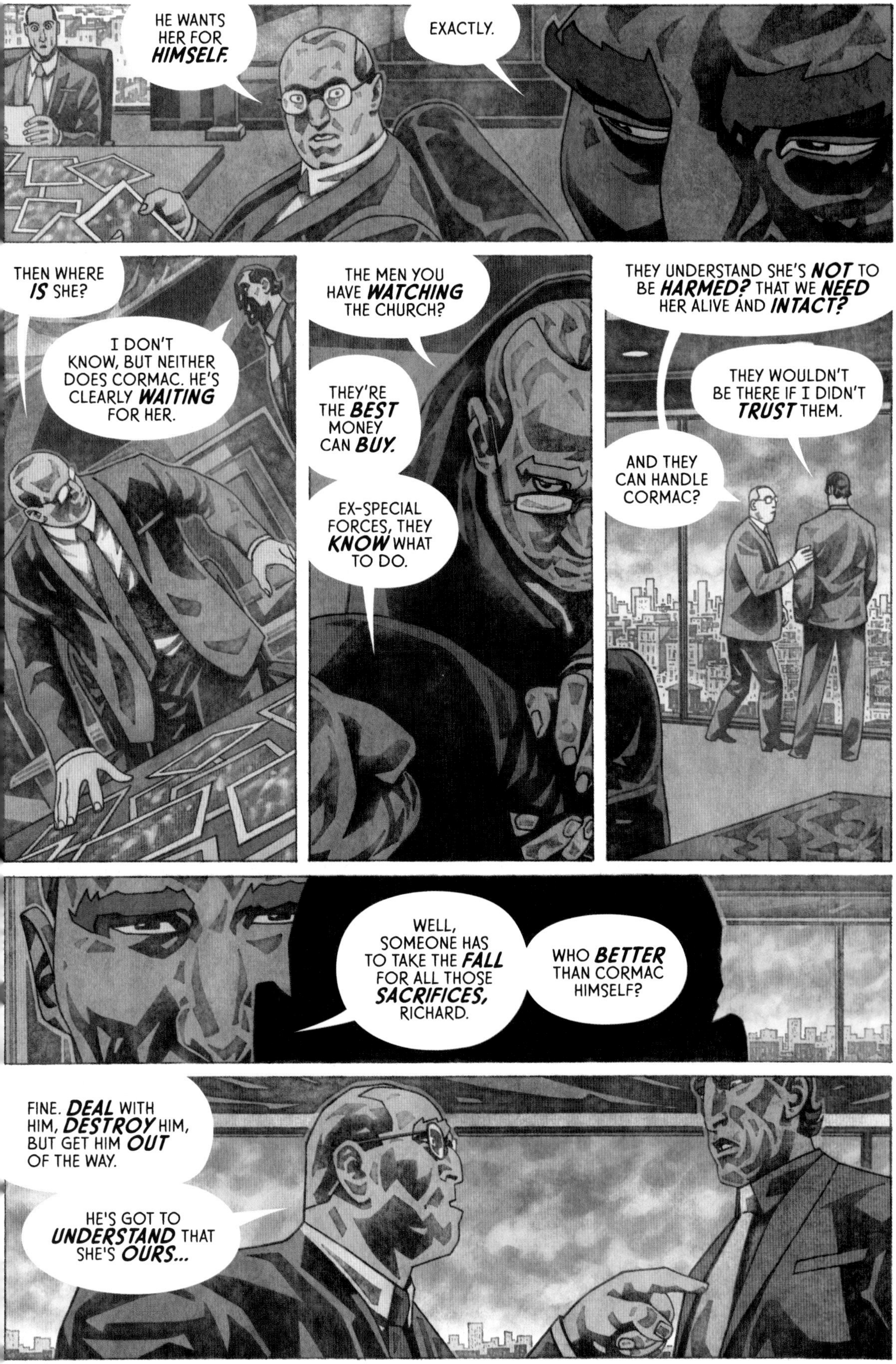

HE WANTS HER FOR HIMSELF.
EXACTLY.
THEN WHERE IS SHE?
I DON'T KNOW, BUT NEITHER DOES CORMAC. HE'S CLEARLY WAITING FOR HER.
THE MEN YOU HAVE WATCHING THE CHURCH?
THEY'RE THE BEST MONEY CAN BUY.
EX-SPECIAL FORCES, THEY KNOW WHAT TO DO.
THEY UNDERSTAND SHE'S NOT TO BE HARMED? THAT WE NEED HER ALIVE AND INTACT?
THEY WOULDN'T BE THERE IF I DIDN'T TRUST THEM.
AND THEY CAN HANDLE CORMAC?
WELL, SOMEONE HAS TO TAKE THE FALL FOR ALL THOSE SACRIFICES, RICHARD.
WHO BETTER THAN CORMAC HIMSELF?
FINE. DEAL WITH HIM, DESTROY HIM, BUT GET HIM OUT OF THE WAY.
HE'S GOT TO UNDERSTAND THAT SHE'S OURS...

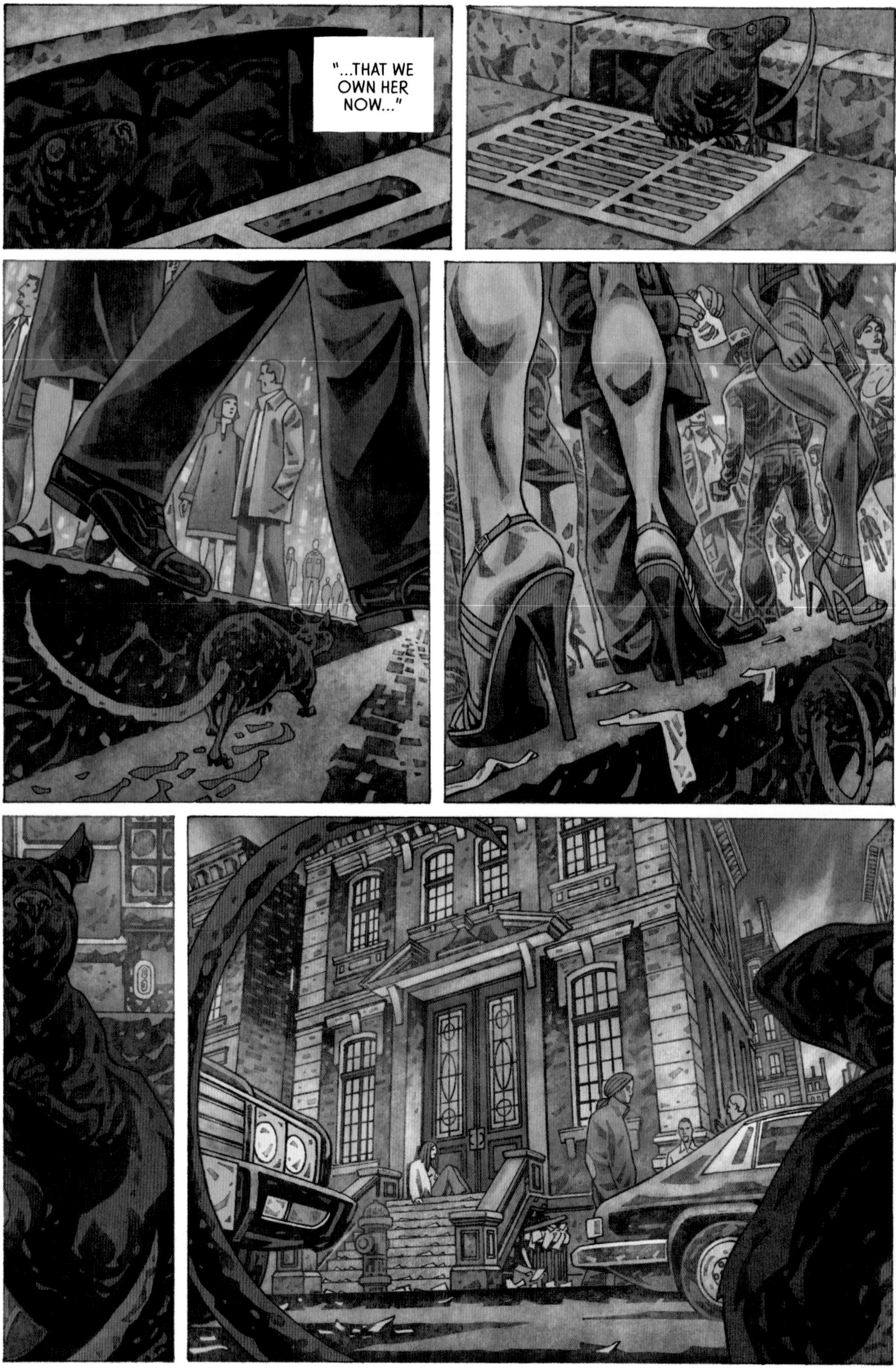
"...THAT WE OWN HER NOW..."

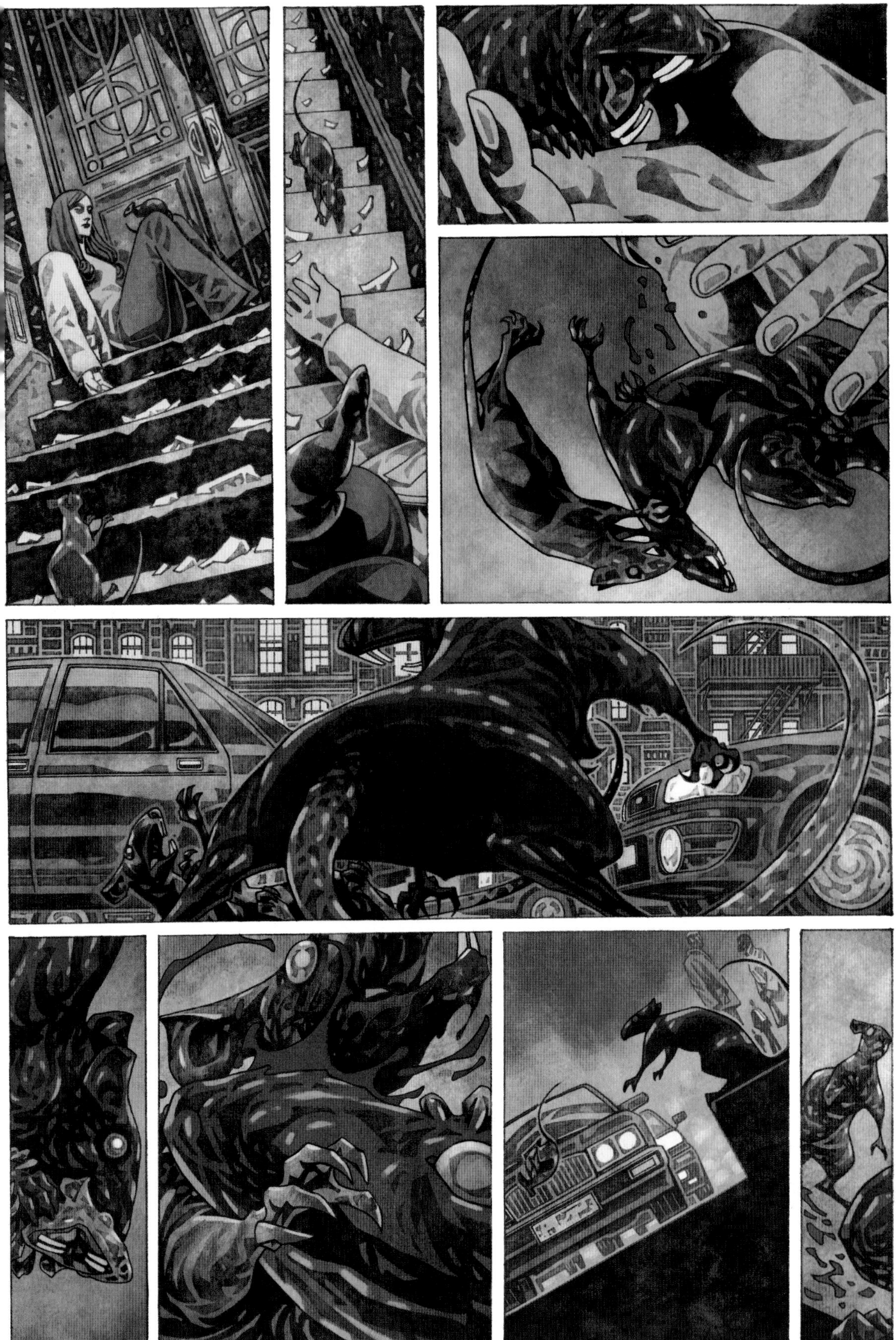

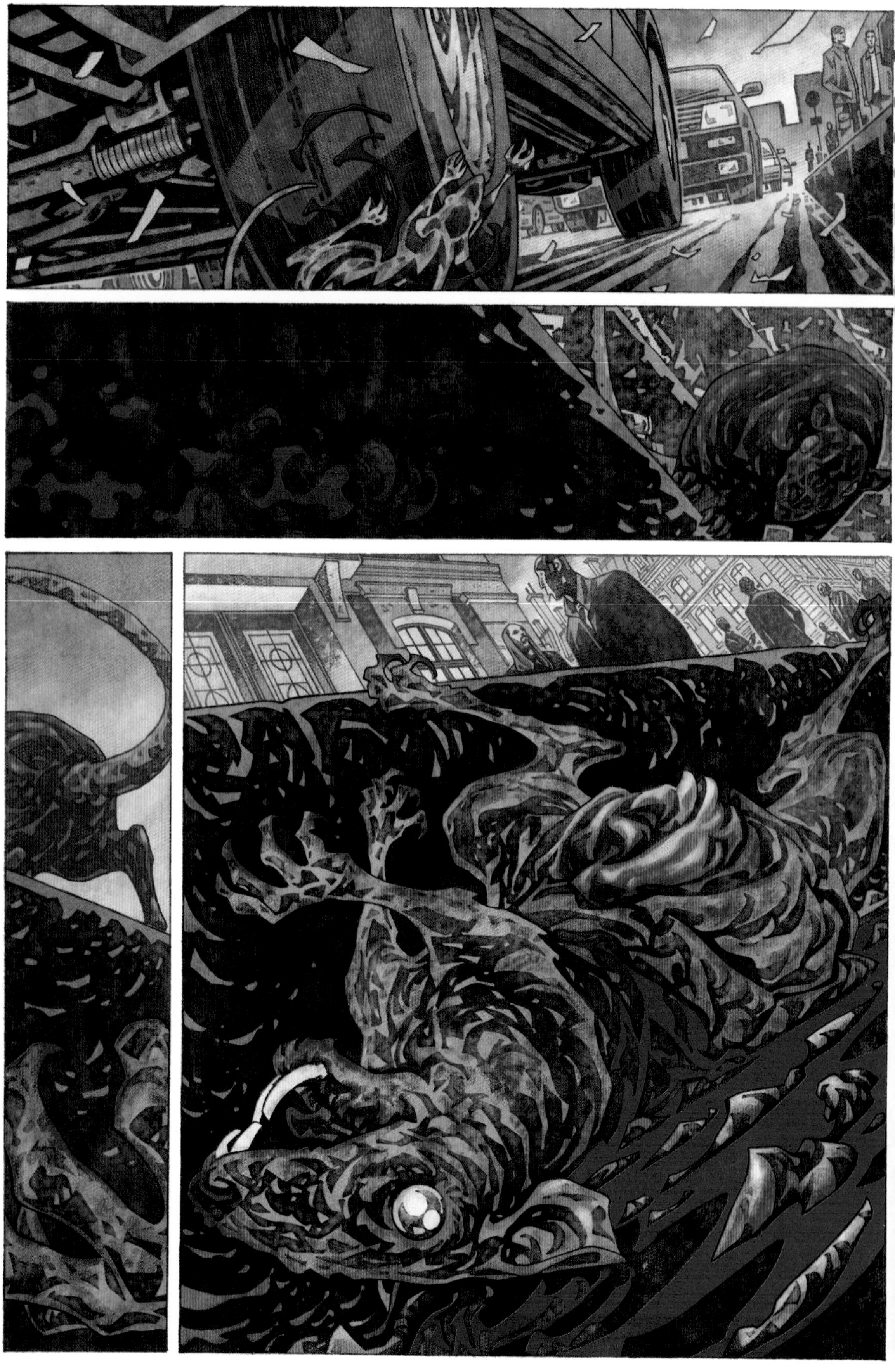

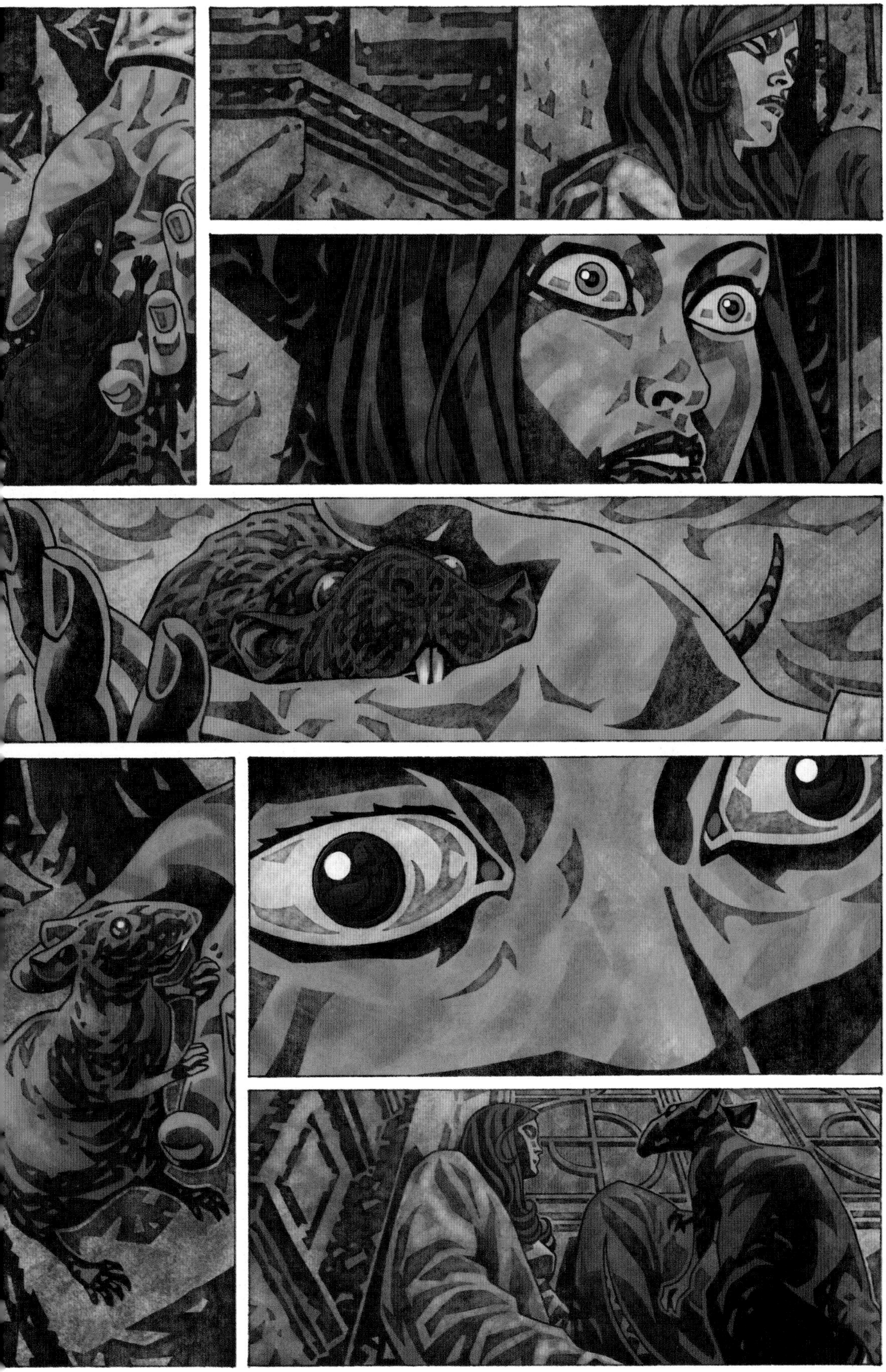

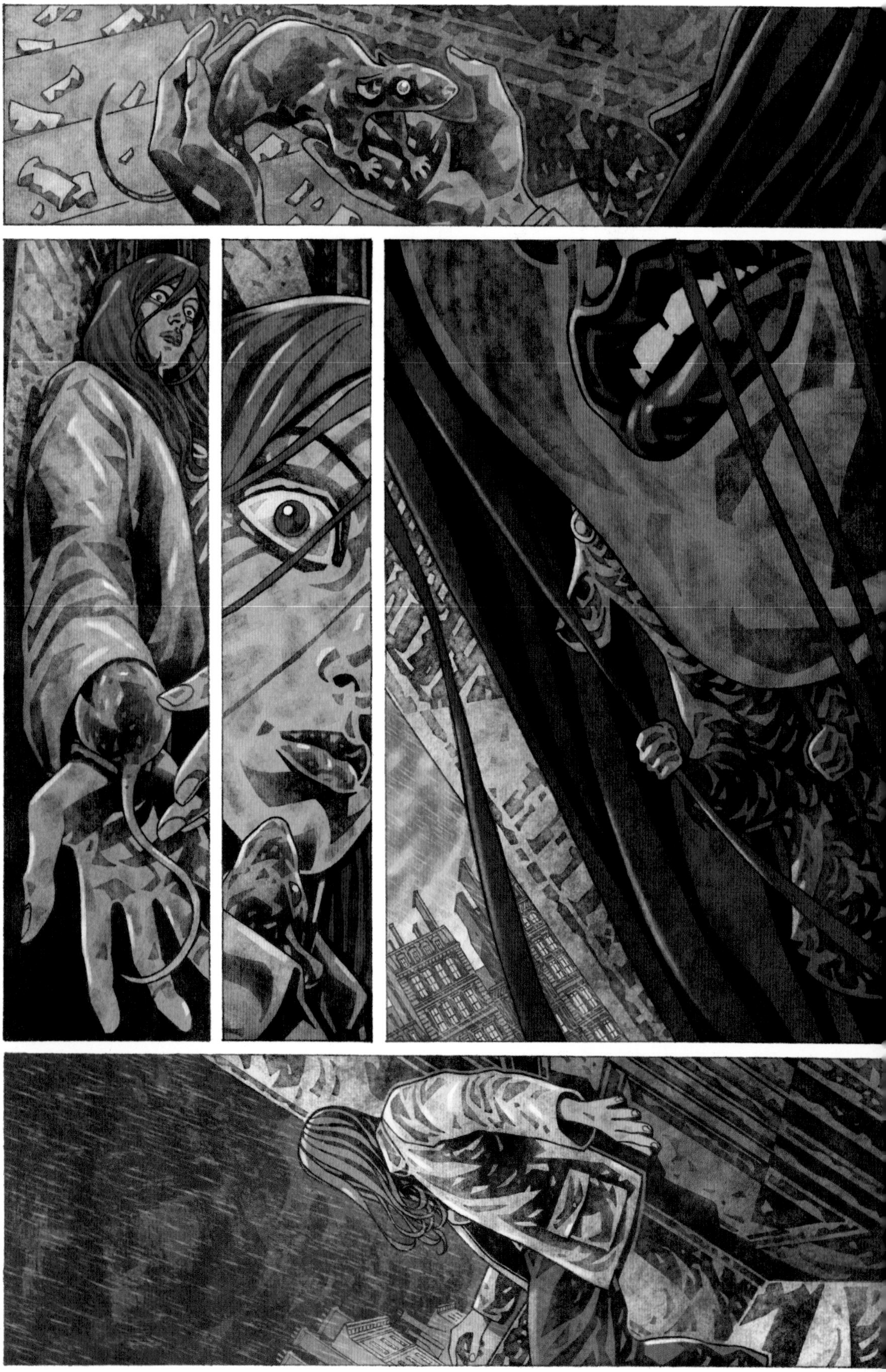

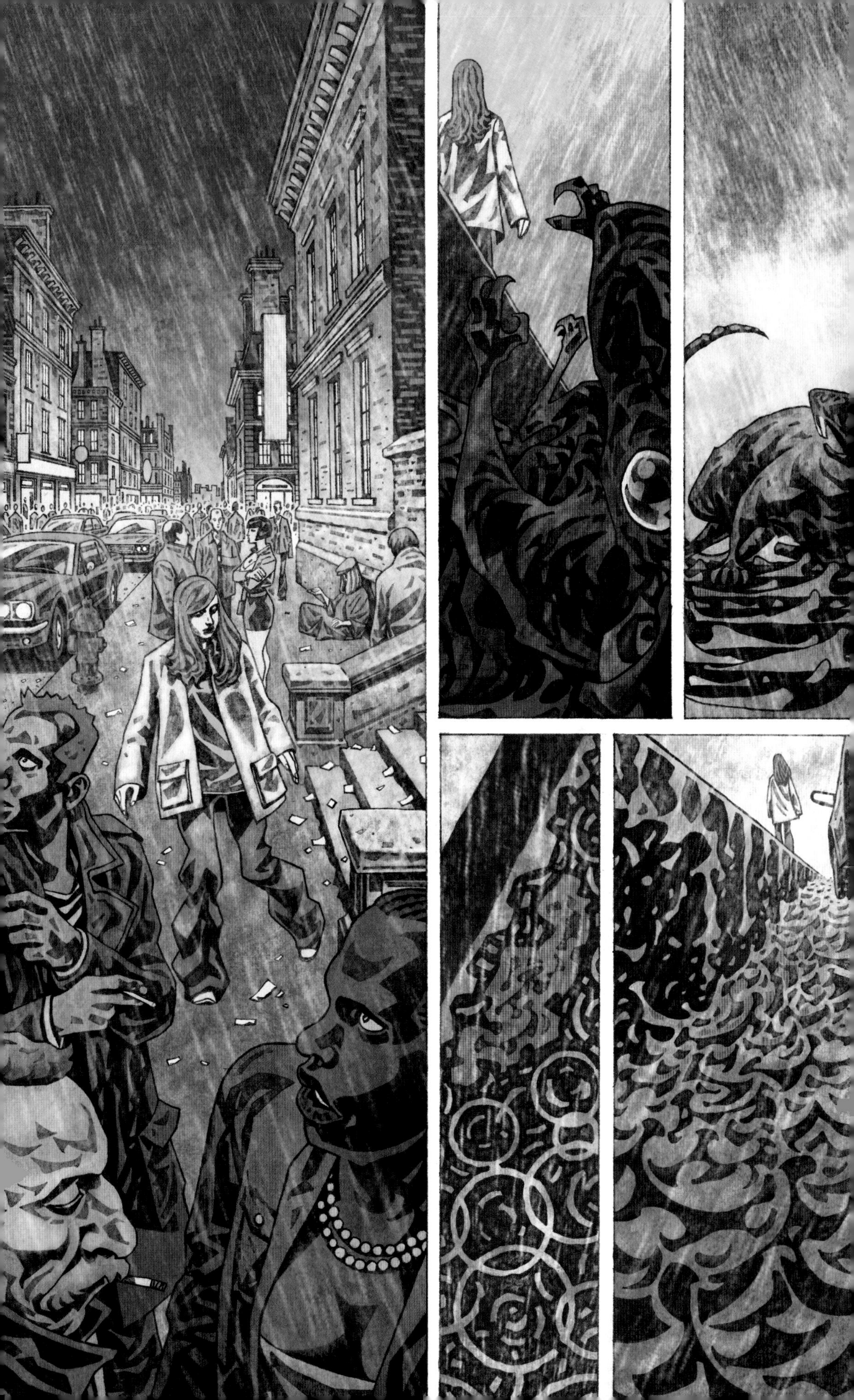

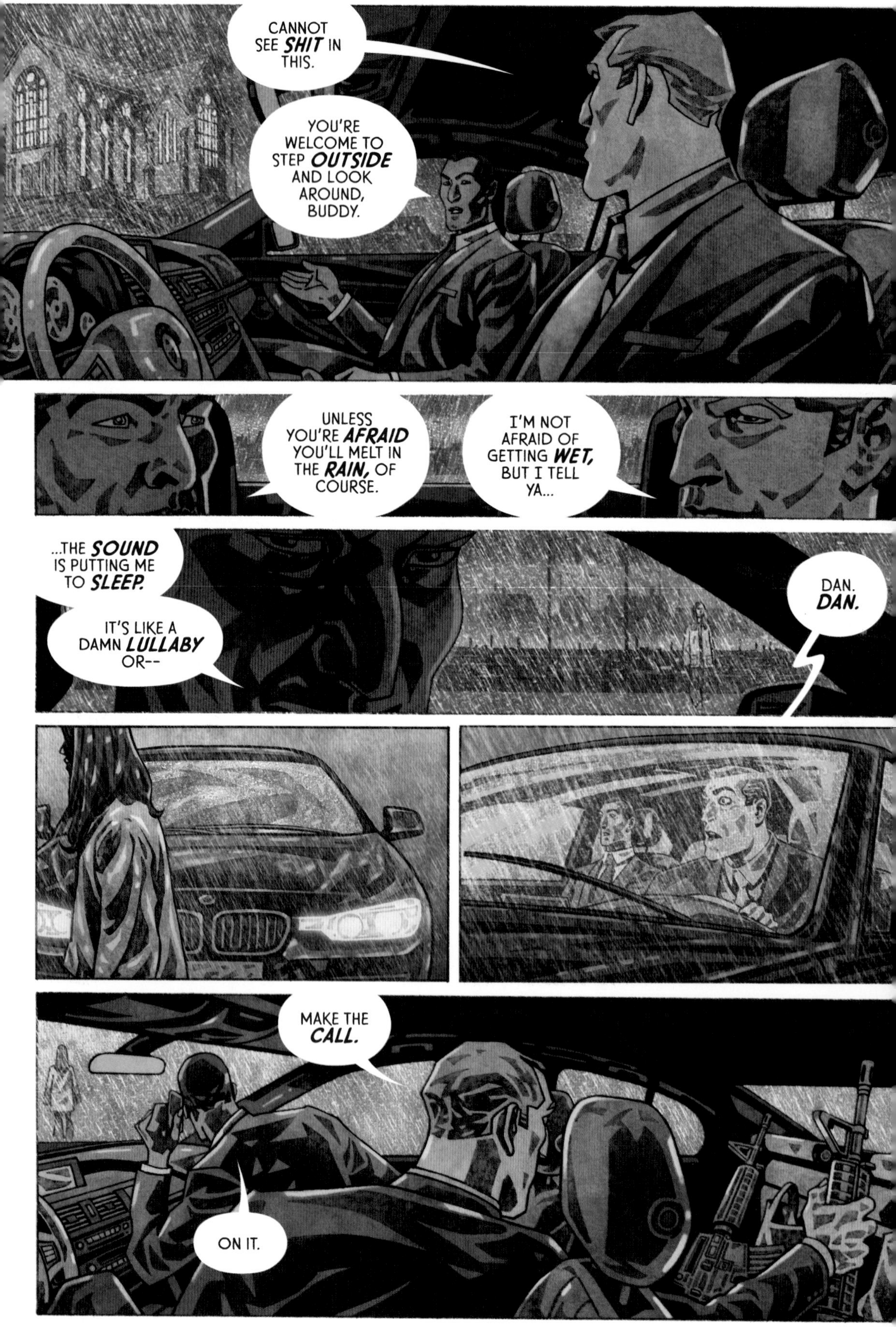
CANNOT SEE SHIT IN THIS.
YOU'RE WELCOME TO STEP OUTSIDE AND LOOK AROUND, BUDDY.
UNLESS YOU'RE AFRAID YOU'LL MELT IN THE RAIN, OF COURSE.
I'M NOT AFRAID OF GETTING WET, BUT I TELL YA...
...THE SOUND IS PUTTING ME TO SLEEP.
IT'S LIKE A DAMN LULLABY OR--
DAN. DAN.
MAKE THE CALL.
ON IT.

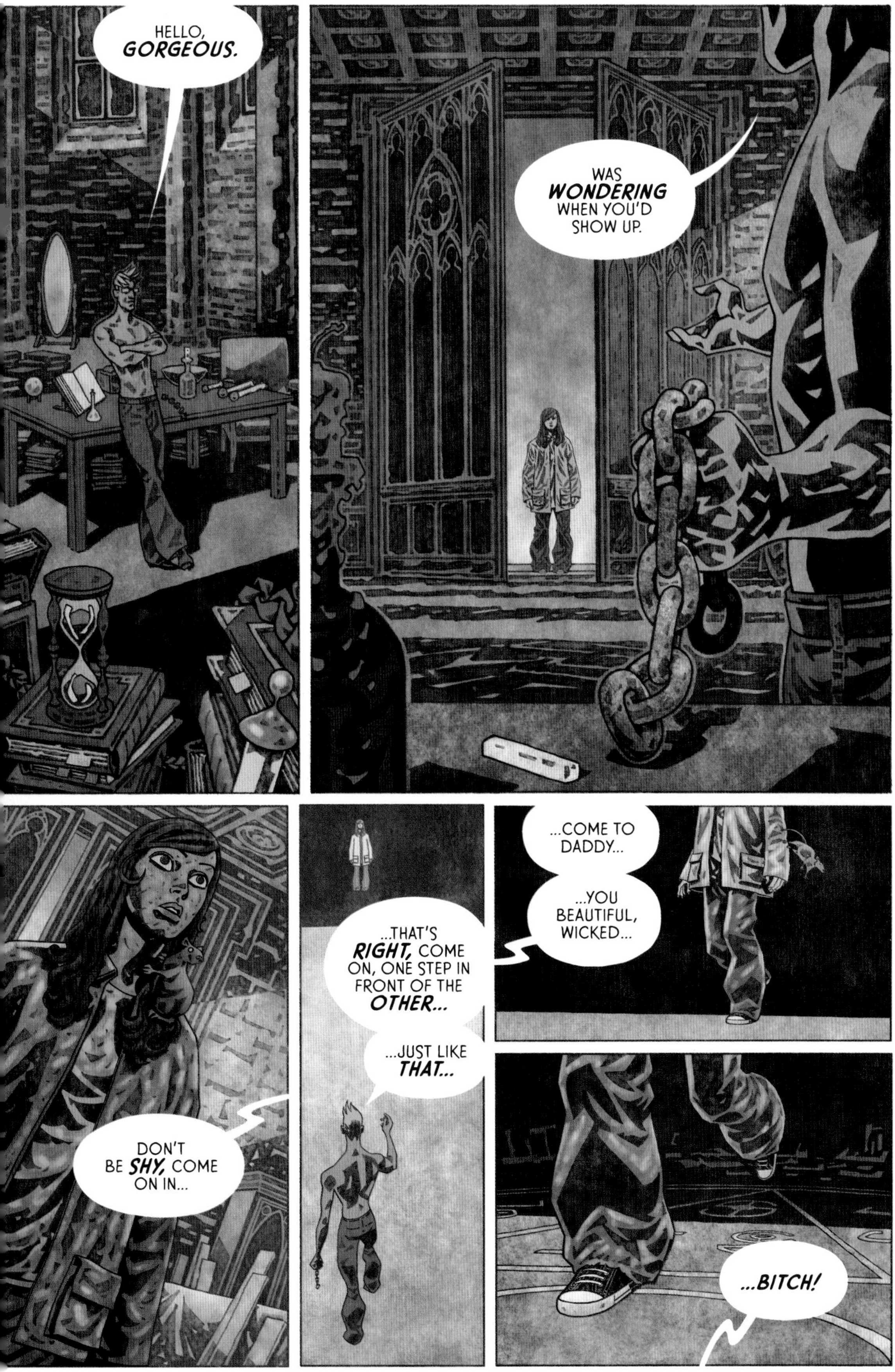
HELLO, GORGEOUS.
WAS WONDERING WHEN YOU'D SHOW UP.
DON'T BE SHY, COME ON IN...
...THAT'S RIGHT, COME ON, ONE STEP IN FRONT OF THE OTHER...
...JUST LIKE THAT...
...COME TO DADDY...
...YOU BEAUTIFUL, WICKED...
...BITCH!

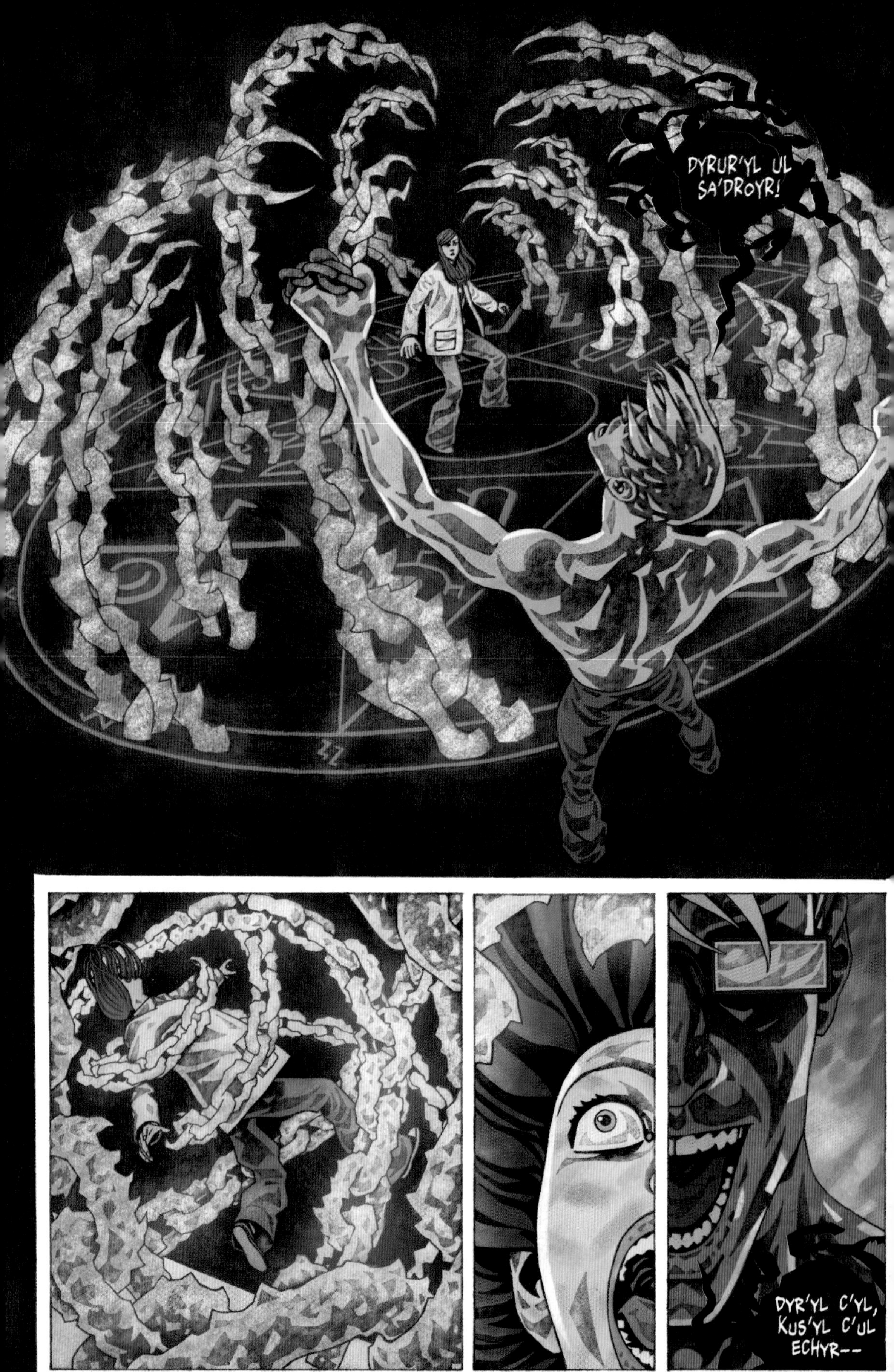
DYRUR'YL UL SA'DROYR!
DYR'YL C'YL, KUS'YL C'UL ECHYR--

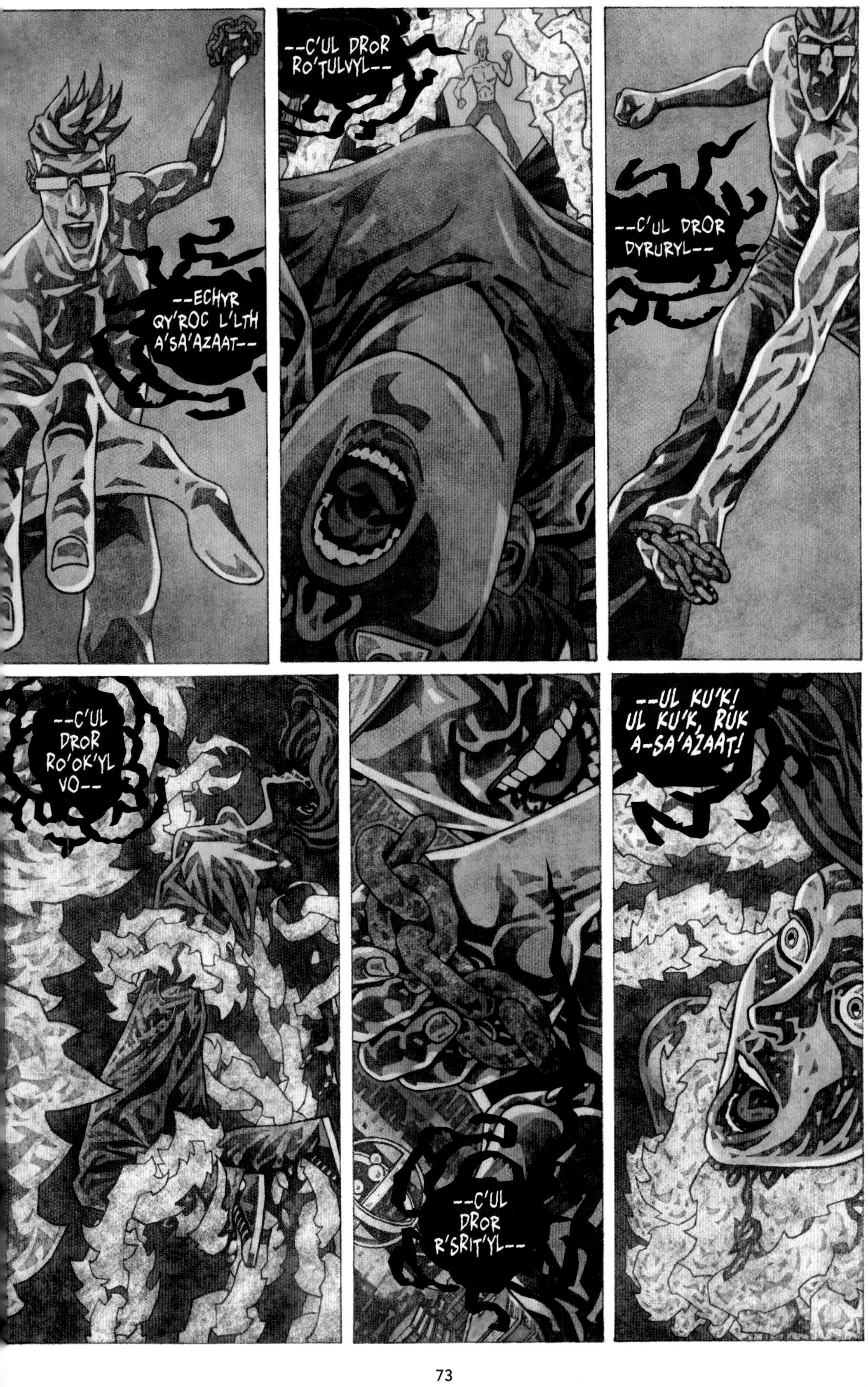
--ECHYR QY'ROC L'LTH A'SA'AZAAT--
--C'UL DROR RO'TULVYL--
--C'UL DROR DYRURYL--
--C'UL DROR RO'OK'YL VO--
--C'UL DROR R'SRIT'YL--
--UL KU'K! UL KU'K, RUK A-SA'AZAAT!

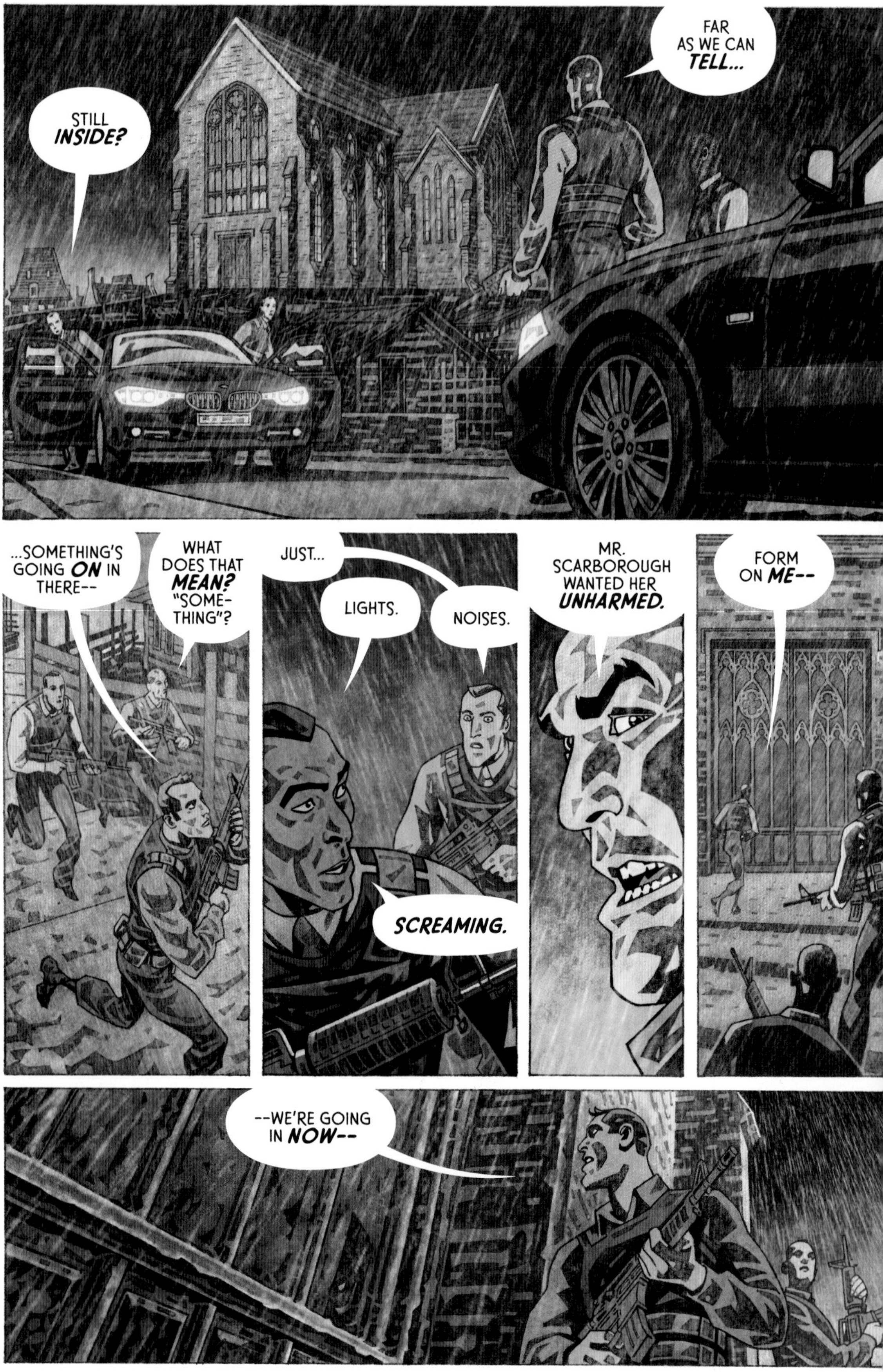
STILL INSIDE?
FAR AS WE CAN TELL...
...SOMETHING'S GOING ON IN THERE--
WHAT DOES THAT MEAN? "SOME-THING"?
JUST...
LIGHTS.
NOISES.
SCREAMING.
MR. SCARBOROUGH WANTED HER UNHARMED.
FORM ON ME--
--WE'RE GOING IN NOW--

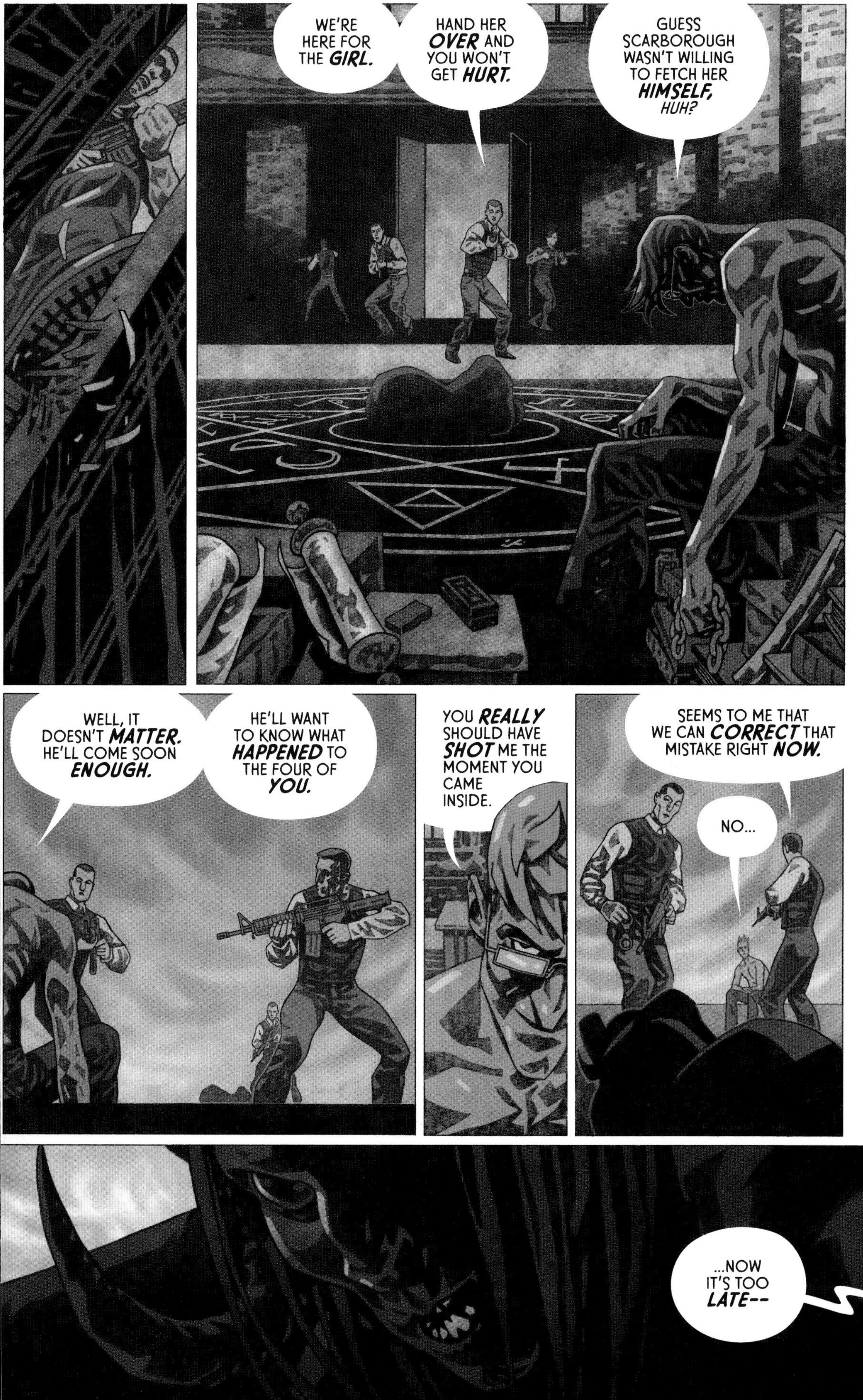
WE'RE HERE FOR THE GIRL.
HAND HER OVER AND YOU WON'T GET HURT.
GUESS SCARBOROUGH WASN'T WILLING TO FETCH HER HIMSELF, HUH?
WELL, IT DOESN'T MATTER. HE'LL COME SOON ENOUGH.
HE'LL WANT TO KNOW WHAT HAPPENED TO THE FOUR OF YOU.
YOU REALLY SHOULD HAVE SHOT ME THE MOMENT YOU CAME INSIDE.
SEEMS TO ME THAT WE CAN CORRECT THAT MISTAKE RIGHT NOW.
NO...
...NOW IT'S TOO LATE--

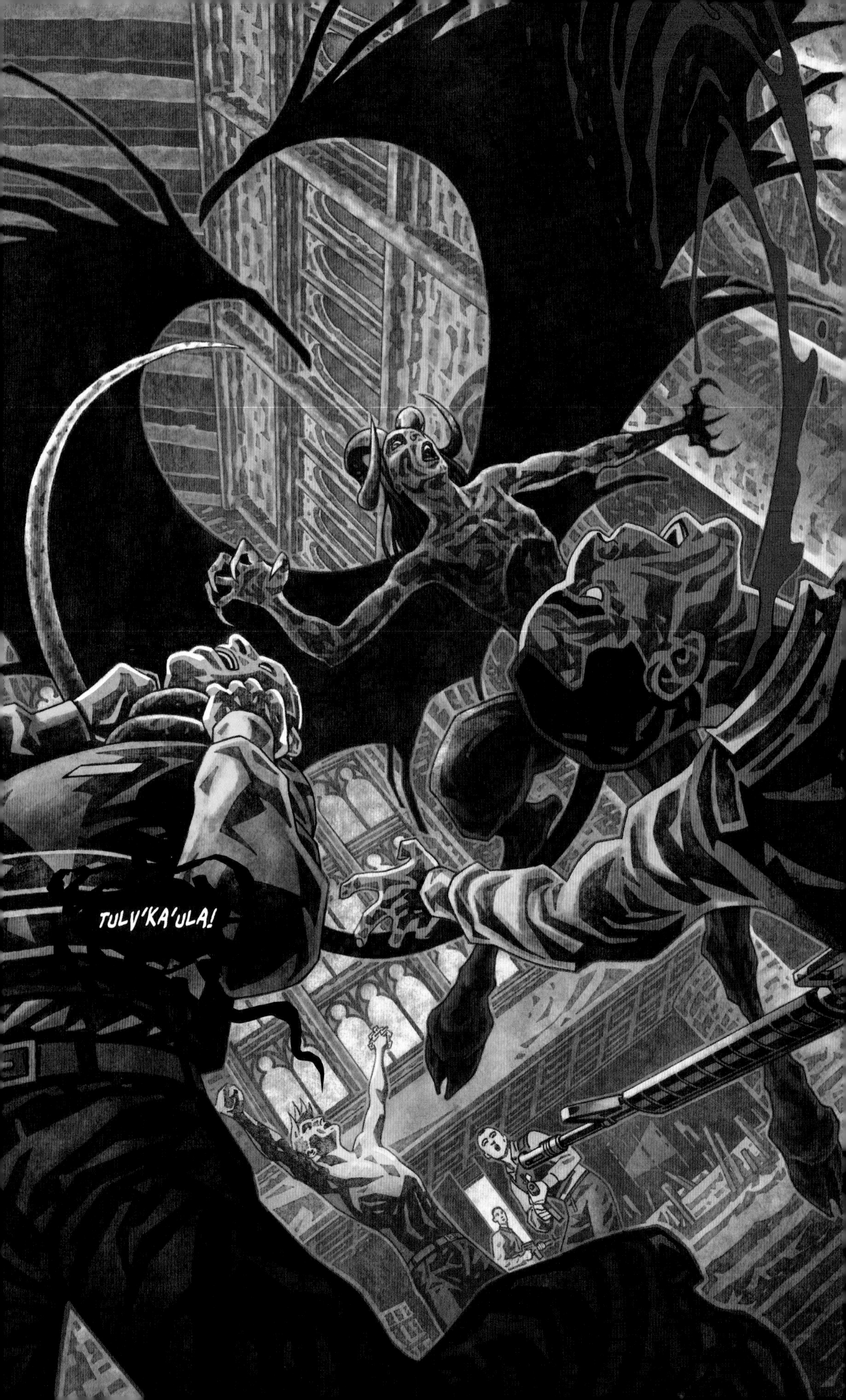
TULV'KA'ULA!

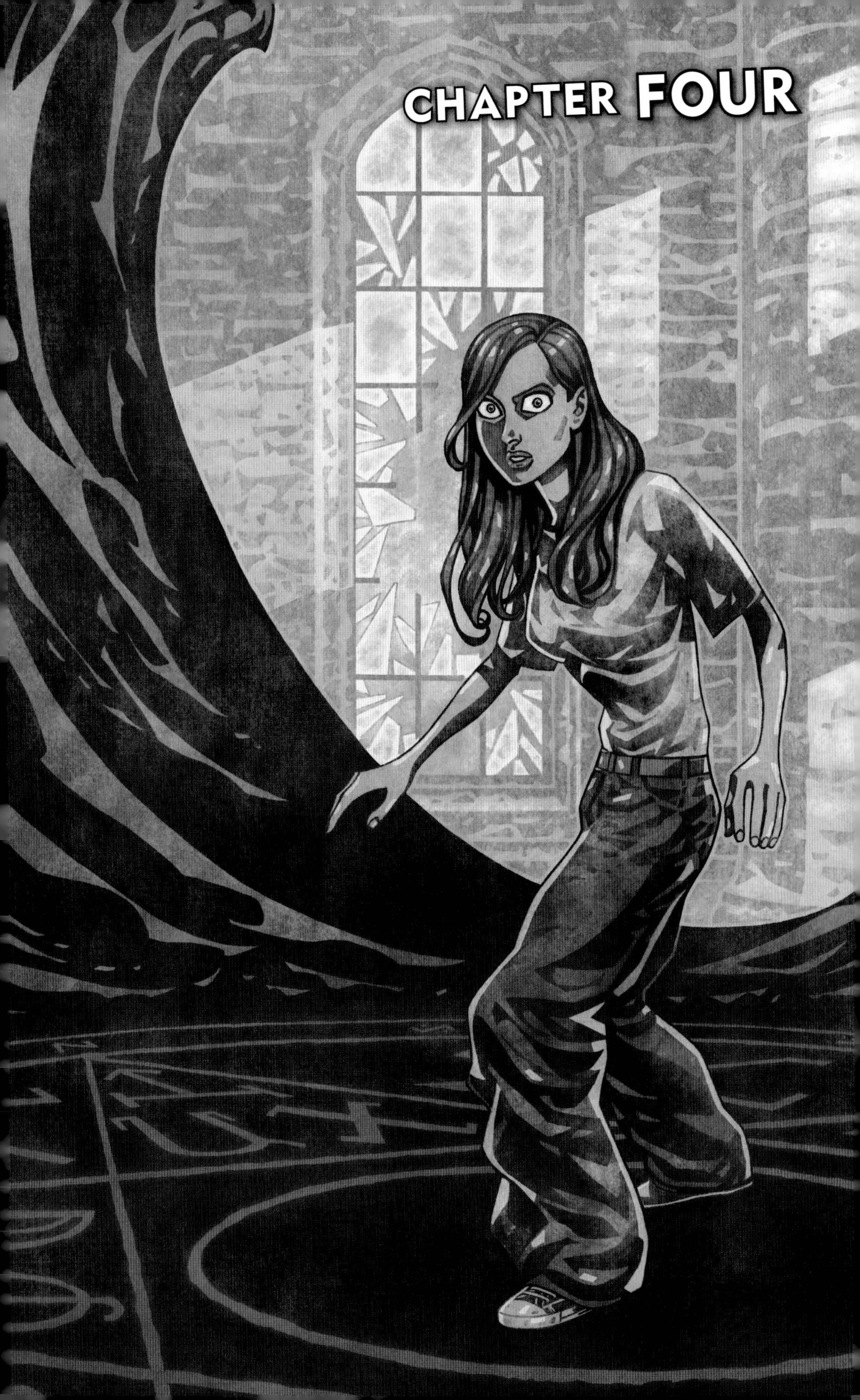
CHAPTER FOUR

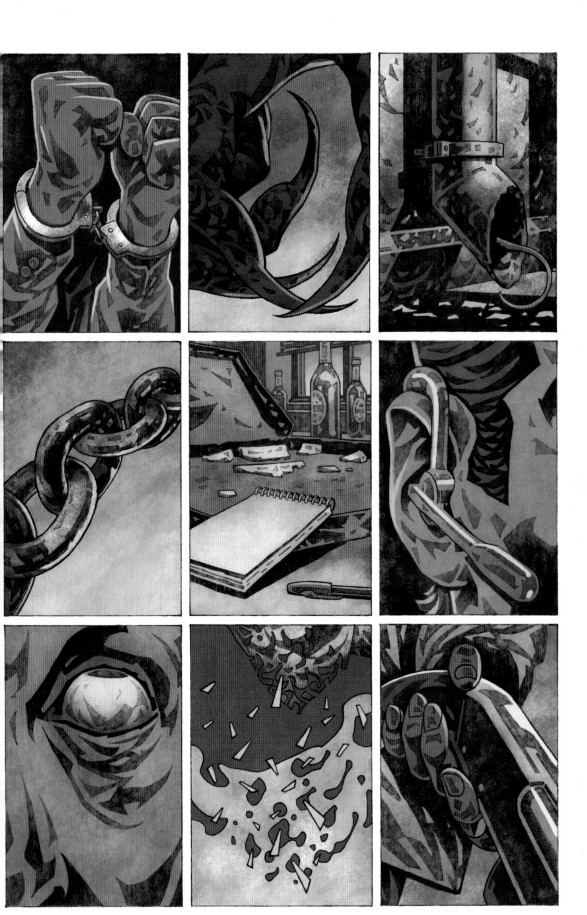

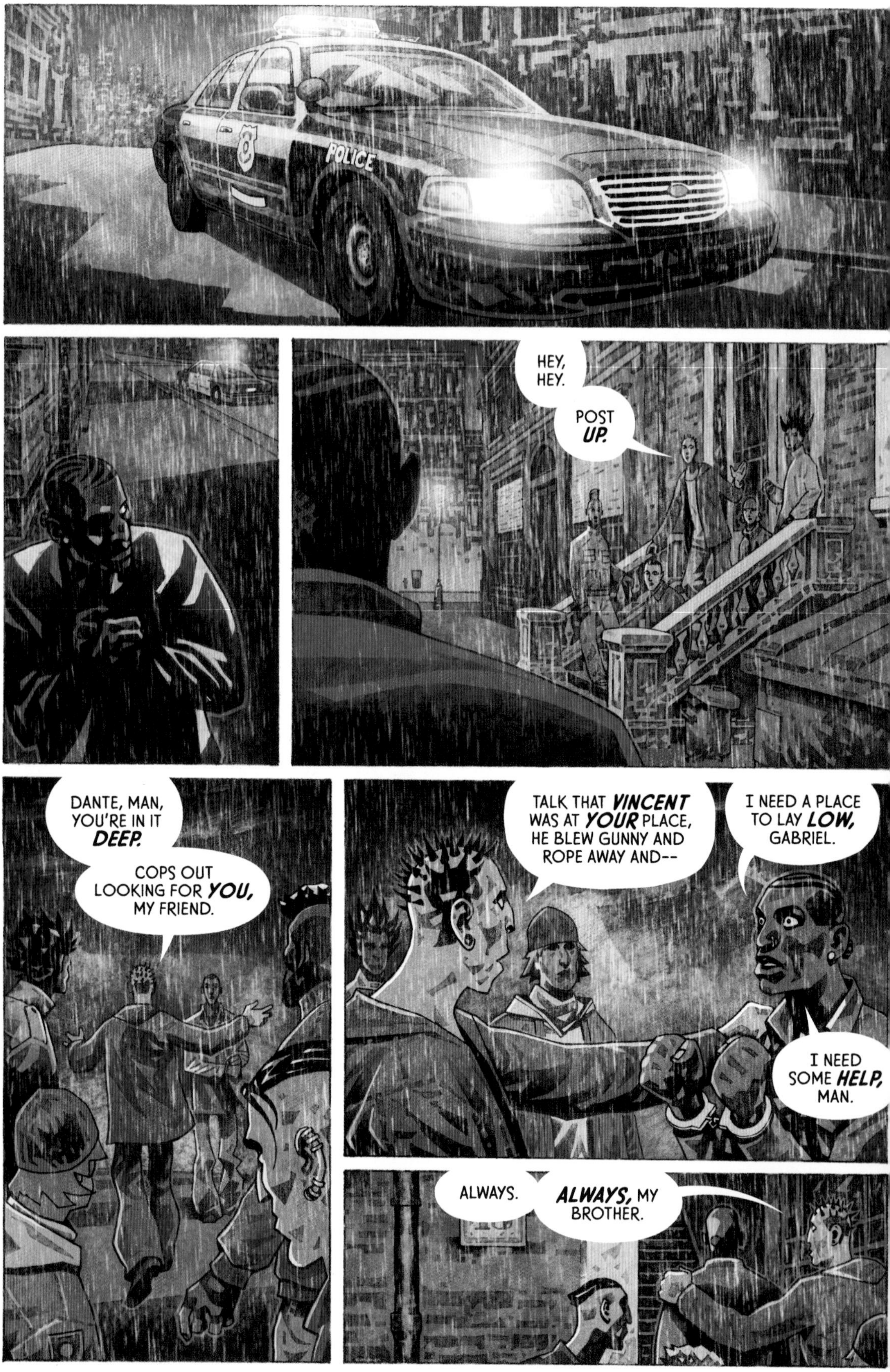
HEY, HEY.
POST UP.
DANTE, MAN, YOU'RE IN IT DEEP.
COPS OUT LOOKING FOR YOU, MY FRIEND.
TALK THAT VINCENT WAS AT YOUR PLACE, HE BLEW GUNNY AND ROPE AWAY AND--
I NEED A PLACE TO LAY LOW, GABRIEL.
I NEED SOME HELP, MAN.
ALWAYS.
ALWAYS, MY BROTHER.

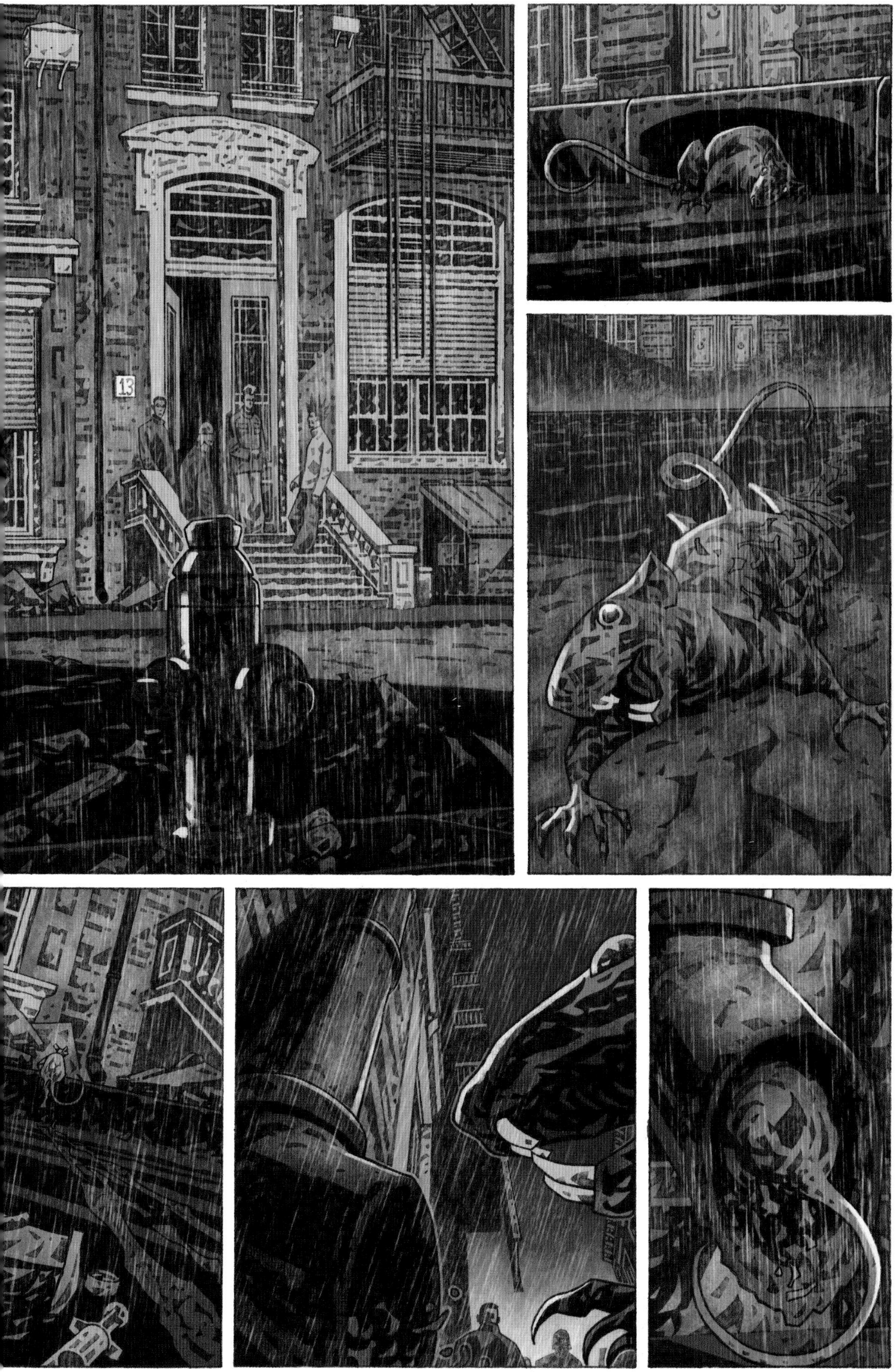
13

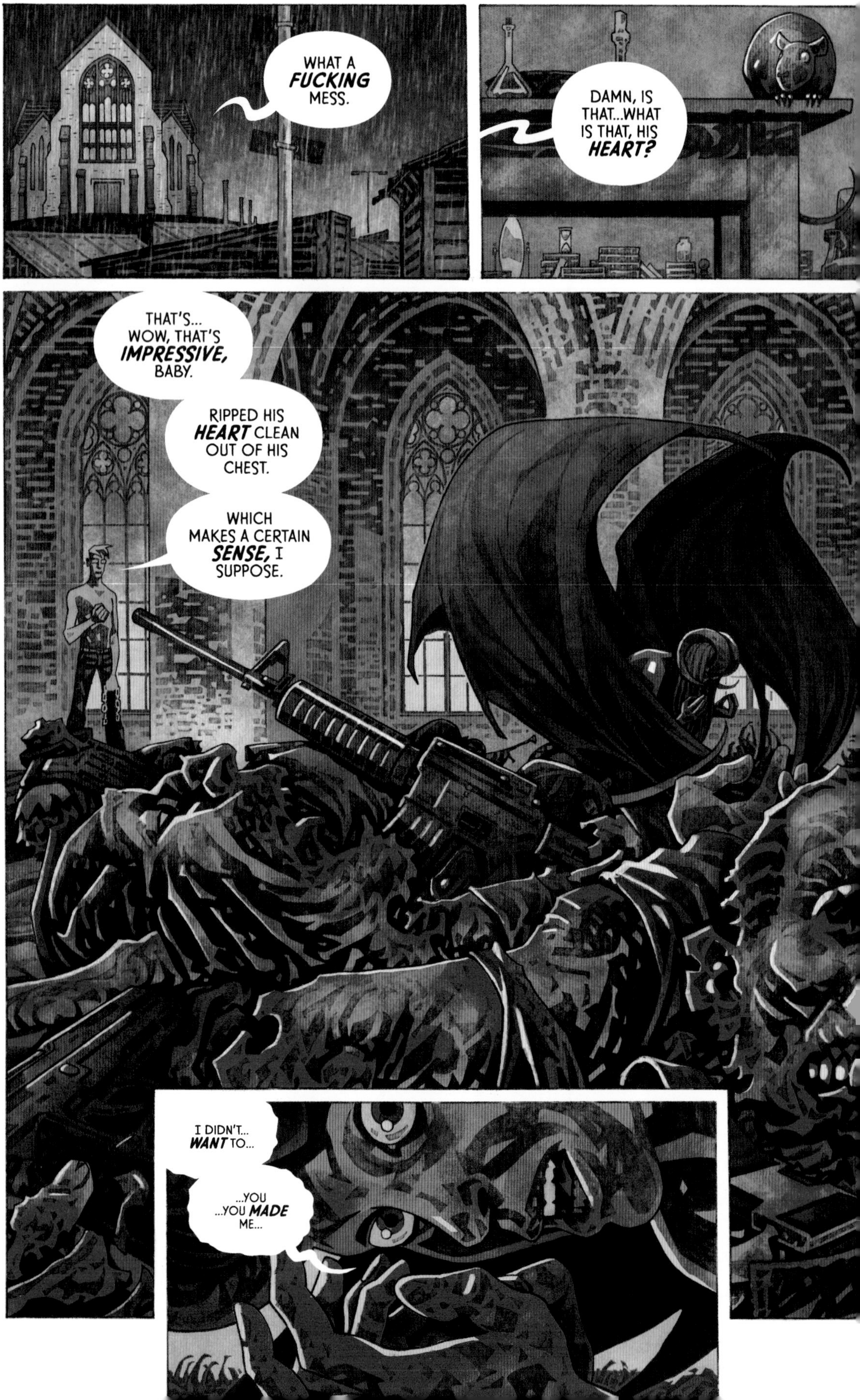
WHAT A FUCKING MESS.
DAMN, IS THAT...WHAT IS THAT, HIS HEART?
THAT'S... WOW, THAT'S IMPRESSIVE, BABY.
RIPPED HIS HEART CLEAN OUT OF HIS CHEST.
WHICH MAKES A CERTAIN SENSE, I SUPPOSE.
I DIDN'T... WANT TO...
...YOU ...YOU MADE ME...

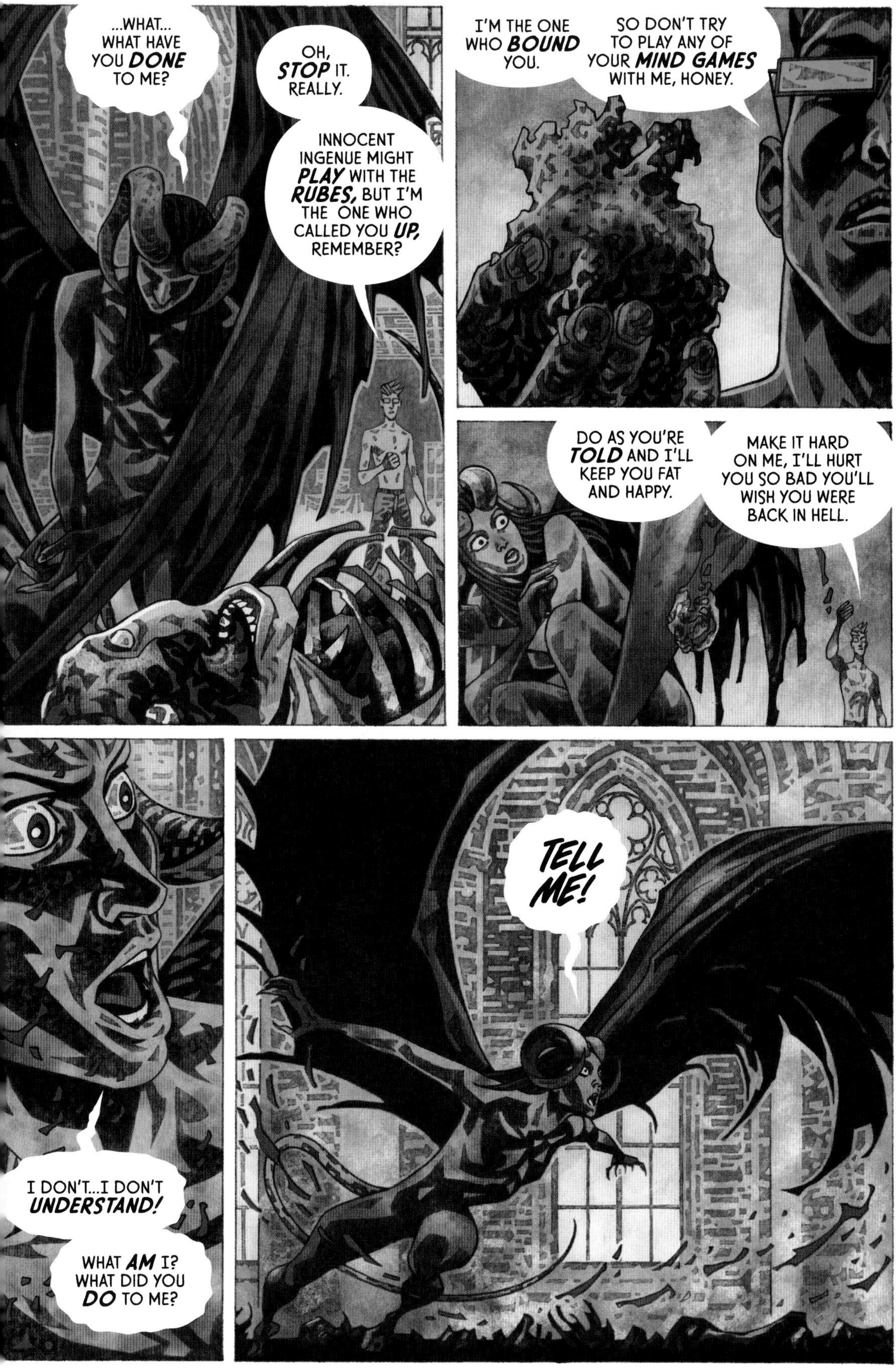
...WHAT... WHAT HAVE YOU DONE TO ME?
OH, STOP IT. REALLY.
INNOCENT INGENUE MIGHT PLAY WITH THE RUBES, BUT I'M THE ONE WHO CALLED YOU UP, REMEMBER?
I'M THE ONE WHO BOUND YOU.
SO DON'T TRY TO PLAY ANY OF YOUR MIND GAMES WITH ME, HONEY.
DO AS YOU'RE TOLD AND I'LL KEEP YOU FAT AND HAPPY.
MAKE IT HARD ON ME, I'LL HURT YOU SO BAD YOU'LL WISH YOU WERE BACK IN HELL.
I DON'T...I DON'T UNDERSTAND!
WHAT AM I? WHAT DID YOU DO TO ME?
TELL ME!

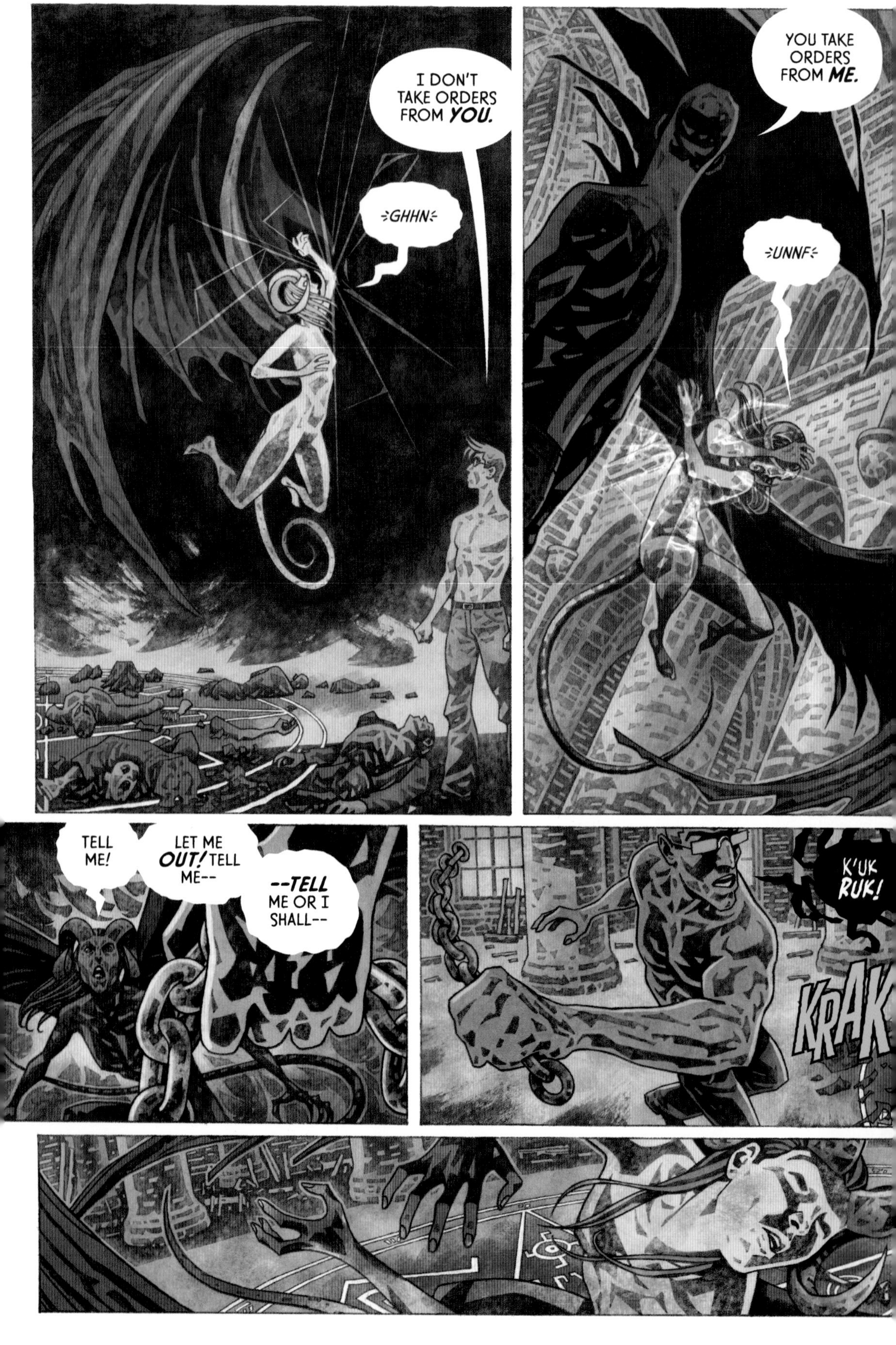
I DON'T TAKE ORDERS FROM *YOU.*
=GHHN=
YOU TAKE ORDERS FROM *ME.*
=UNNF=
TELL ME!
LET ME *OUT!* TELL ME--
--TELL ME OR I SHALL--
K'UK RUK!
KRAK

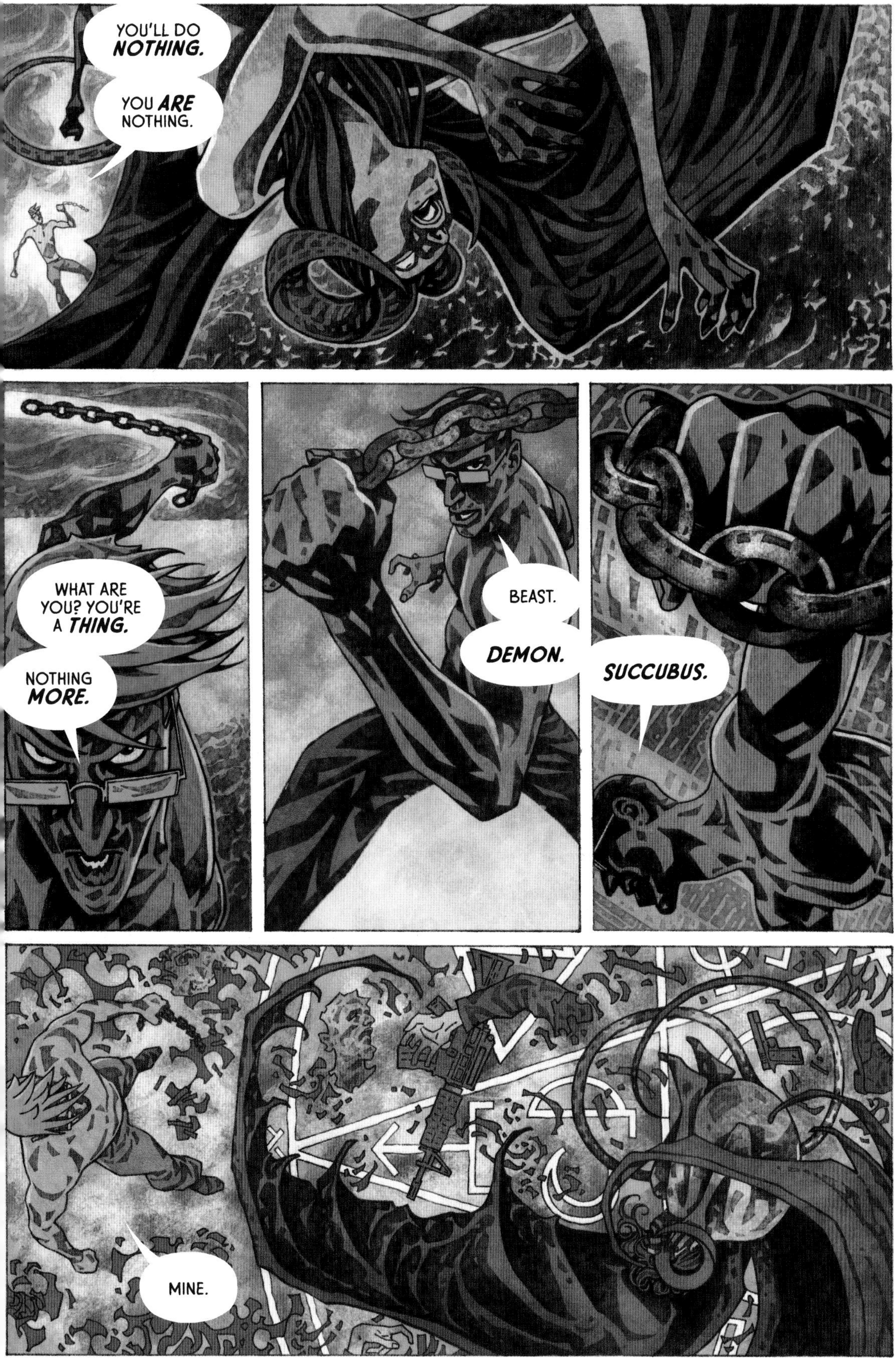
YOU'LL DO NOTHING.
YOU ARE NOTHING.
WHAT ARE YOU? YOU'RE A THING.
NOTHING MORE.
BEAST.
DEMON.
SUCCUBUS.
MINE.

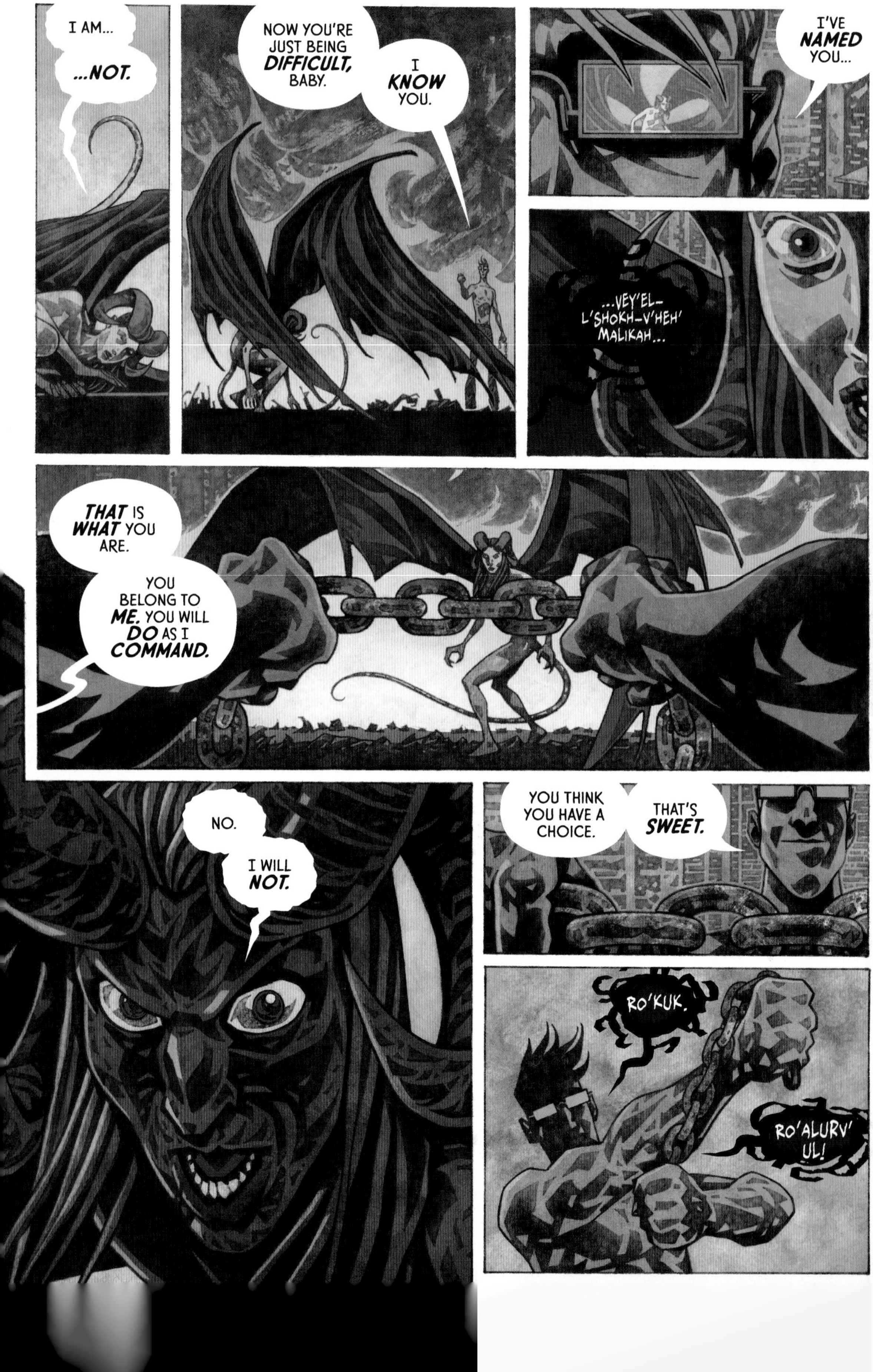
I AM...
...NOT.
NOW YOU'RE JUST BEING DIFFICULT, BABY.
I KNOW YOU.
I'VE NAMED YOU...
...VEY'EL-L'SHOKH-V'HEH' MALIKAH...
THAT IS WHAT YOU ARE.
YOU BELONG TO ME. YOU WILL DO AS I COMMAND.
NO.
I WILL NOT.
YOU THINK YOU HAVE A CHOICE.
THAT'S SWEET.
RO'KUK.
RO'ALURV'UL!

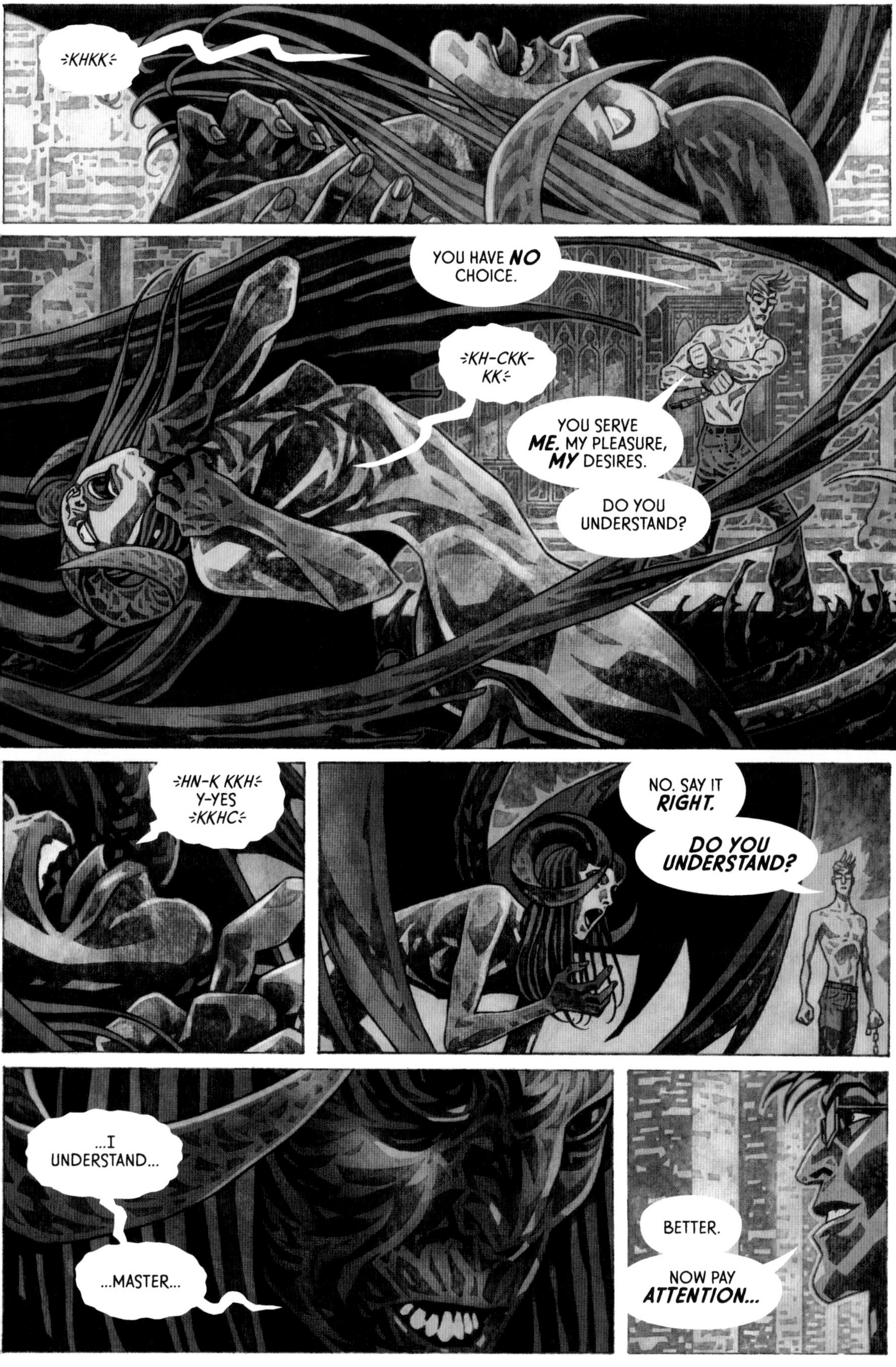

=KHKK=
YOU HAVE NO CHOICE.
=KH-CKK-KK=
YOU SERVE ME. MY PLEASURE, MY DESIRES.
DO YOU UNDERSTAND?
=HN-K KKH= Y-YES =KKHC=
NO. SAY IT RIGHT.
DO YOU UNDERSTAND?
...I UNDERSTAND...
...MASTER...
BETTER.
NOW PAY ATTENTION...

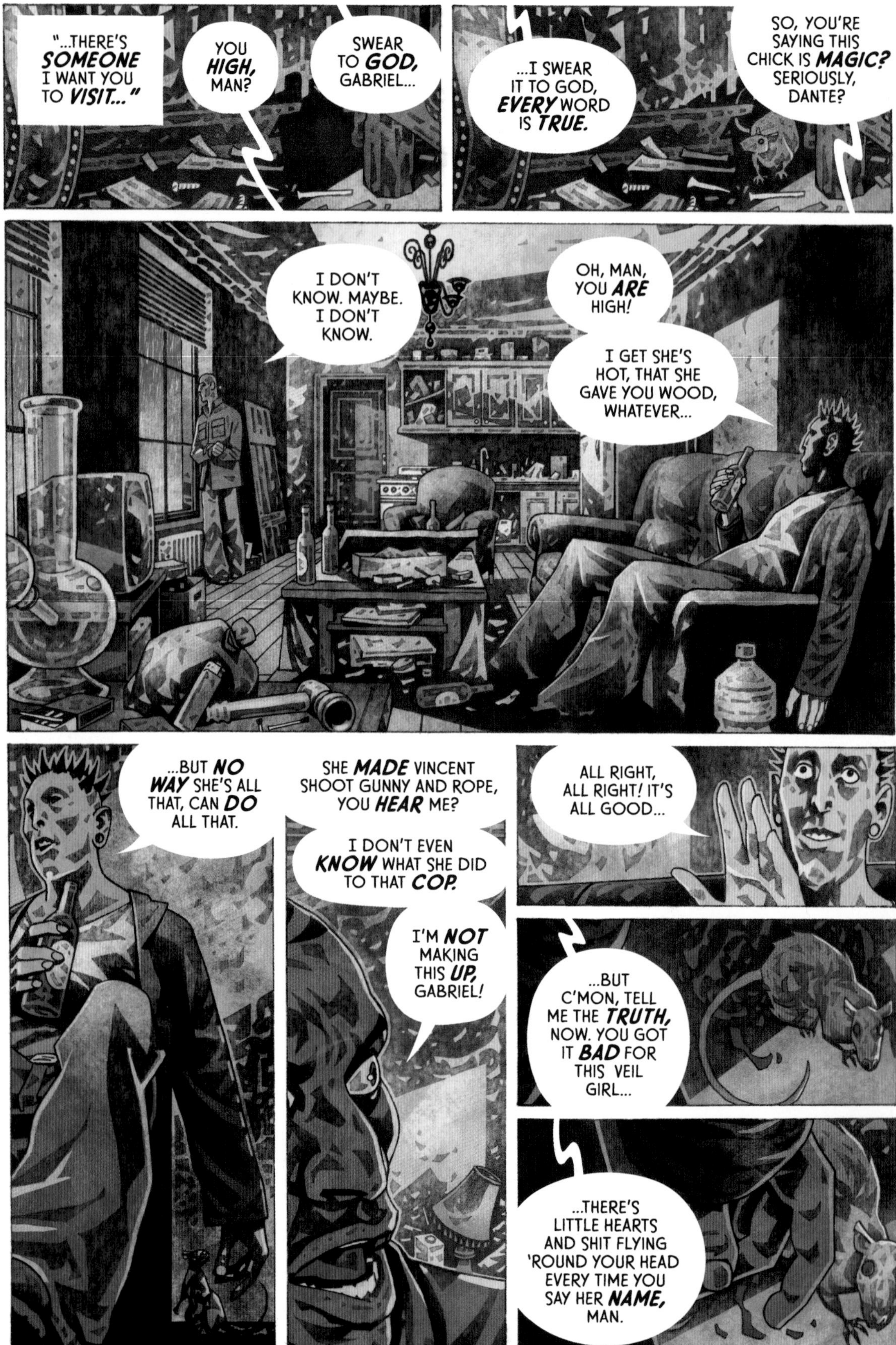
"...THERE'S SOMEONE I WANT YOU TO VISIT..."
YOU HIGH, MAN?
SWEAR TO GOD, GABRIEL...
...I SWEAR IT TO GOD, EVERY WORD IS TRUE.
SO, YOU'RE SAYING THIS CHICK IS MAGIC? SERIOUSLY, DANTE?
I DON'T KNOW. MAYBE. I DON'T KNOW.
OH, MAN, YOU ARE HIGH!
I GET SHE'S HOT, THAT SHE GAVE YOU WOOD, WHATEVER...
...BUT NO WAY SHE'S ALL THAT, CAN DO ALL THAT.
SHE MADE VINCENT SHOOT GUNNY AND ROPE, YOU HEAR ME?
I DON'T EVEN KNOW WHAT SHE DID TO THAT COP.
I'M NOT MAKING THIS UP, GABRIEL!
ALL RIGHT, ALL RIGHT! IT'S ALL GOOD...
...BUT C'MON, TELL ME THE TRUTH, NOW. YOU GOT IT BAD FOR THIS VEIL GIRL...
...THERE'S LITTLE HEARTS AND SHIT FLYING 'ROUND YOUR HEAD EVERY TIME YOU SAY HER NAME, MAN.

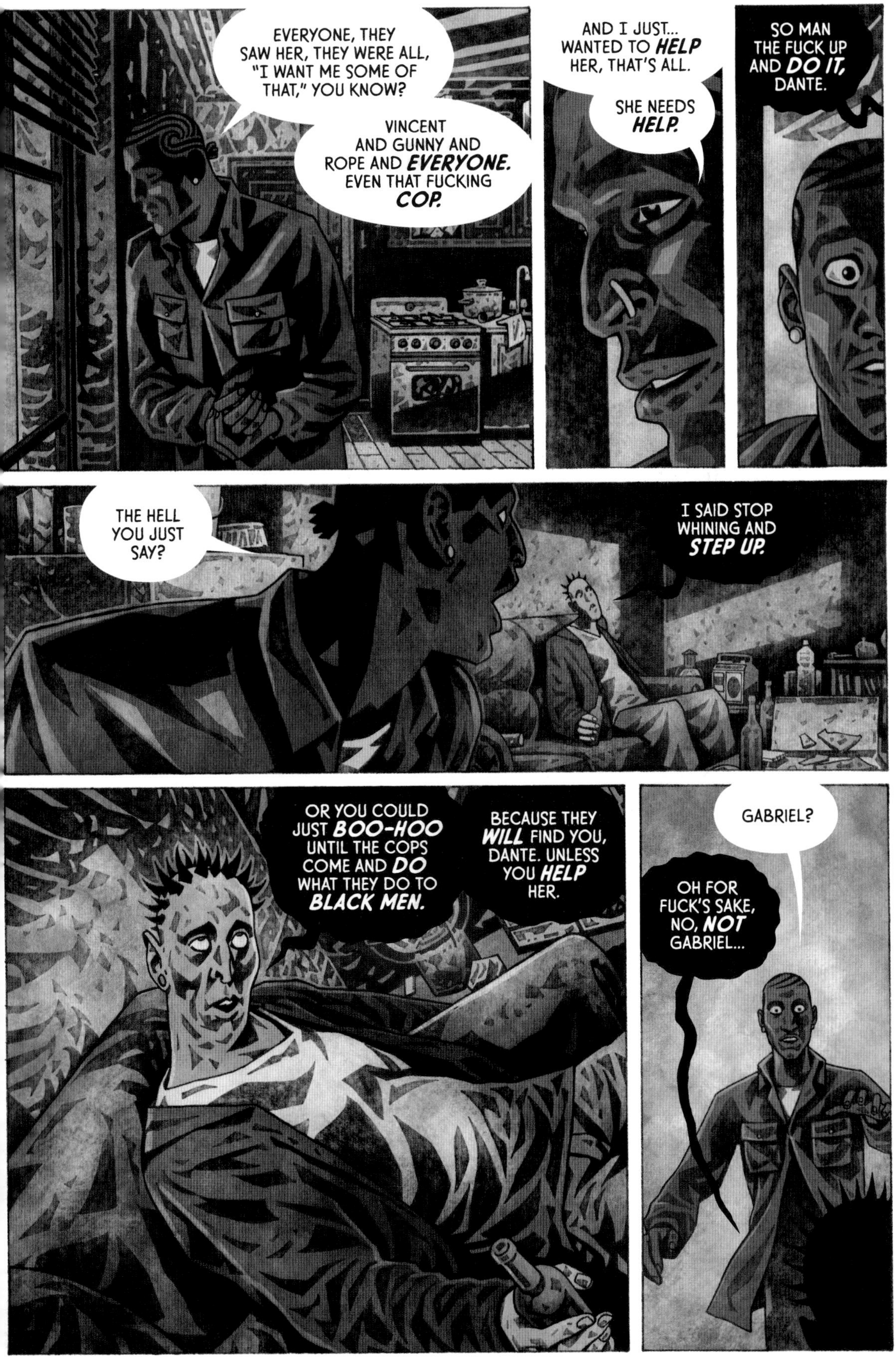
EVERYONE, THEY SAW HER, THEY WERE ALL, "I WANT ME SOME OF THAT," YOU KNOW?
VINCENT AND GUNNY AND ROPE AND EVERYONE. EVEN THAT FUCKING COP.
AND I JUST... WANTED TO HELP HER, THAT'S ALL.
SHE NEEDS HELP.
SO MAN THE FUCK UP AND DO IT, DANTE.
THE HELL YOU JUST SAY?
I SAID STOP WHINING AND STEP UP.
OR YOU COULD JUST BOO-HOO UNTIL THE COPS COME AND DO WHAT THEY DO TO BLACK MEN.
BECAUSE THEY WILL FIND YOU, DANTE. UNLESS YOU HELP HER.
GABRIEL?
OH FOR FUCK'S SAKE, NO, NOT GABRIEL...

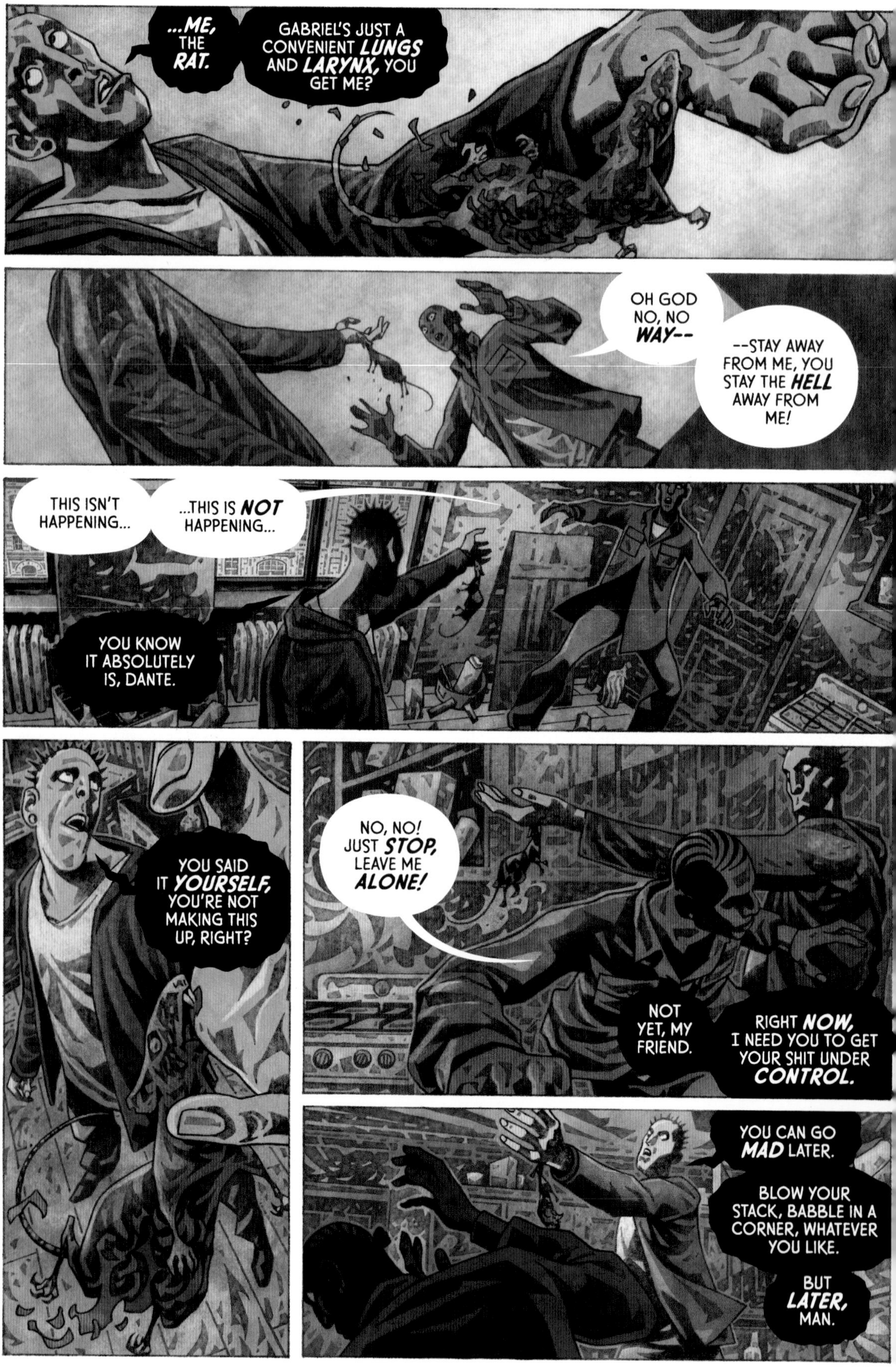
...ME, THE RAT.
GABRIEL'S JUST A CONVENIENT LUNGS AND LARYNX, YOU GET ME?
OH GOD NO, NO WAY--
--STAY AWAY FROM ME, YOU STAY THE HELL AWAY FROM ME!
THIS ISN'T HAPPENING...
...THIS IS NOT HAPPENING...
YOU KNOW IT ABSOLUTELY IS, DANTE.
YOU SAID IT YOURSELF, YOU'RE NOT MAKING THIS UP, RIGHT?
NO, NO! JUST STOP, LEAVE ME ALONE!
NOT YET, MY FRIEND.
RIGHT NOW, I NEED YOU TO GET YOUR SHIT UNDER CONTROL.
YOU CAN GO MAD LATER.
BLOW YOUR STACK, BABBLE IN A CORNER, WHATEVER YOU LIKE.
BUT LATER, MAN.

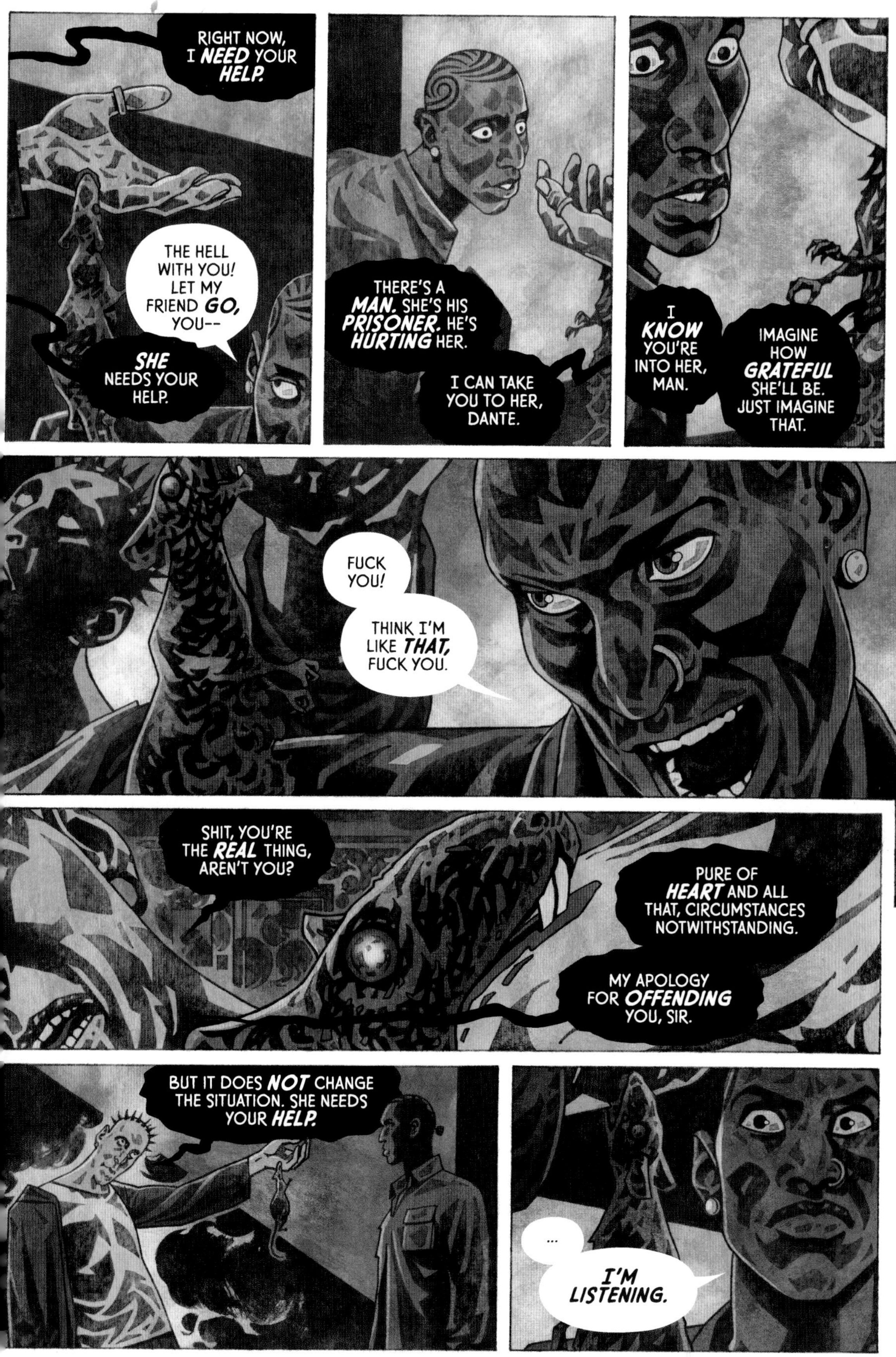
RIGHT NOW, I NEED YOUR HELP.
THE HELL WITH YOU! LET MY FRIEND GO, YOU--
SHE NEEDS YOUR HELP.
THERE'S A MAN. SHE'S HIS PRISONER. HE'S HURTING HER.
I CAN TAKE YOU TO HER, DANTE.
I KNOW YOU'RE INTO HER, MAN.
IMAGINE HOW GRATEFUL SHE'LL BE. JUST IMAGINE THAT.
FUCK YOU!
THINK I'M LIKE THAT, FUCK YOU.
SHIT, YOU'RE THE REAL THING, AREN'T YOU?
PURE OF HEART AND ALL THAT, CIRCUMSTANCES NOTWITHSTANDING.
MY APOLOGY FOR OFFENDING YOU, SIR.
BUT IT DOES NOT CHANGE THE SITUATION. SHE NEEDS YOUR HELP.
...
I'M LISTENING.

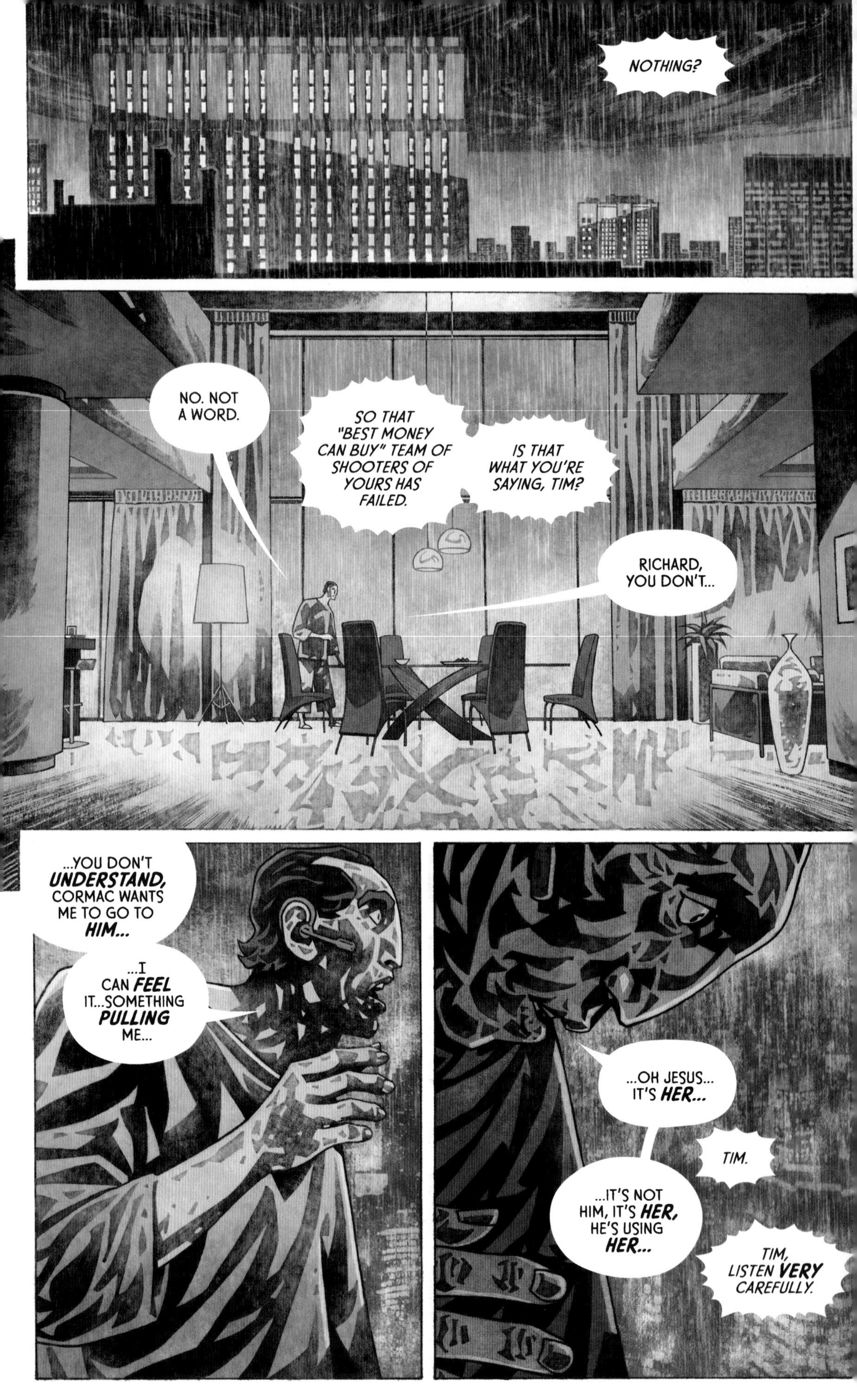
NOTHING?
NO. NOT A WORD.
SO THAT "BEST MONEY CAN BUY" TEAM OF SHOOTERS OF YOURS HAS FAILED.
IS THAT WHAT YOU'RE SAYING, TIM?
RICHARD, YOU DON'T...
...YOU DON'T UNDERSTAND, CORMAC WANTS ME TO GO TO HIM...
...I CAN FEEL IT...SOMETHING PULLING ME...
...OH JESUS... IT'S HER...
TIM.
...IT'S NOT HIM, IT'S HER, HE'S USING HER...
TIM, LISTEN VERY CAREFULLY.

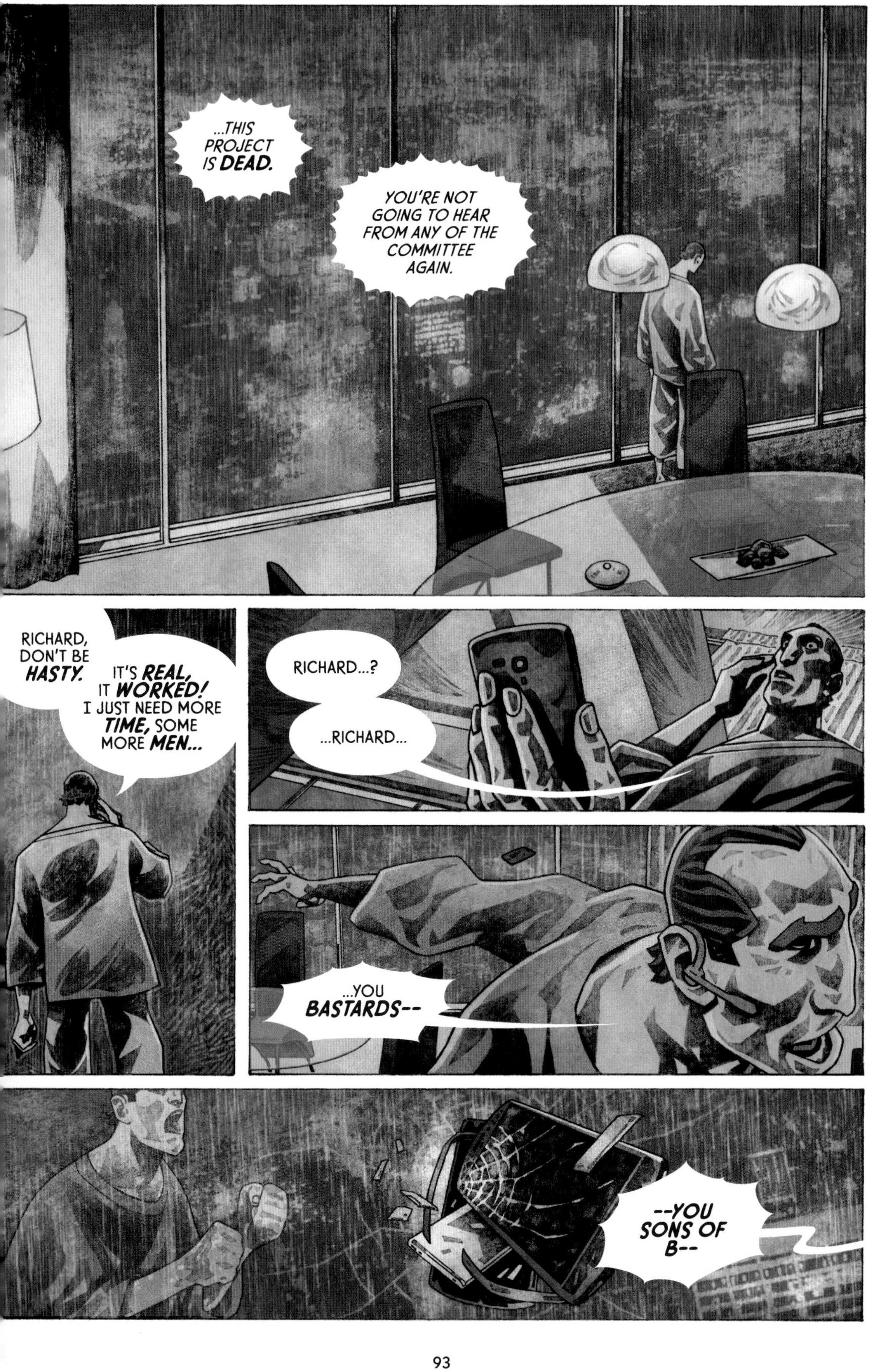
...THIS PROJECT IS DEAD.
YOU'RE NOT GOING TO HEAR FROM ANY OF THE COMMITTEE AGAIN.
RICHARD, DON'T BE HASTY.
IT'S REAL, IT WORKED! I JUST NEED MORE TIME, SOME MORE MEN...
RICHARD...?
...RICHARD...
...YOU BASTARDS--
--YOU SONS OF B--

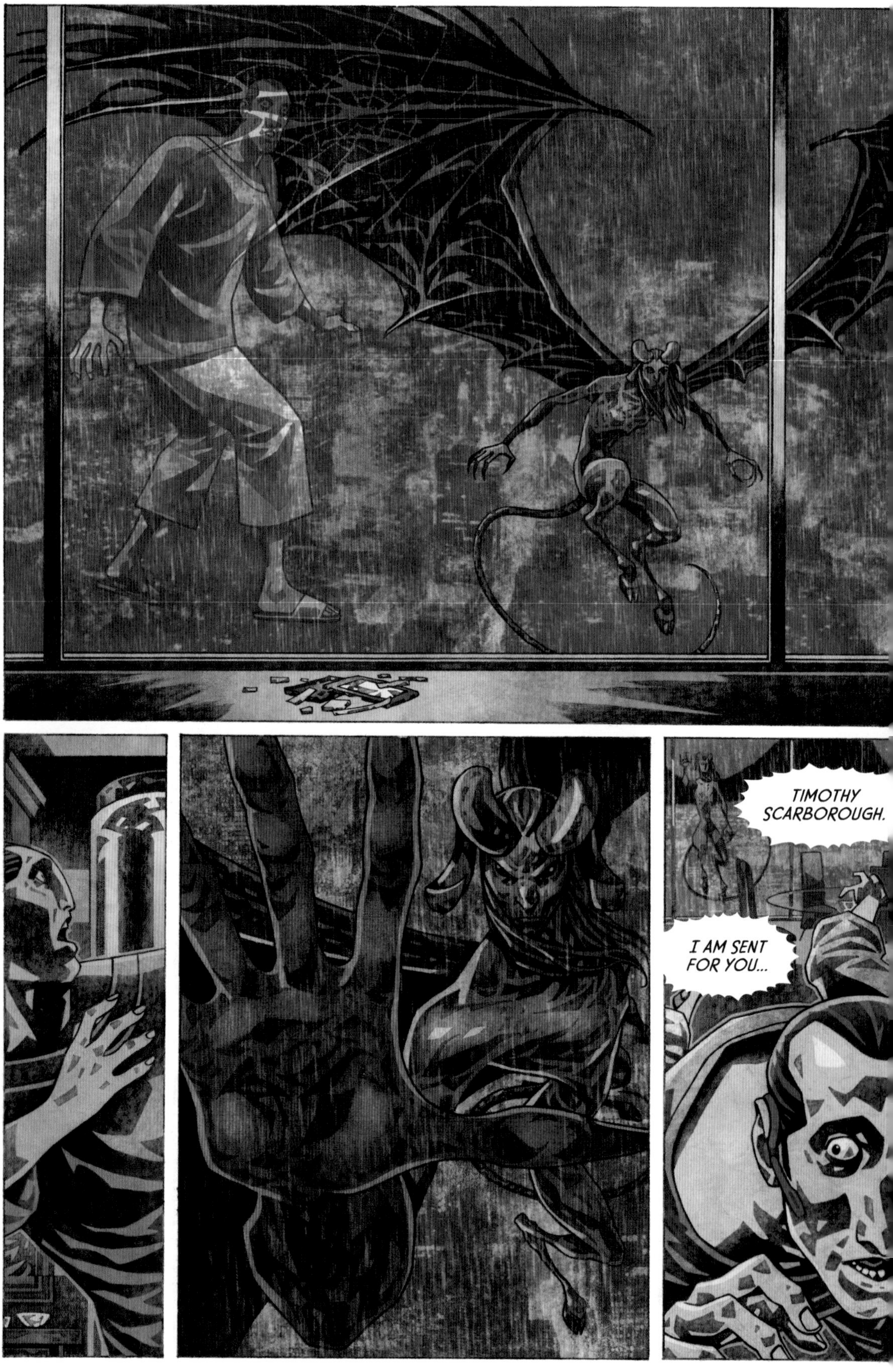
TIMOTHY
SCARBOROUGH.
I AM SENT
FOR YOU...

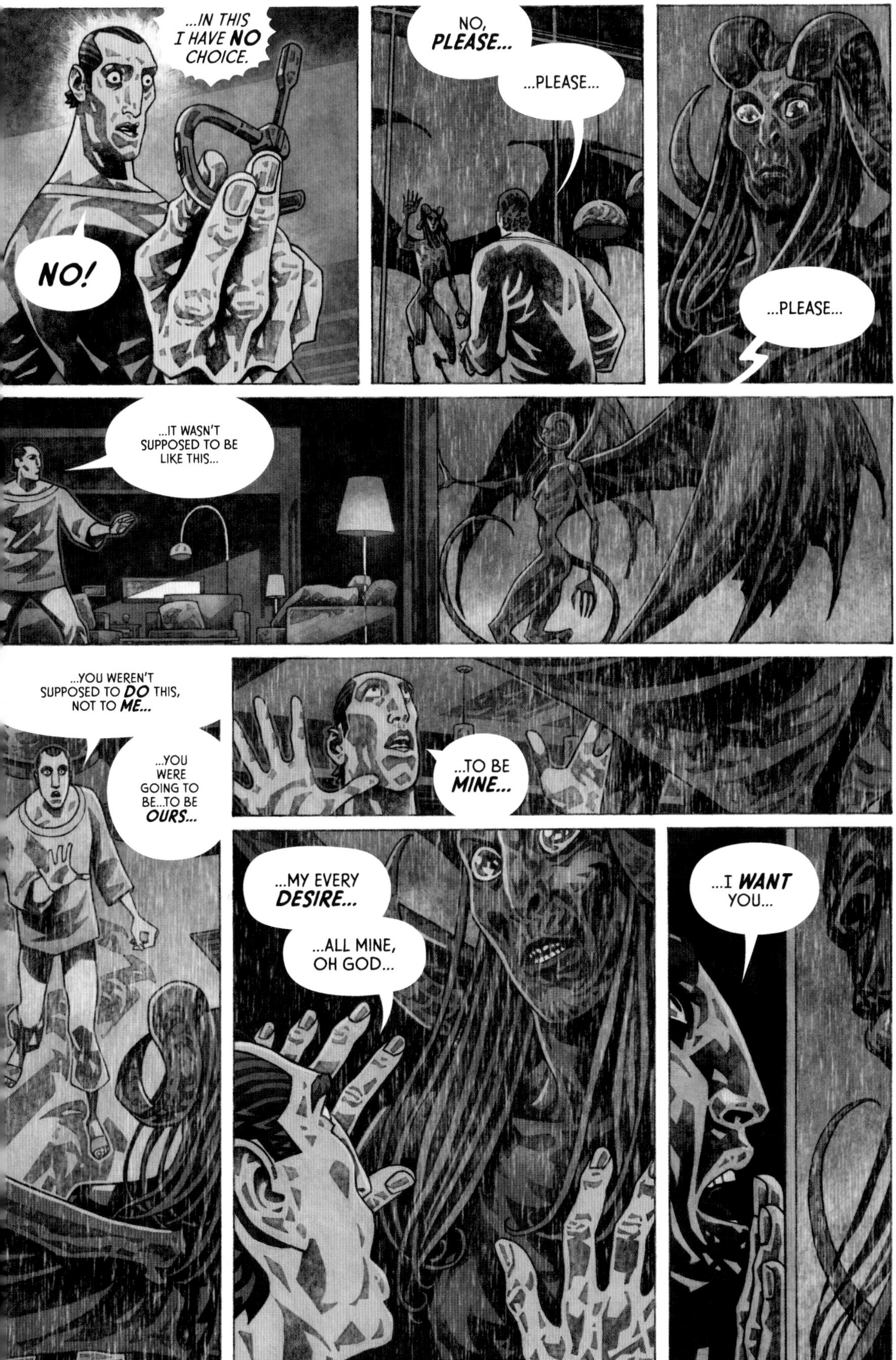
...IN THIS I HAVE NO CHOICE.
NO!
NO, PLEASE...
...PLEASE...
...PLEASE...
...IT WASN'T SUPPOSED TO BE LIKE THIS...
...YOU WEREN'T SUPPOSED TO DO THIS, NOT TO ME...
...YOU WERE GOING TO BE...TO BE OURS...
...TO BE MINE...
...MY EVERY DESIRE...
...ALL MINE, OH GOD...
...I WANT YOU...

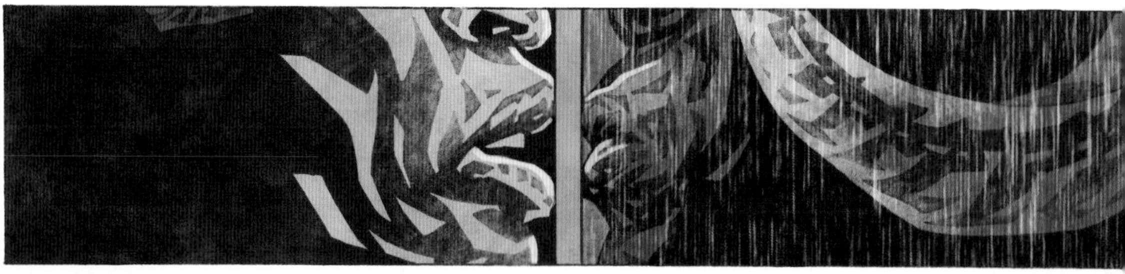

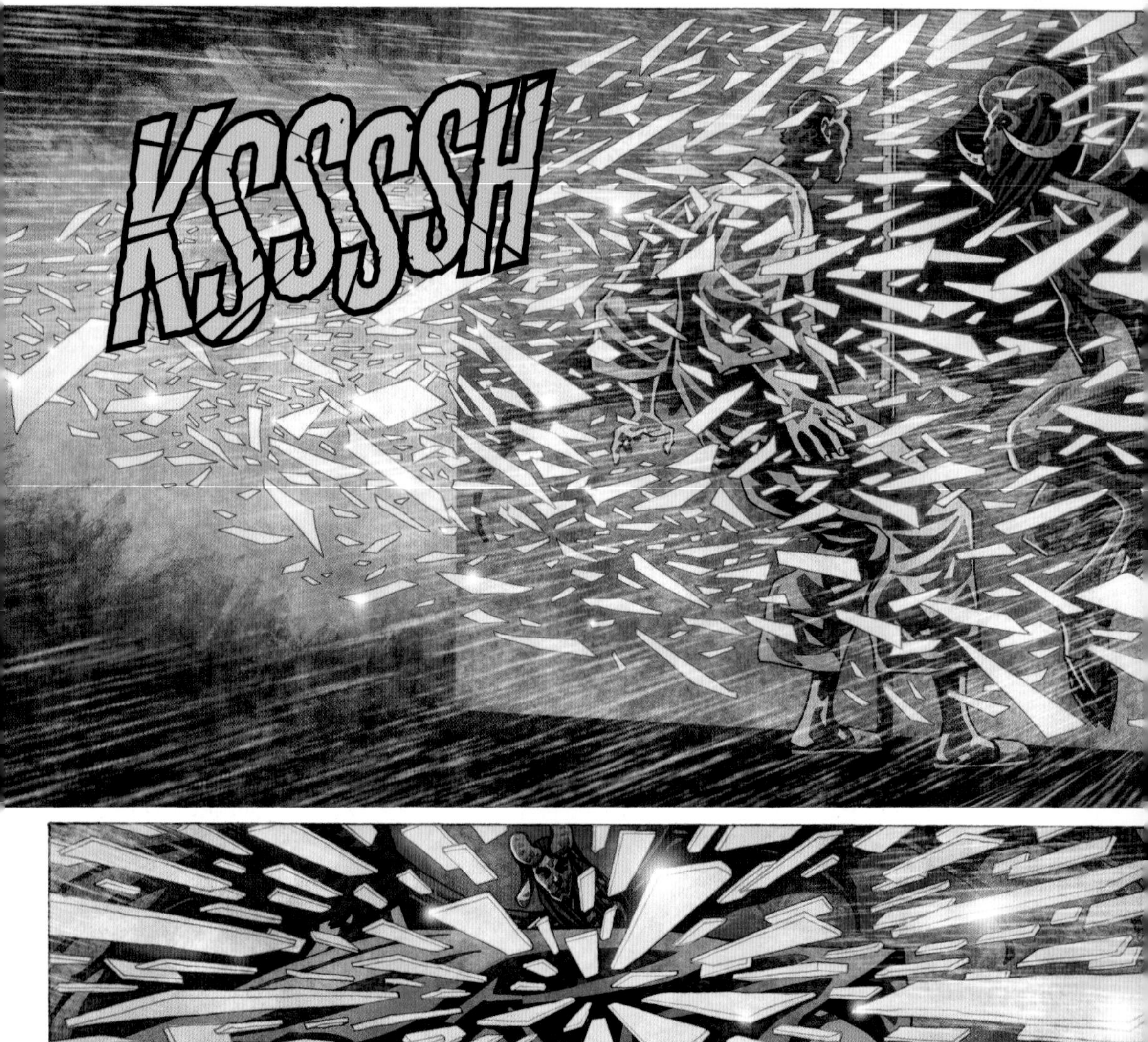
KSSSSH

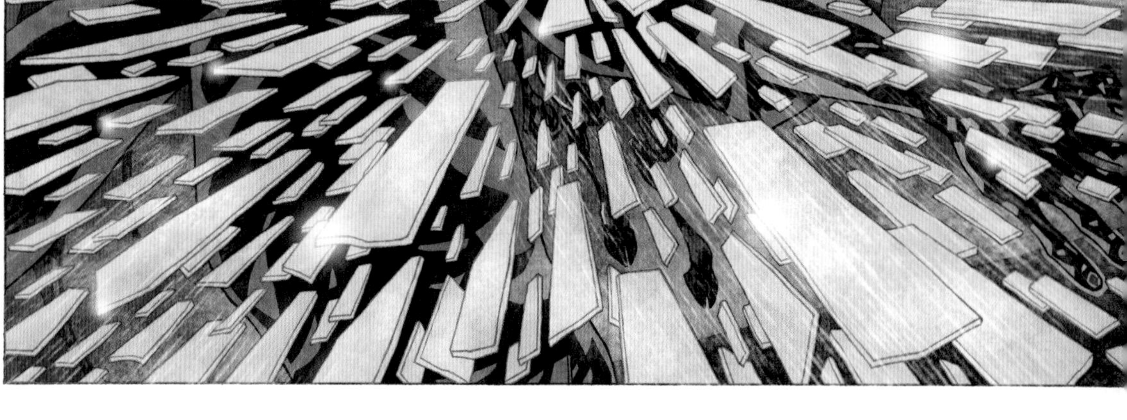

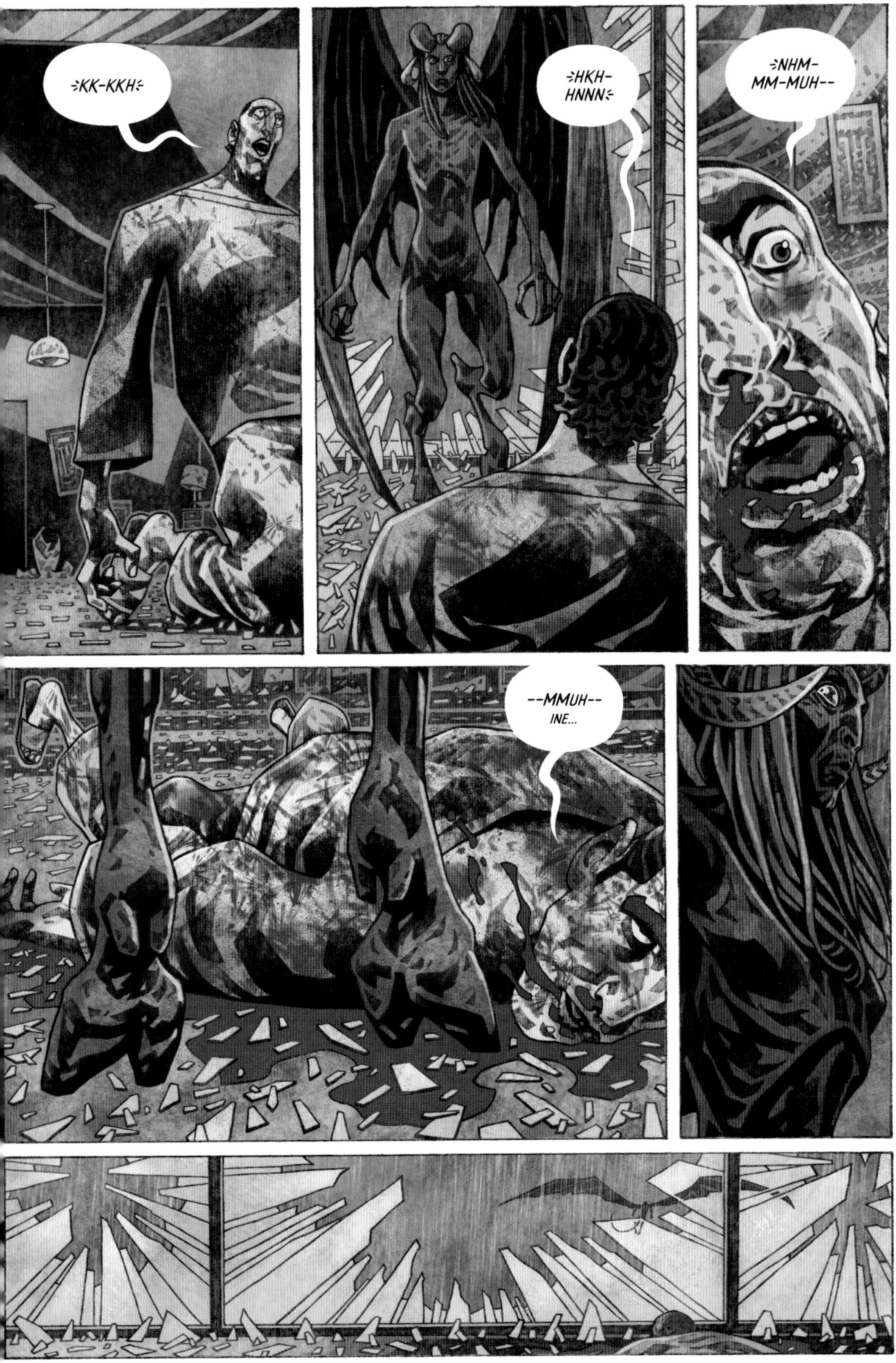

KK-KKH
HKH-
HNNN
NHM-
MM-MUH--
--MMUH--
INE...

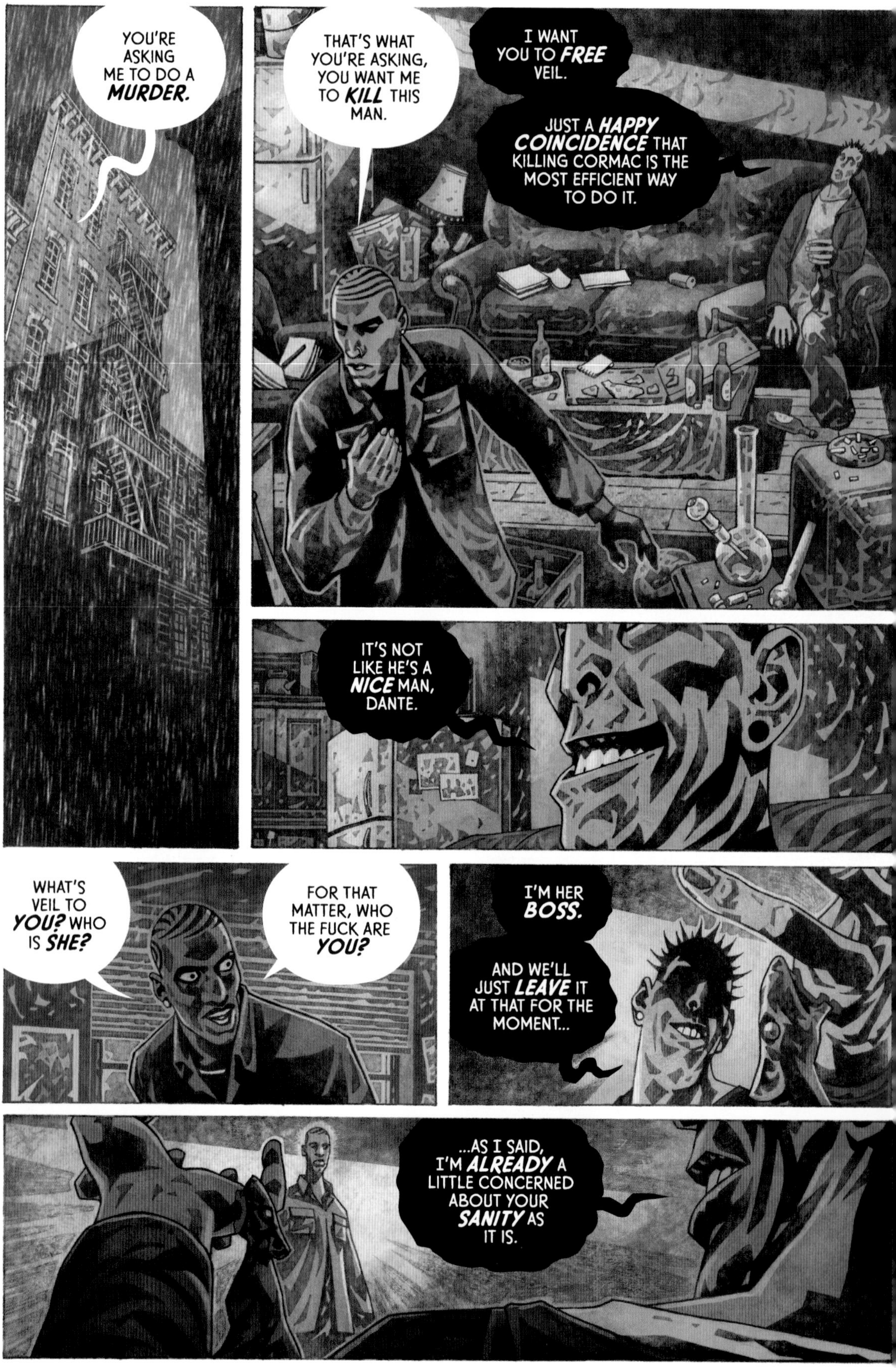

YOU'RE ASKING ME TO DO A MURDER.
THAT'S WHAT YOU'RE ASKING, YOU WANT ME TO KILL THIS MAN.
I WANT YOU TO FREE VEIL.
JUST A HAPPY COINCIDENCE THAT KILLING CORMAC IS THE MOST EFFICIENT WAY TO DO IT.
IT'S NOT LIKE HE'S A NICE MAN, DANTE.
WHAT'S VEIL TO YOU? WHO IS SHE?
FOR THAT MATTER, WHO THE FUCK ARE YOU?
I'M HER BOSS.
AND WE'LL JUST LEAVE IT AT THAT FOR THE MOMENT...
...AS I SAID, I'M ALREADY A LITTLE CONCERNED ABOUT YOUR SANITY AS IT IS.

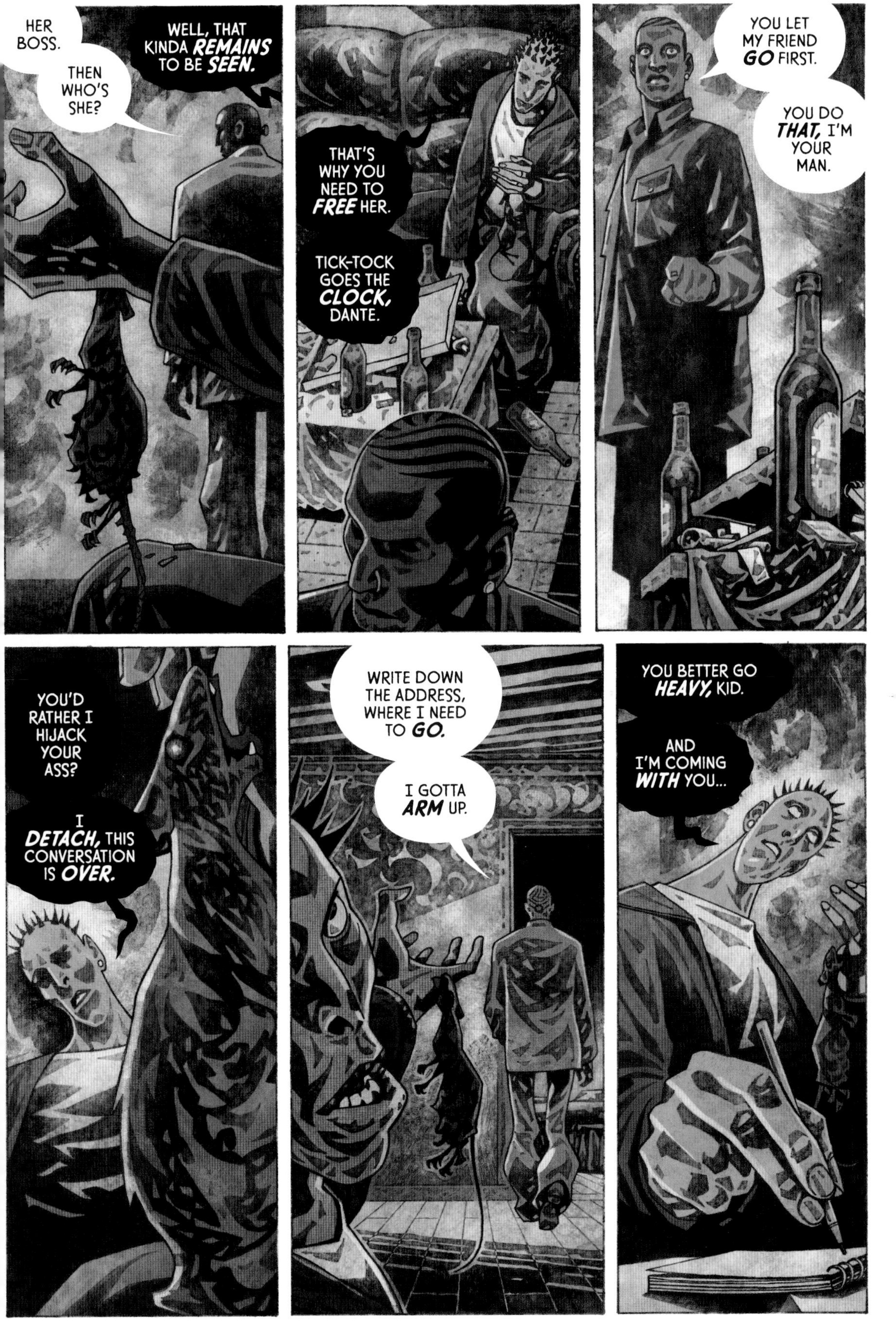

HER BOSS.
THEN WHO'S SHE?
WELL, THAT KINDA REMAINS TO BE SEEN.
THAT'S WHY YOU NEED TO FREE HER.
TICK-TOCK GOES THE CLOCK, DANTE.
YOU LET MY FRIEND GO FIRST.
YOU DO THAT, I'M YOUR MAN.
YOU'D RATHER I HIJACK YOUR ASS?
I DETACH, THIS CONVERSATION IS OVER.
WRITE DOWN THE ADDRESS, WHERE I NEED TO GO.
I GOTTA ARM UP.
YOU BETTER GO HEAVY, KID.
AND I'M COMING WITH YOU...

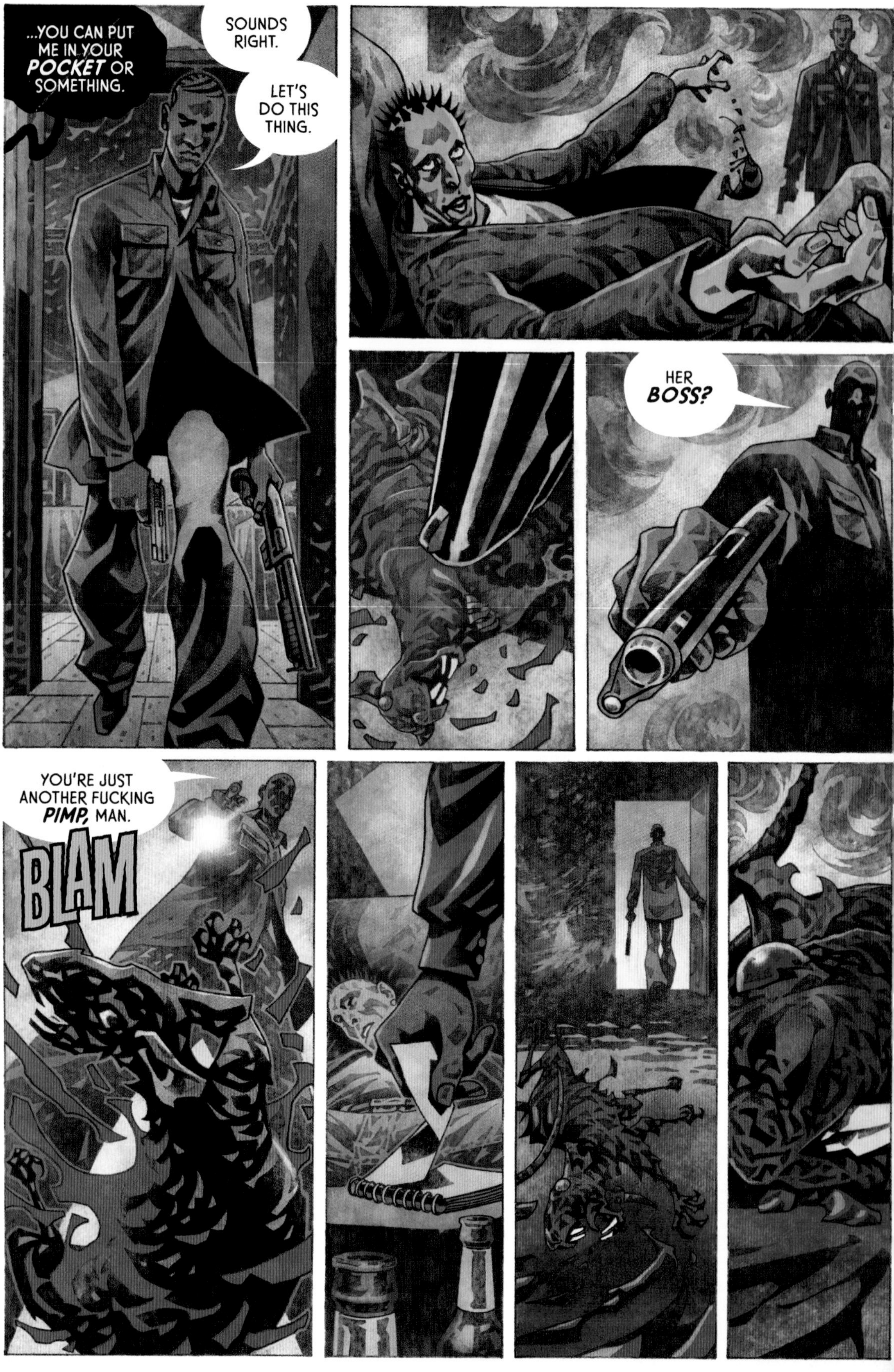
...YOU CAN PUT ME IN YOUR POCKET OR SOMETHING.
SOUNDS RIGHT.
LET'S DO THIS THING.
HER BOSS?
YOU'RE JUST ANOTHER FUCKING PIMP, MAN.
BLAM

CHAPTER FIVE

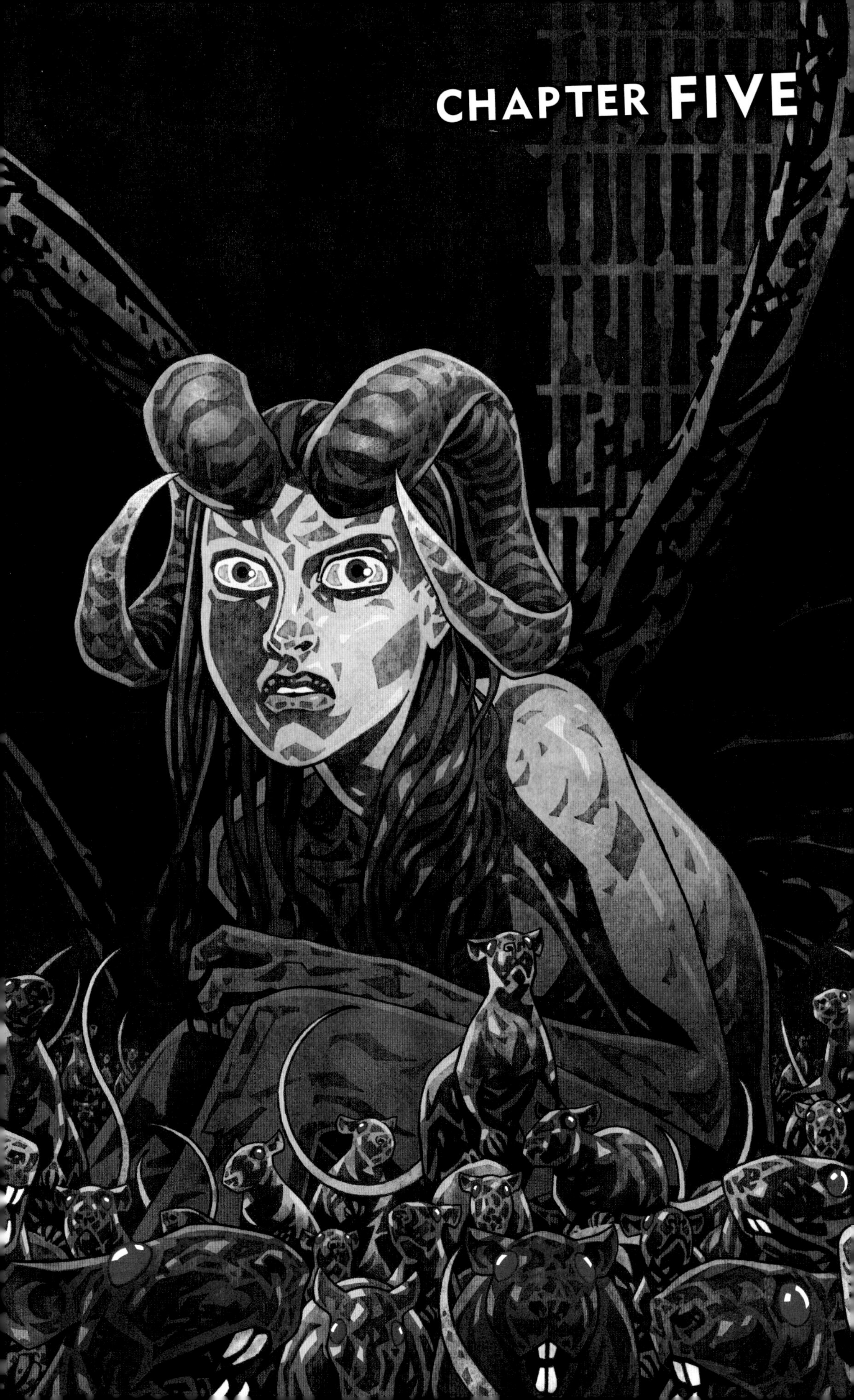

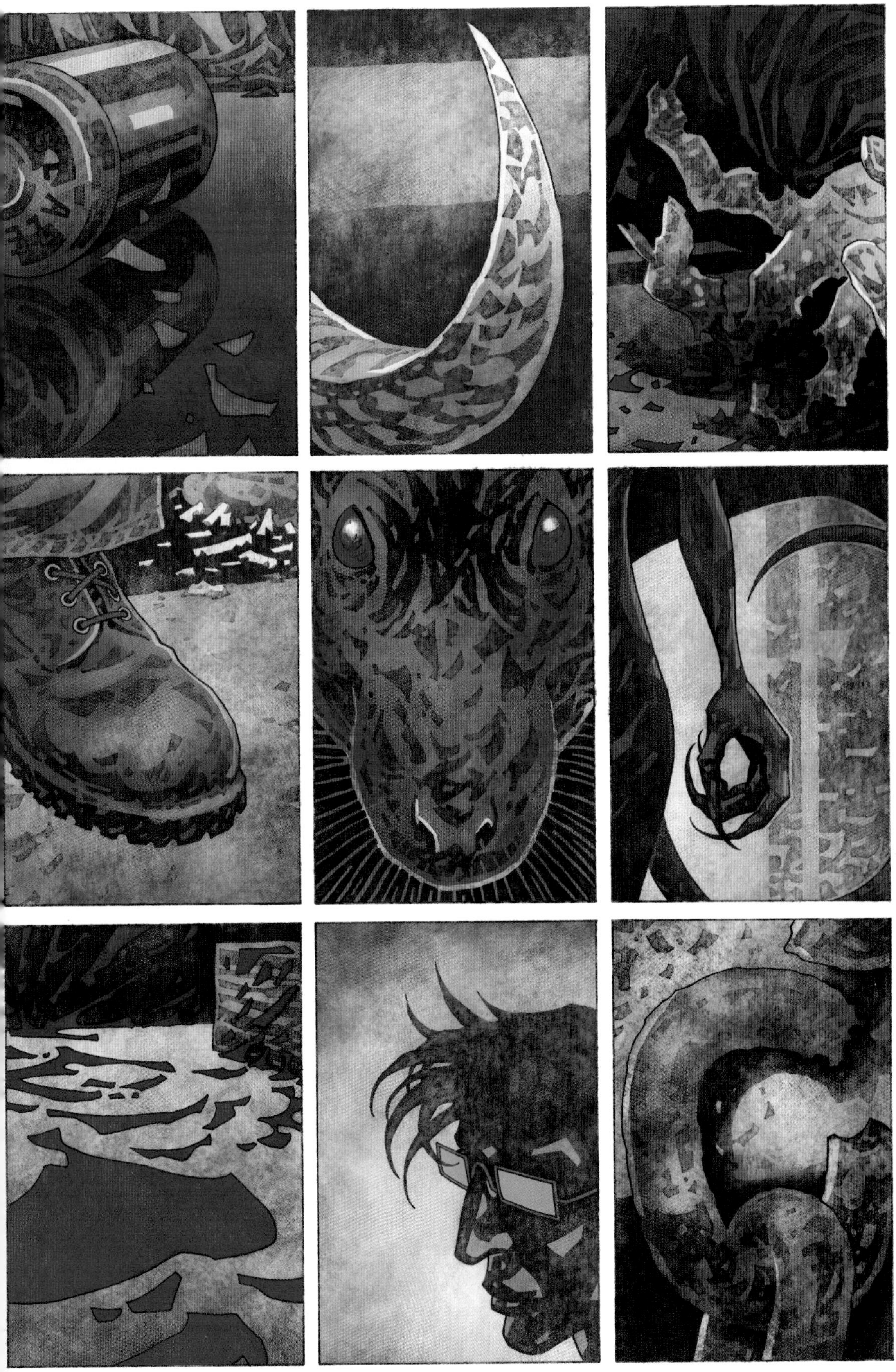

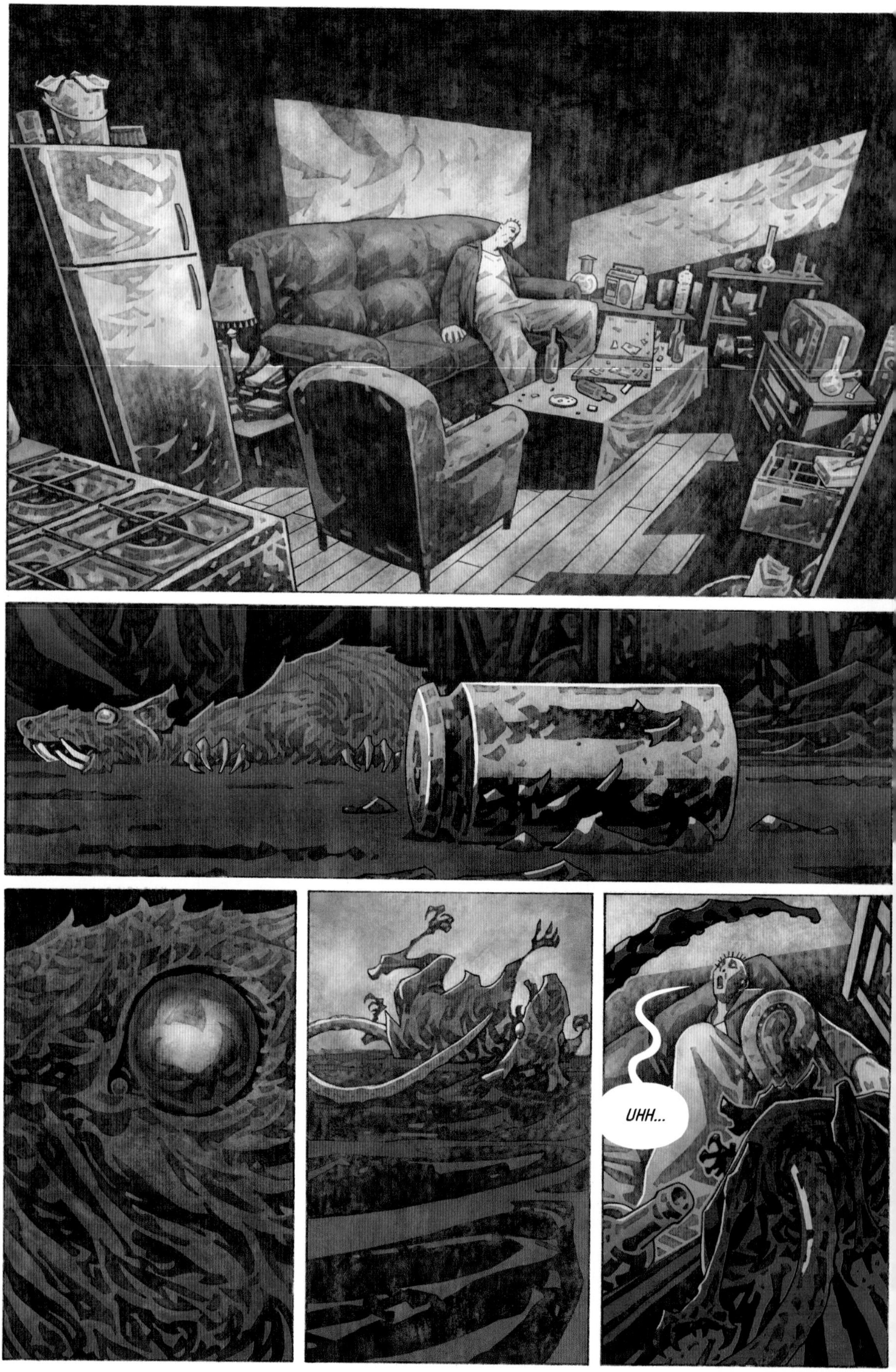
UHH...

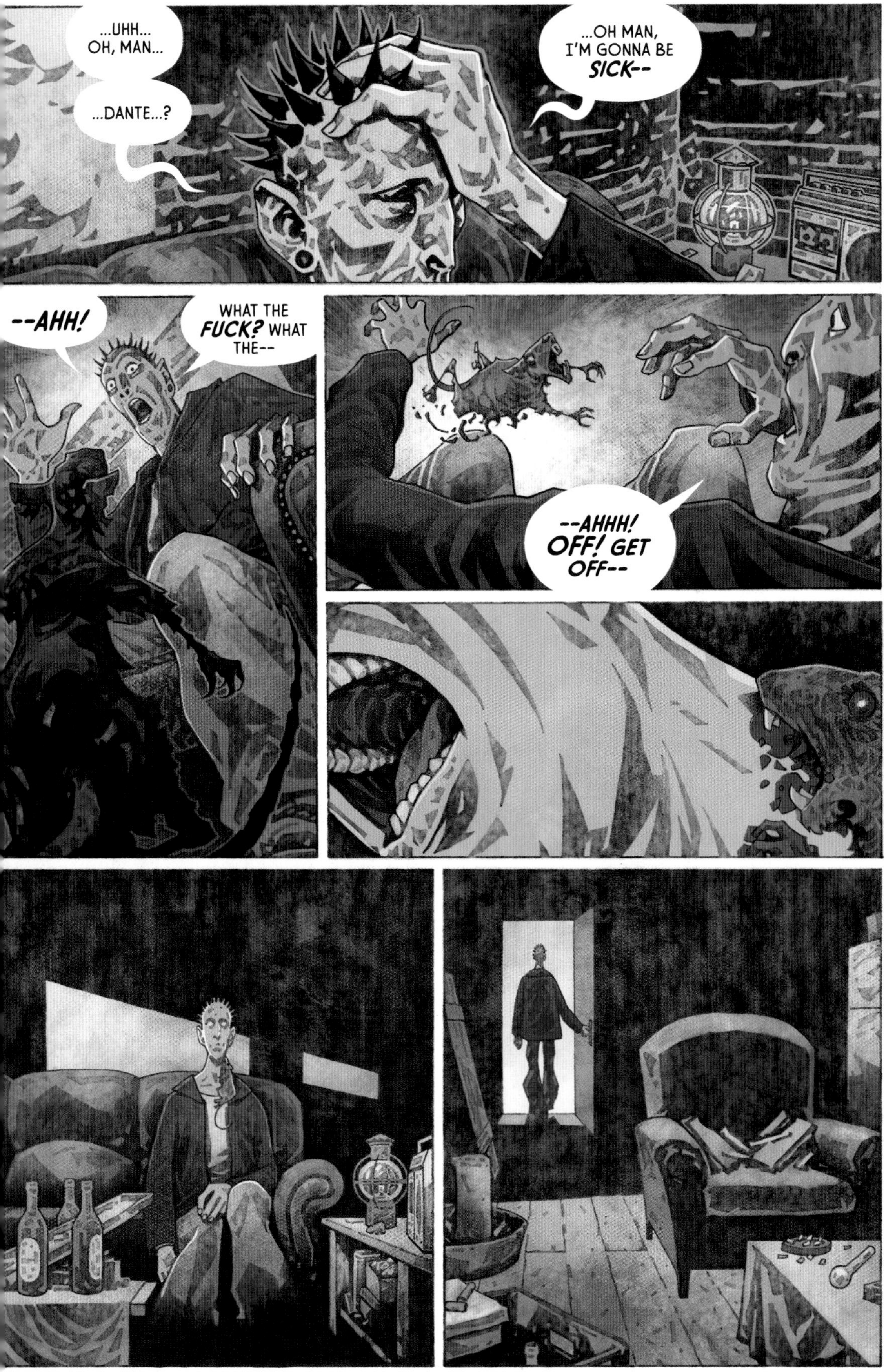
...UHH...
OH, MAN...
...DANTE...?
...OH MAN, I'M GONNA BE SICK--
--AHH!
WHAT THE FUCK? WHAT THE--
--AHHH! OFF! GET OFF--

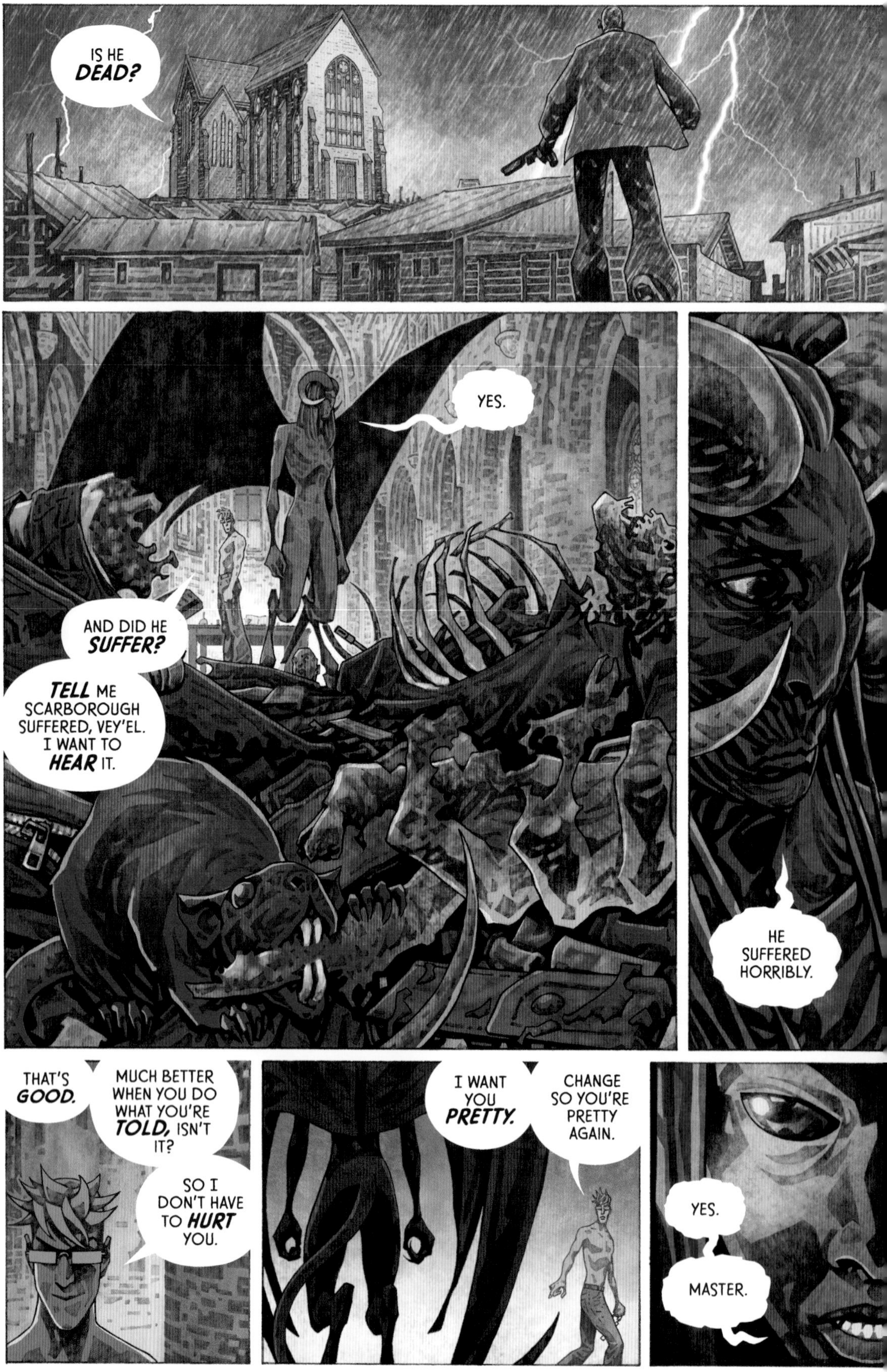
IS HE DEAD?
YES.
AND DID HE SUFFER?
TELL ME SCARBOROUGH SUFFERED, VEY'EL. I WANT TO HEAR IT.
HE SUFFERED HORRIBLY.
THAT'S GOOD.
MUCH BETTER WHEN YOU DO WHAT YOU'RE TOLD, ISN'T IT?
SO I DON'T HAVE TO HURT YOU.
I WANT YOU PRETTY.
CHANGE SO YOU'RE PRETTY AGAIN.
YES.
MASTER.

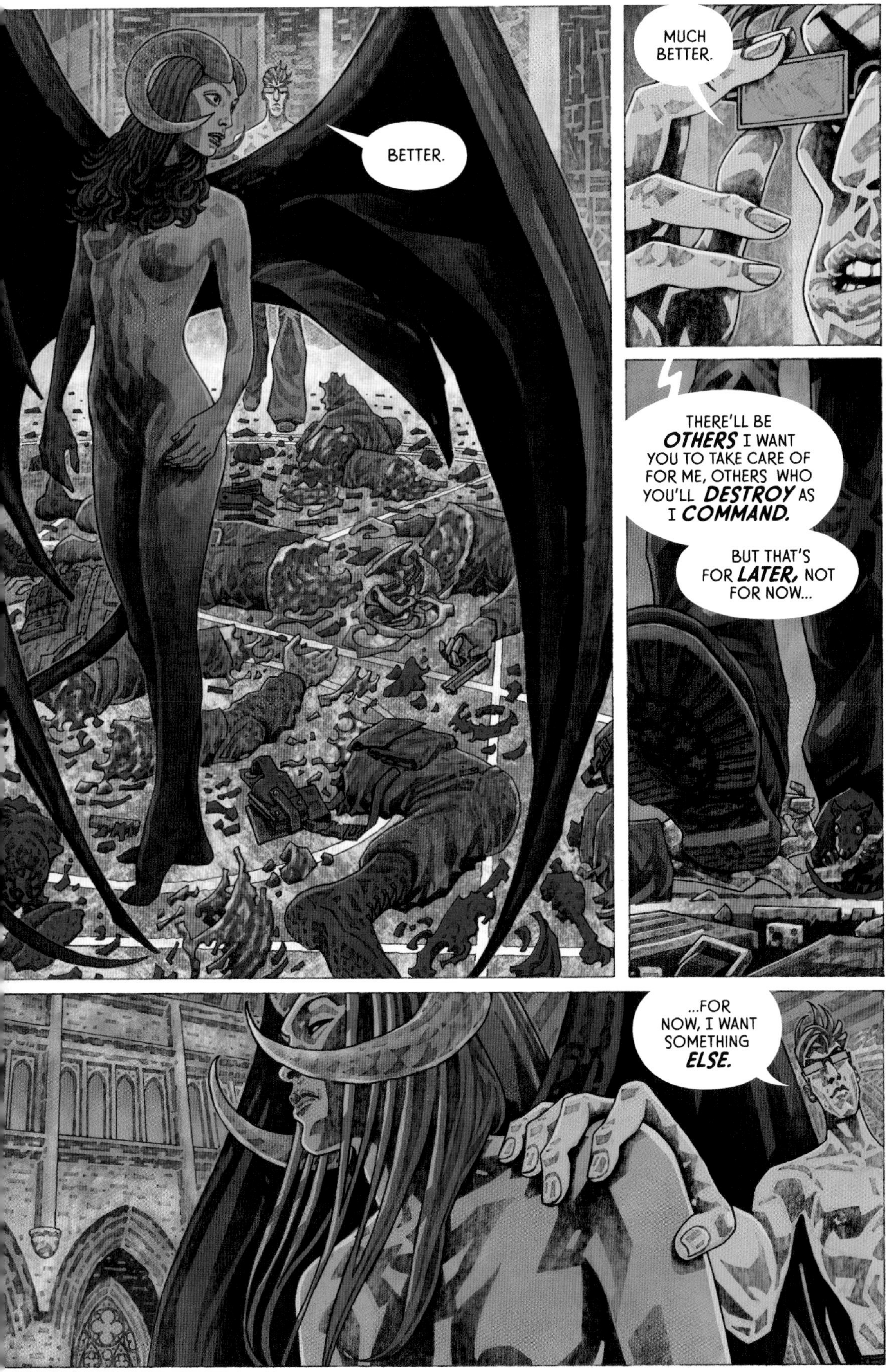
BETTER.
MUCH BETTER.
THERE'LL BE OTHERS I WANT YOU TO TAKE CARE OF FOR ME, OTHERS WHO YOU'LL DESTROY AS I COMMAND.
BUT THAT'S FOR LATER, NOT FOR NOW...
...FOR NOW, I WANT SOMETHING ELSE.

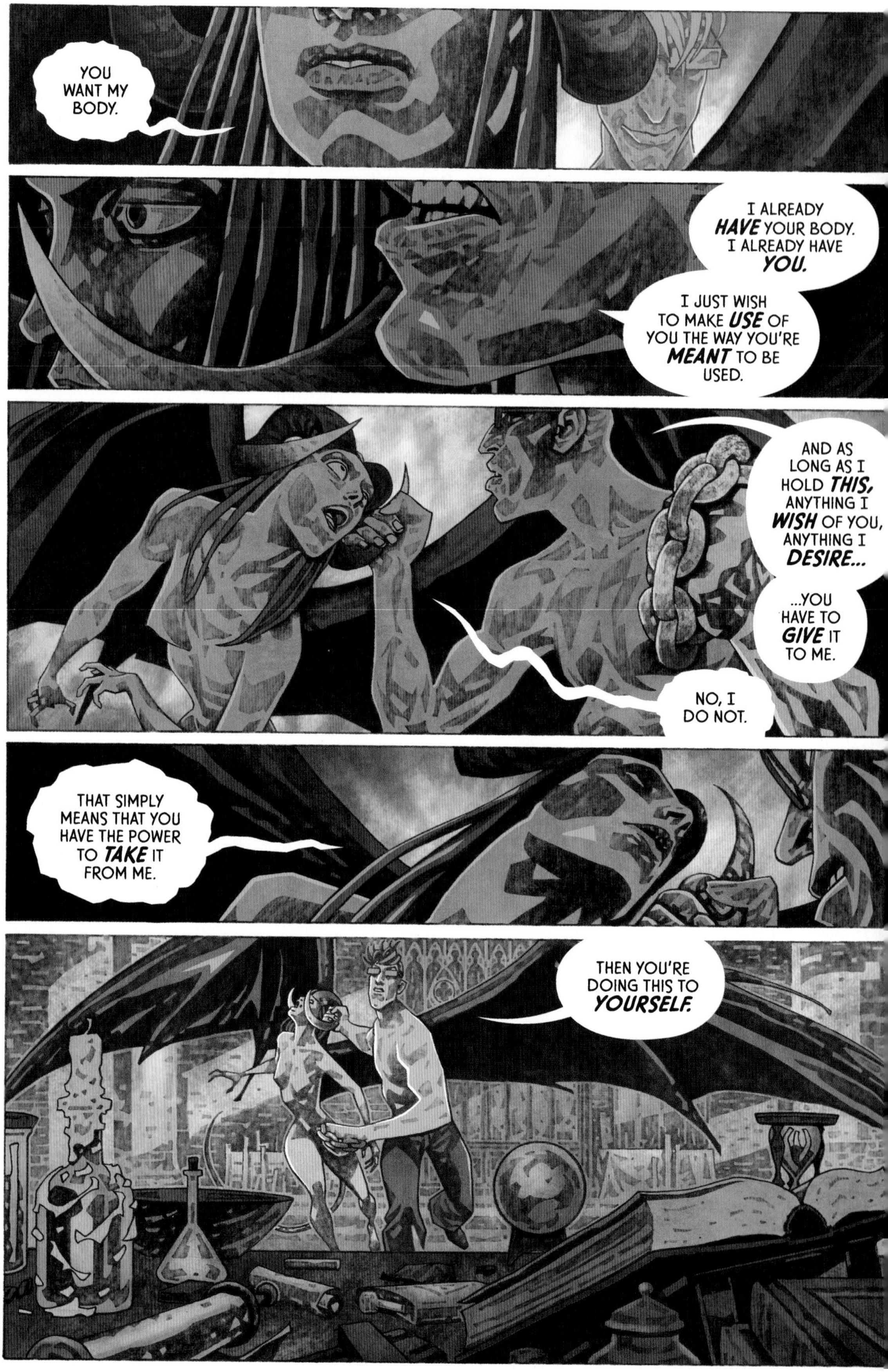
YOU WANT MY BODY.
I ALREADY HAVE YOUR BODY. I ALREADY HAVE YOU.
I JUST WISH TO MAKE USE OF YOU THE WAY YOU'RE MEANT TO BE USED.
AND AS LONG AS I HOLD THIS, ANYTHING I WISH OF YOU, ANYTHING I DESIRE...
...YOU HAVE TO GIVE IT TO ME.
NO, I DO NOT.
THAT SIMPLY MEANS THAT YOU HAVE THE POWER TO TAKE IT FROM ME.
THEN YOU'RE DOING THIS TO YOURSELF.

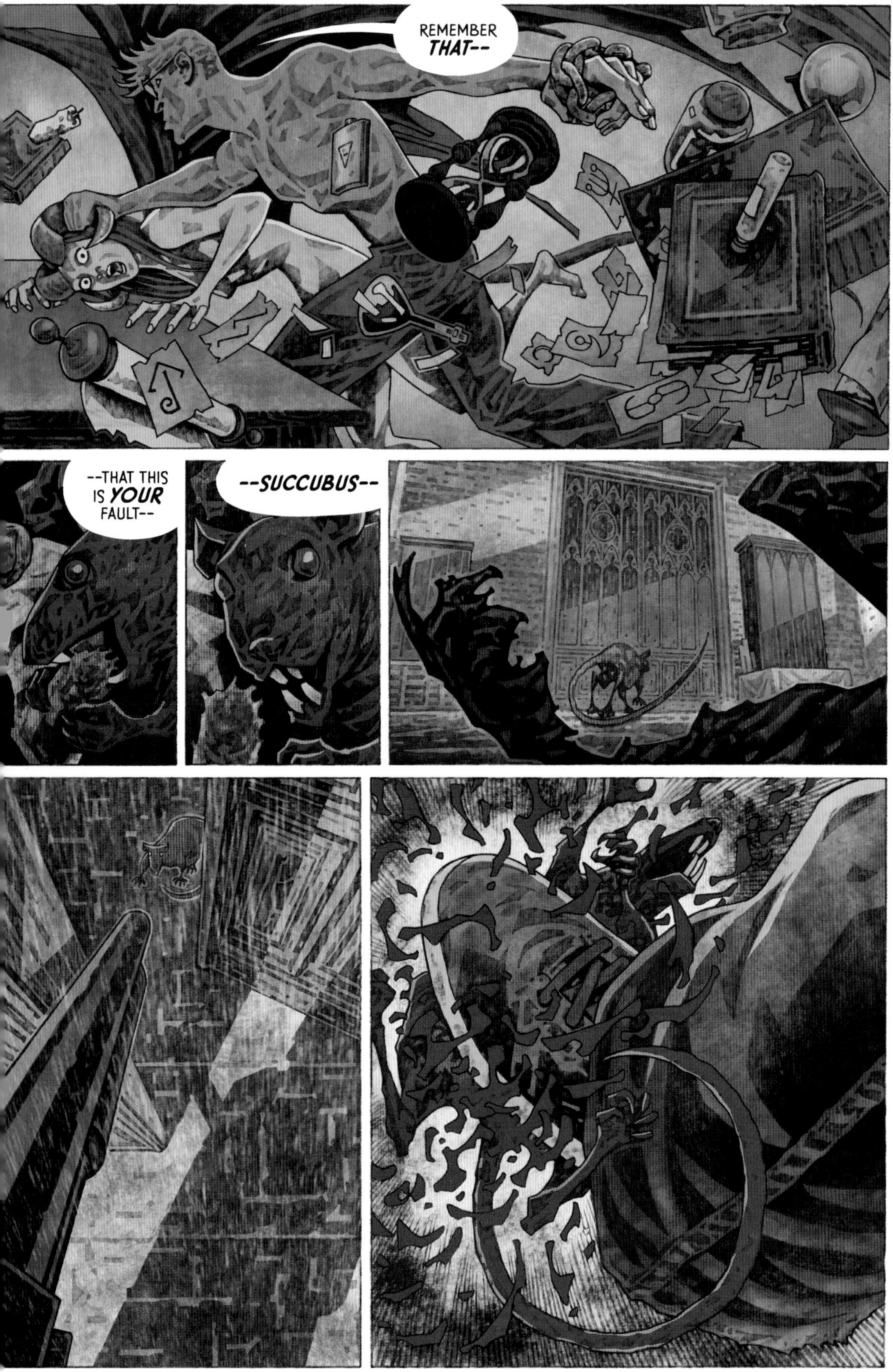
REMEMBER *THAT*--
--THAT THIS IS *YOUR* FAULT--
--SUCCUBUS--

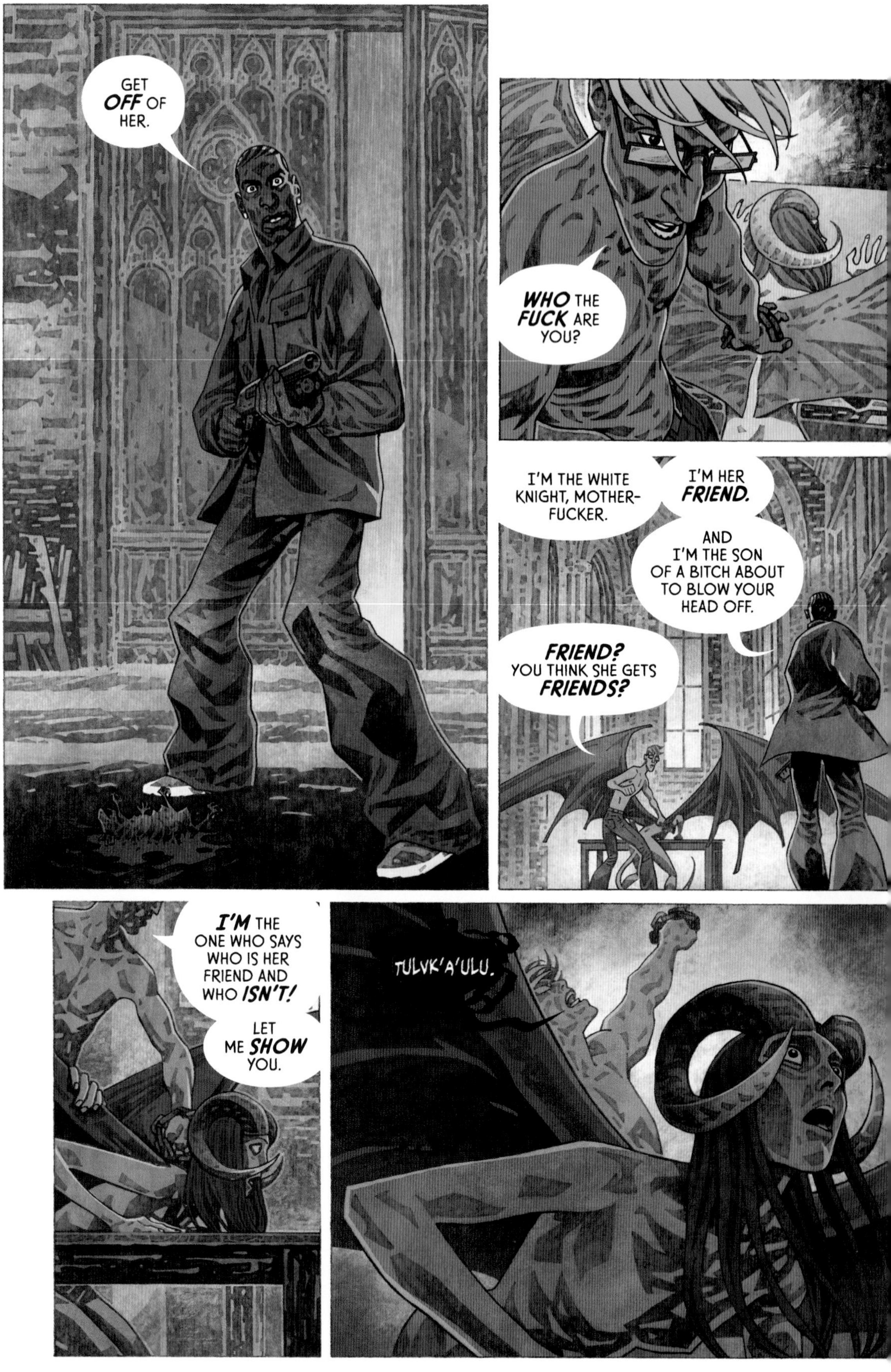
GET OFF OF HER.
WHO THE FUCK ARE YOU?
I'M THE WHITE KNIGHT, MOTHER-FUCKER.
I'M HER FRIEND.
AND I'M THE SON OF A BITCH ABOUT TO BLOW YOUR HEAD OFF.
FRIEND? YOU THINK SHE GETS FRIENDS?
I'M THE ONE WHO SAYS WHO IS HER FRIEND AND WHO ISN'T!
LET ME SHOW YOU.
TULVK'A'ULU.

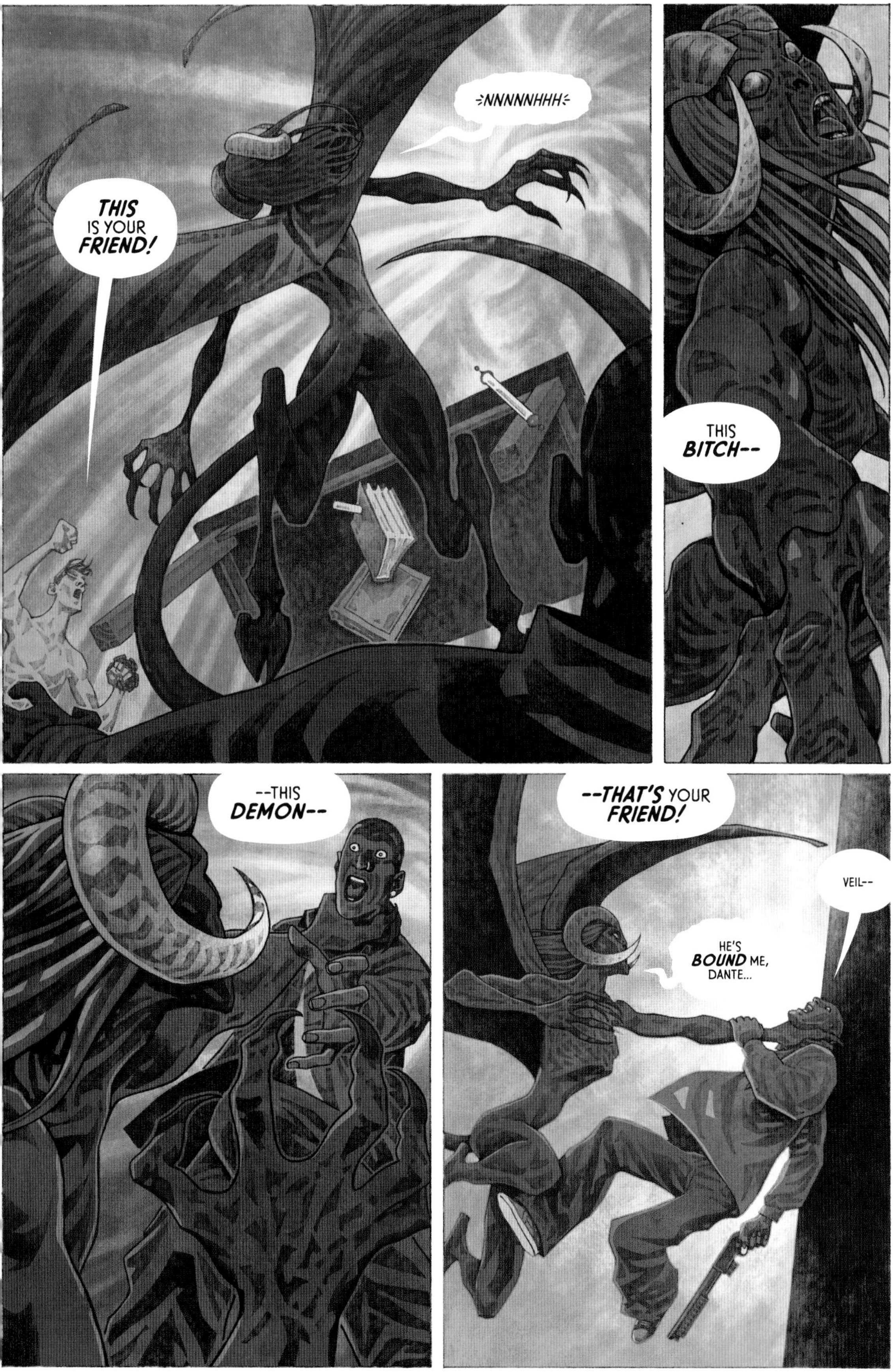
THIS IS YOUR FRIEND!
=NNNNNHHH=
THIS BITCH--
--THIS DEMON--
--THAT'S YOUR FRIEND!
VEIL--
HE'S BOUND ME, DANTE...

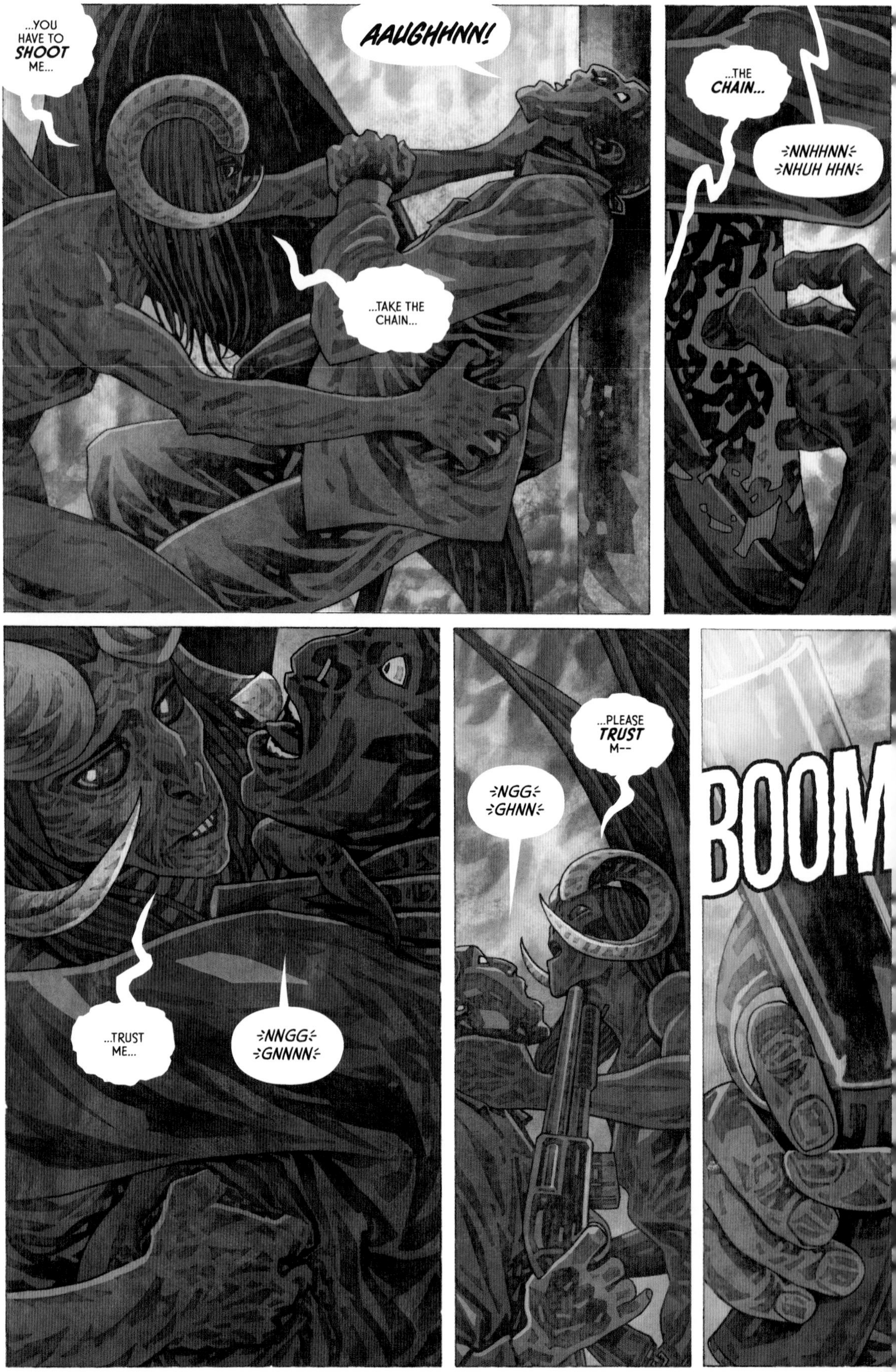
...YOU HAVE TO SHOOT ME...
AAUGHHNN!
...TAKE THE CHAIN...
...THE CHAIN...
NNHHNN NHUH HHN
...TRUST ME...
NNGG GNNNN
...PLEASE TRUST M--
NGG GHNN
BOOM

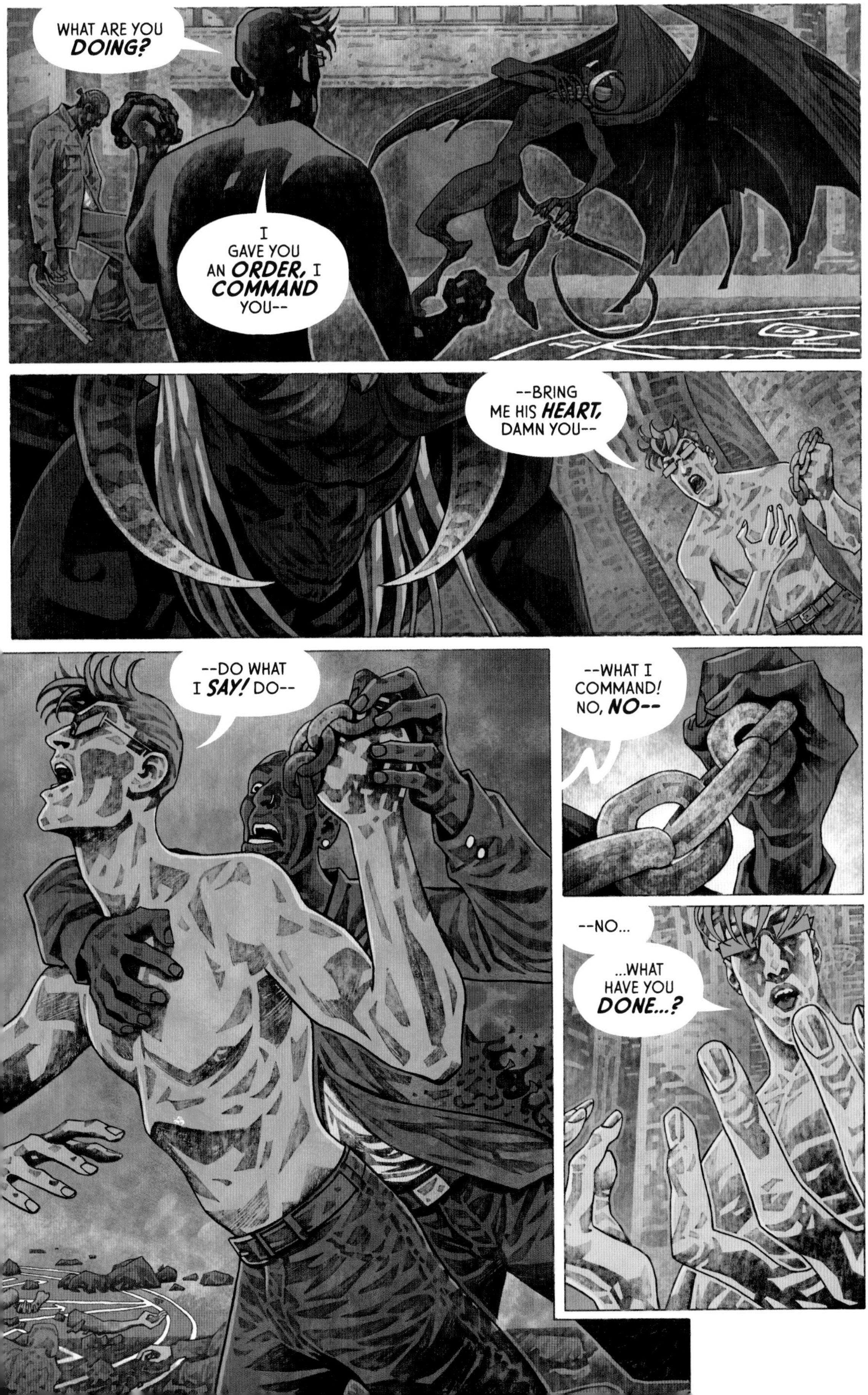
WHAT ARE YOU DOING?
I GAVE YOU AN ORDER, I COMMAND YOU--
--BRING ME HIS HEART, DAMN YOU--
--DO WHAT I SAY! DO--
--WHAT I COMMAND! NO, NO--
--NO...
...WHAT HAVE YOU DONE...?

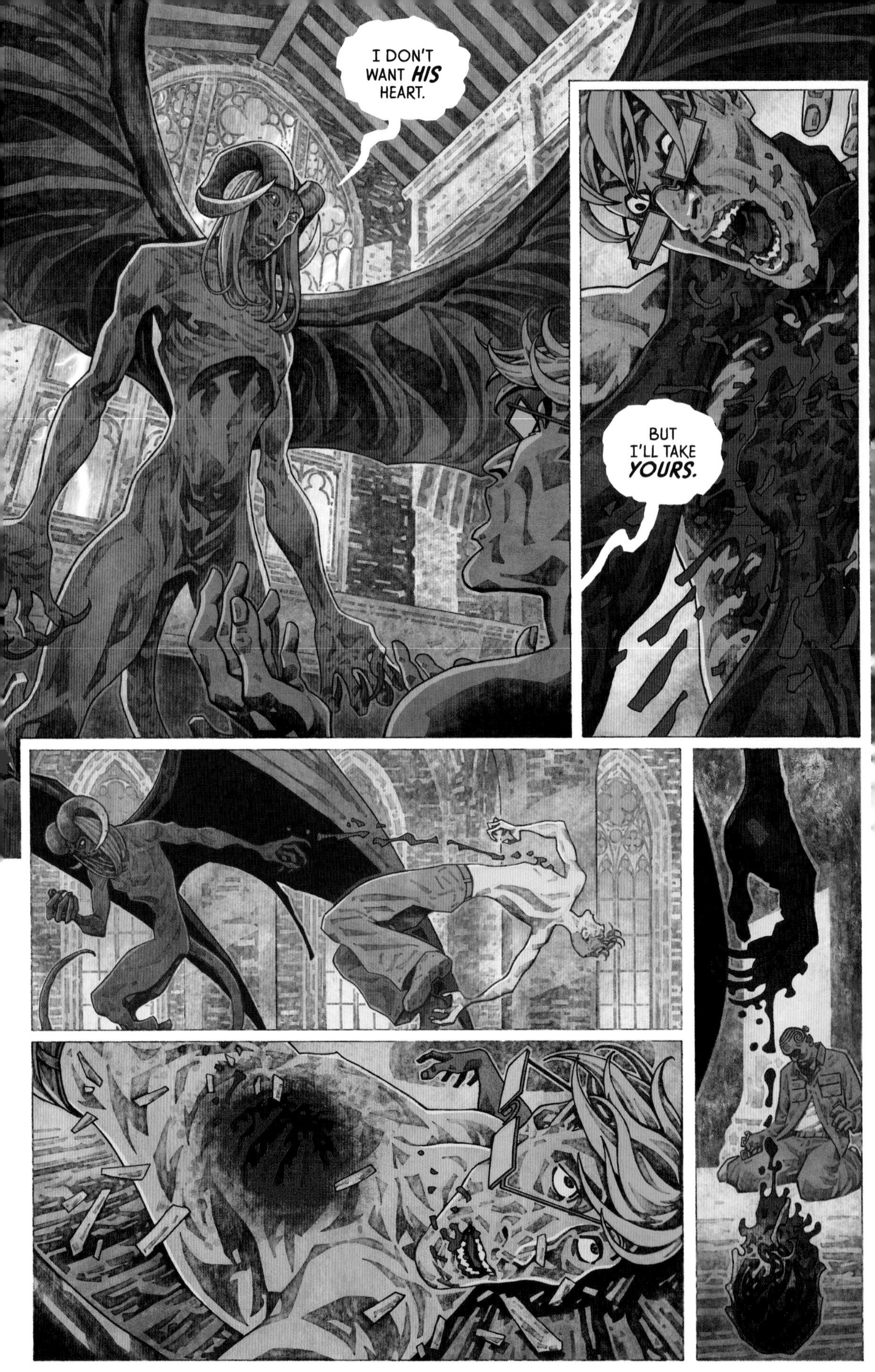
I DON'T WANT *HIS* HEART.
BUT I'LL TAKE *YOURS.*

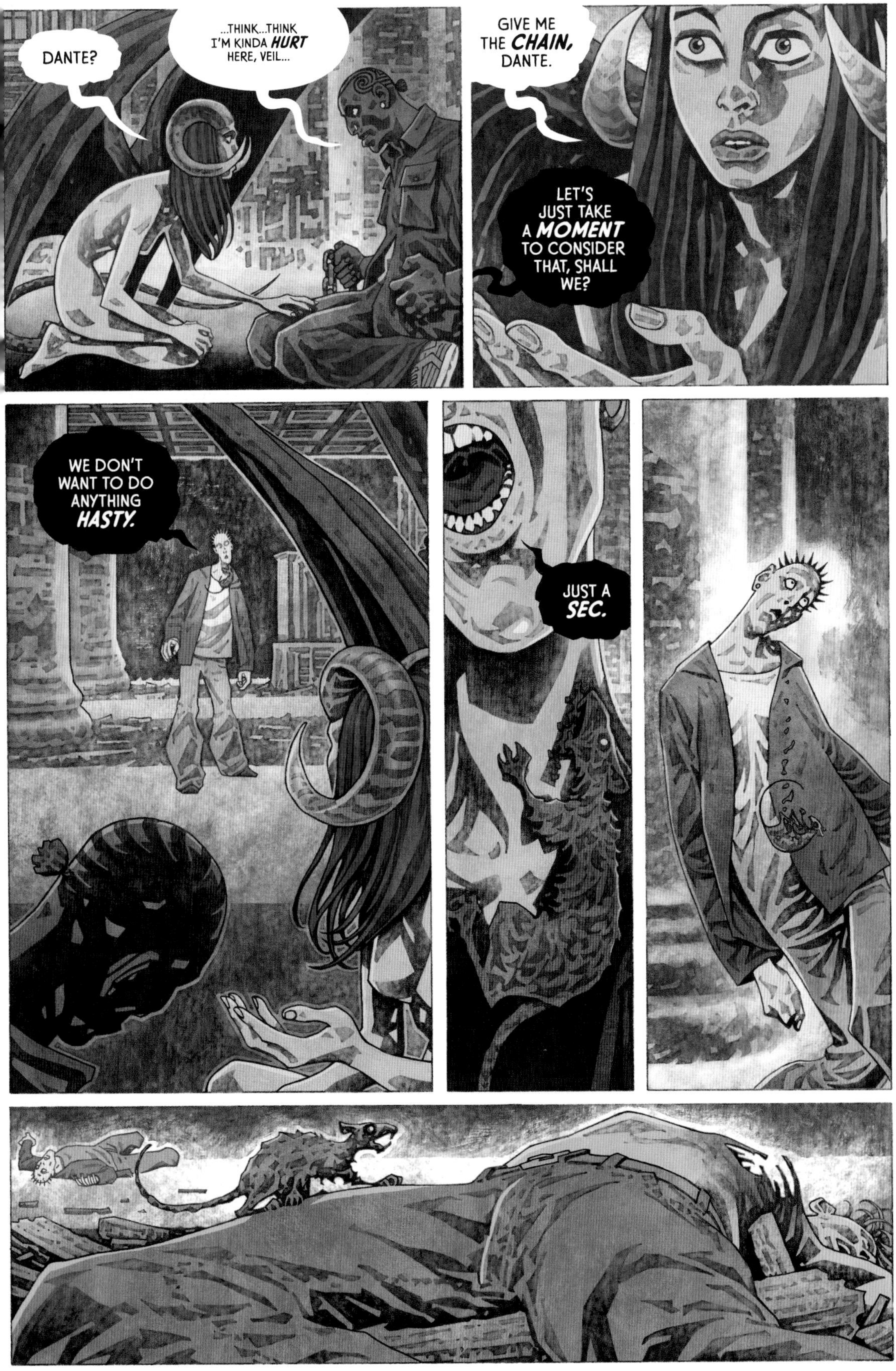
DANTE?
...THINK...THINK I'M KINDA HURT HERE, VEIL...
GIVE ME THE CHAIN, DANTE.
LET'S JUST TAKE A MOMENT TO CONSIDER THAT, SHALL WE?
WE DON'T WANT TO DO ANYTHING HASTY.
JUST A SEC.

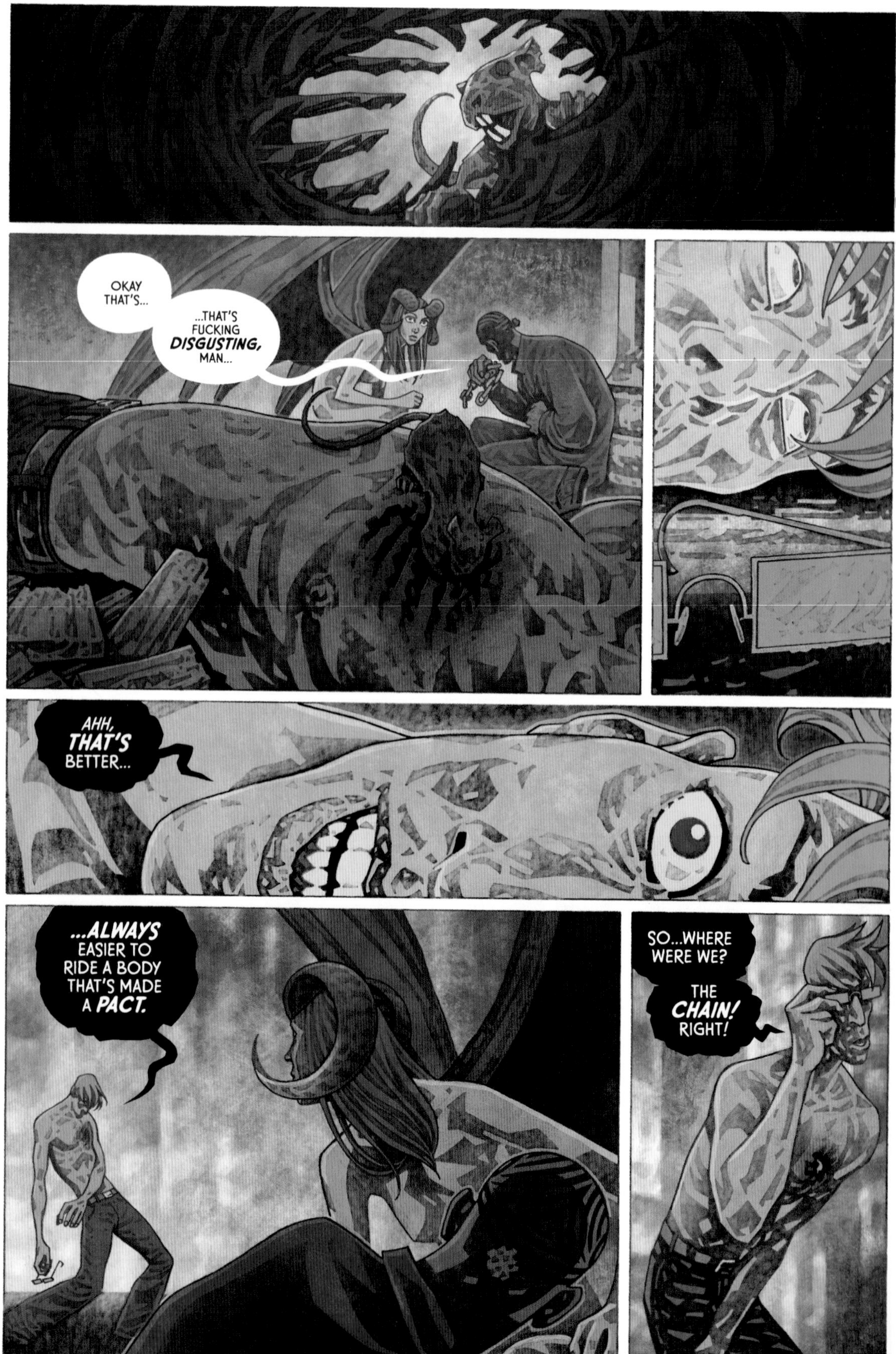
OKAY THAT'S...
...THAT'S FUCKING DISGUSTING, MAN...
AHH, THAT'S BETTER...
...ALWAYS EASIER TO RIDE A BODY THAT'S MADE A PACT.
SO...WHERE WERE WE?
THE CHAIN! RIGHT!

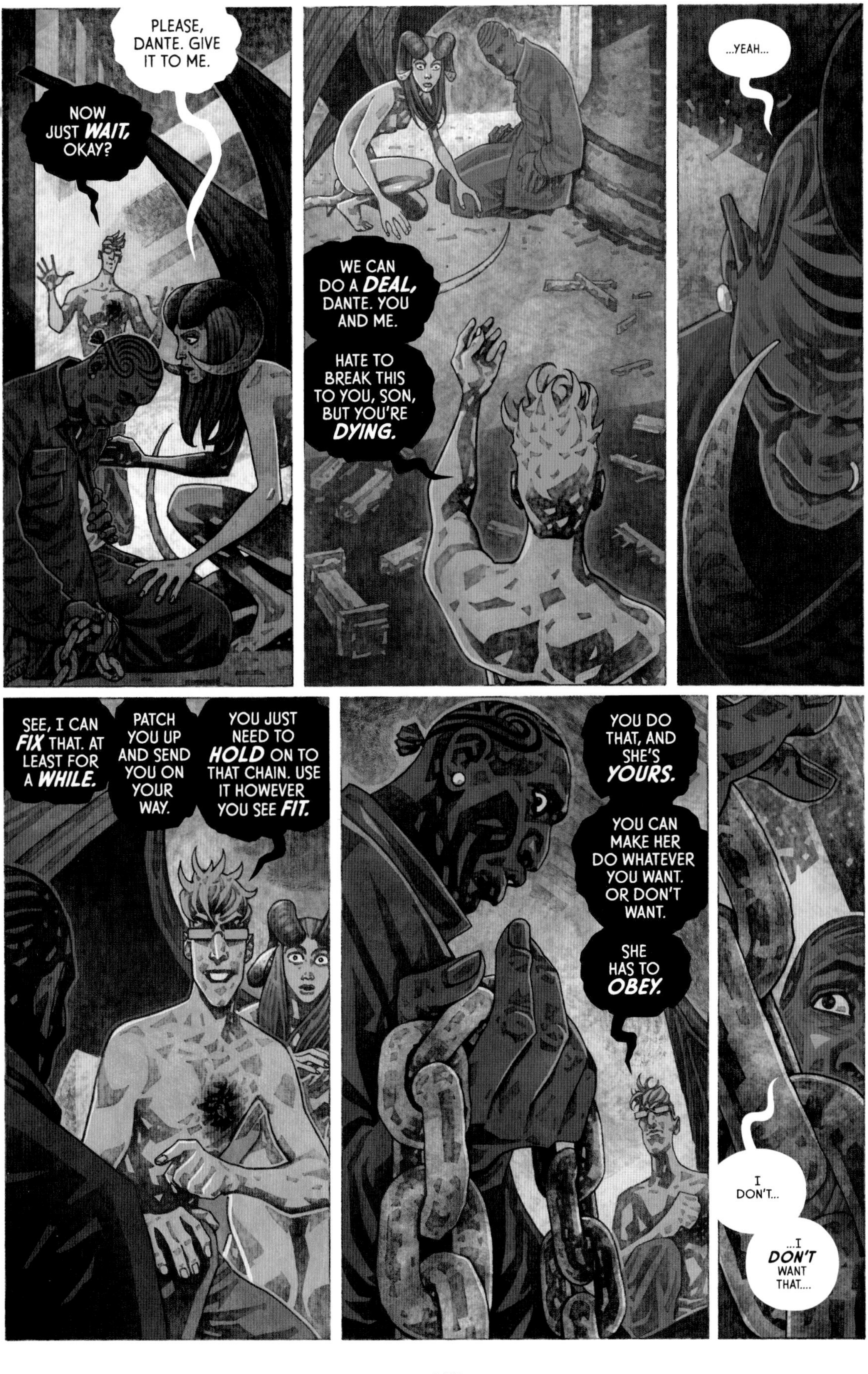
PLEASE, DANTE. GIVE IT TO ME.
NOW JUST WAIT, OKAY?
WE CAN DO A DEAL, DANTE. YOU AND ME.
HATE TO BREAK THIS TO YOU, SON, BUT YOU'RE DYING.
...YEAH...
SEE, I CAN FIX THAT. AT LEAST FOR A WHILE.
PATCH YOU UP AND SEND YOU ON YOUR WAY.
YOU JUST NEED TO HOLD ON TO THAT CHAIN. USE IT HOWEVER YOU SEE FIT.
YOU DO THAT, AND SHE'S YOURS.
YOU CAN MAKE HER DO WHATEVER YOU WANT. OR DON'T WANT.
SHE HAS TO OBEY.
I DON'T...
...I DON'T WANT THAT....

...I *NEVER* WANTED THAT FROM YOU.

I KNOW.

OKAY, THEN, HERE'S SOMETHING *ELSE* TO CONSIDER. YOU GIVE THAT TO HER, SHE'LL BE *FREE.*

THINK ABOUT *THAT.* LOOK AT HER AND THINK ABOUT THAT.

SHE'S A *DEMON,* DANTE. SHE'S A *MINION* OF HELL.

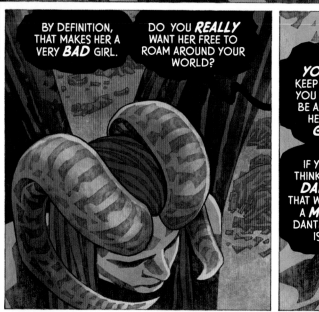

BY DEFINITION, THAT MAKES HER A VERY *BAD* GIRL.

DO YOU *REALLY* WANT HER FREE TO ROAM AROUND YOUR WORLD?

BUT *YOU* COULD KEEP HER IN LINE. YOU MIGHT EVEN BE ABLE TO USE HER TO DO *GOOD.*

IF YOU DON'T... THINK ABOUT HOW *DANGEROUS* THAT WILL BE. YOU'RE A *MORAL* GUY, DANTE, THAT MUCH IS CLEAR...

...BUT *SOMEONE'S* GOT TO *CONTROL* HER.

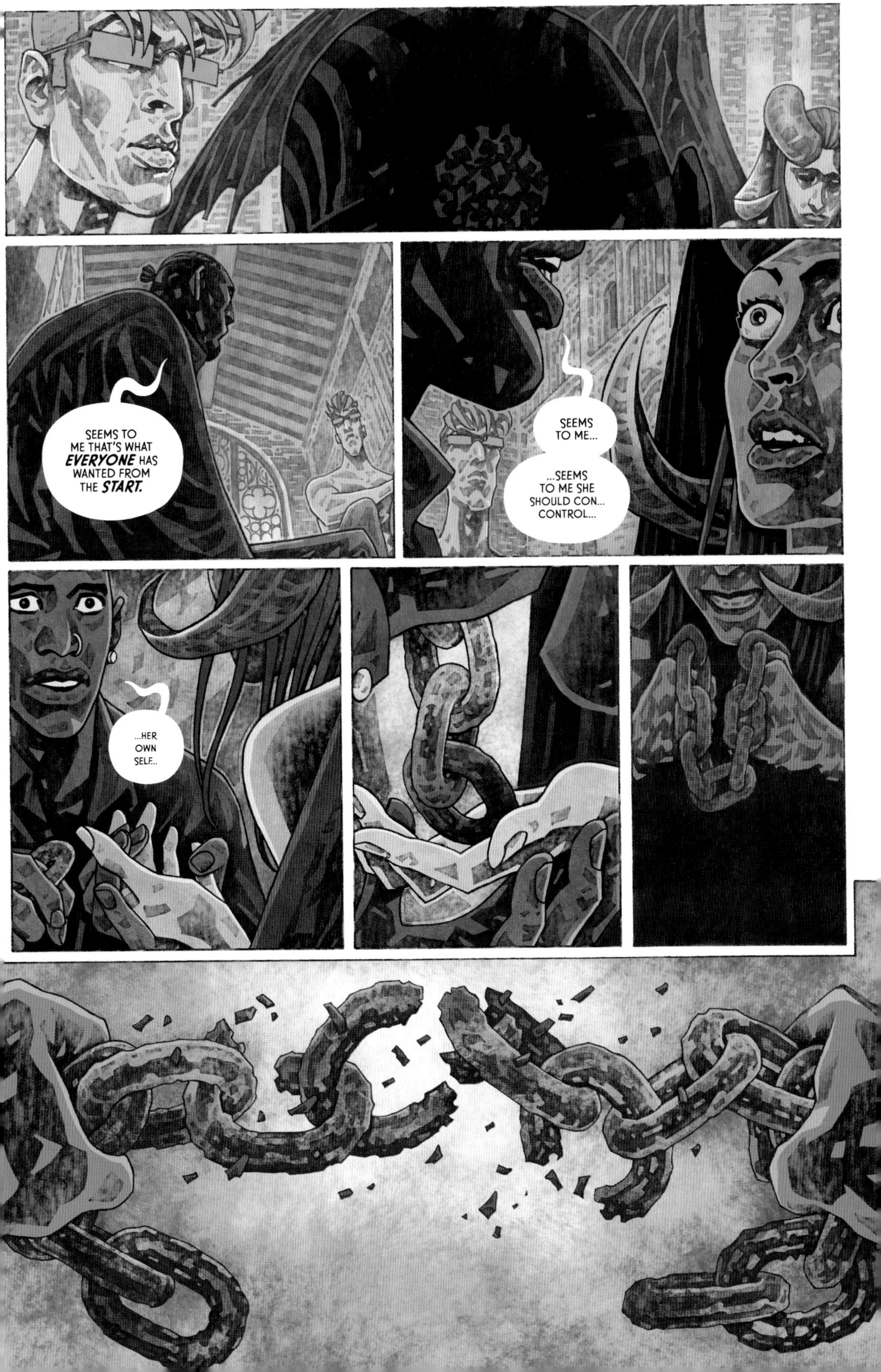
SEEMS TO ME THAT'S WHAT ***EVERYONE*** HAS WANTED FROM THE ***START.***
SEEMS TO ME...
...SEEMS TO ME SHE SHOULD CON... CONTROL...
...HER OWN SELF...

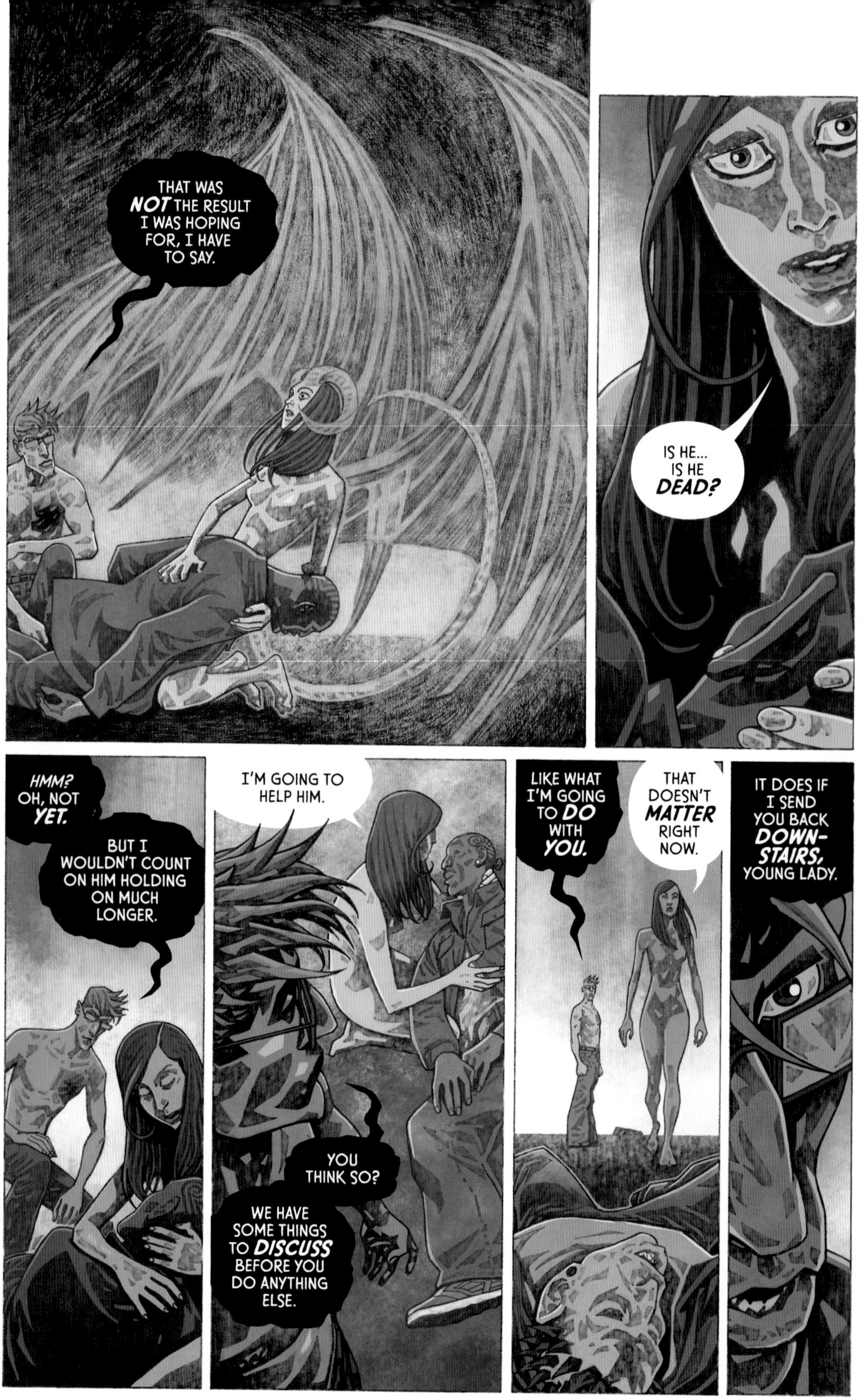
THAT WAS NOT THE RESULT I WAS HOPING FOR, I HAVE TO SAY.
IS HE... IS HE DEAD?
HMM? OH, NOT YET.
BUT I WOULDN'T COUNT ON HIM HOLDING ON MUCH LONGER.
I'M GOING TO HELP HIM.
YOU THINK SO?
WE HAVE SOME THINGS TO DISCUSS BEFORE YOU DO ANYTHING ELSE.
LIKE WHAT I'M GOING TO DO WITH YOU.
THAT DOESN'T MATTER RIGHT NOW.
IT DOES IF I SEND YOU BACK DOWN-STAIRS, YOUNG LADY.

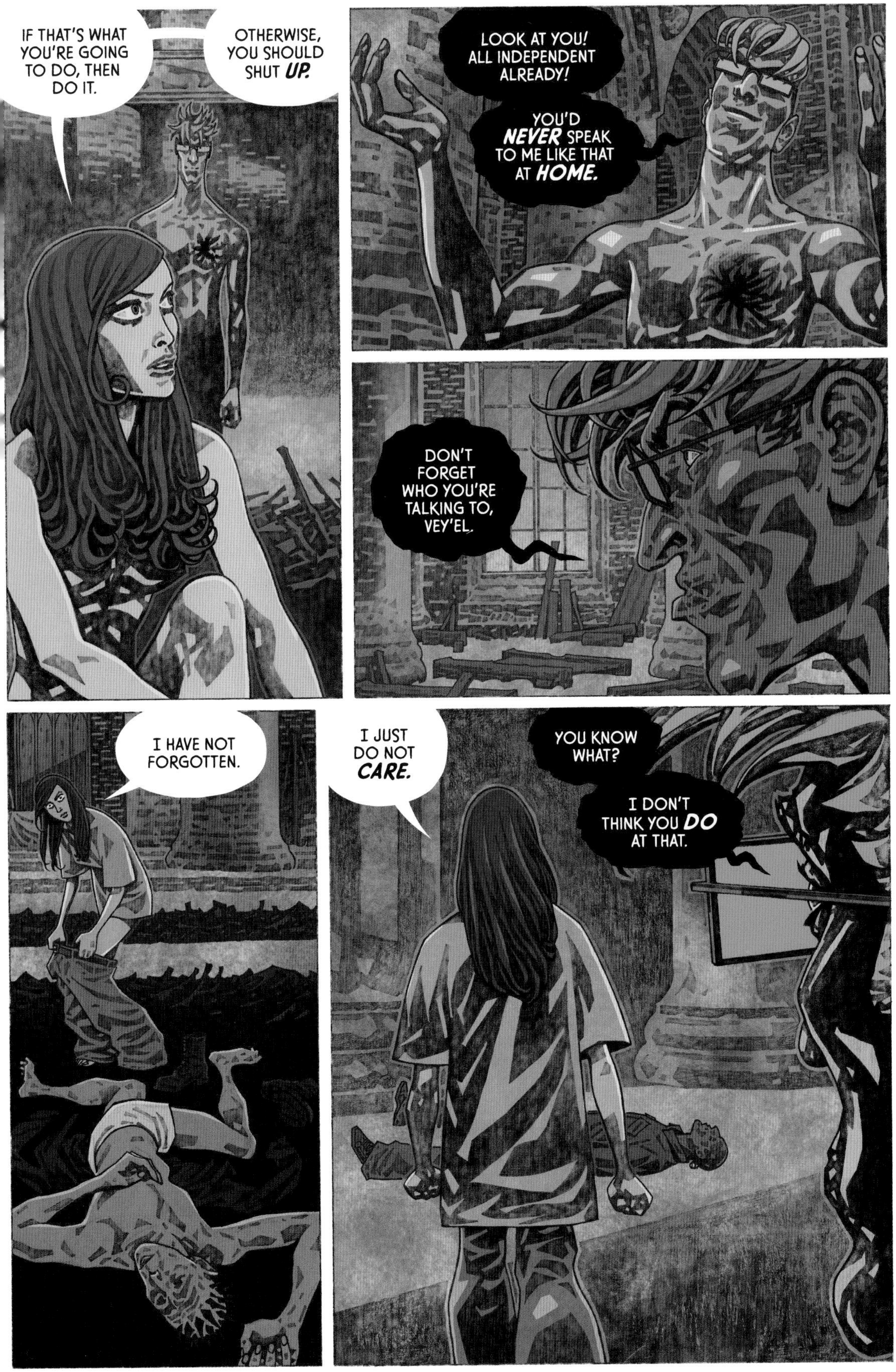
IF THAT'S WHAT YOU'RE GOING TO DO, THEN DO IT.
OTHERWISE, YOU SHOULD SHUT *UP.*
LOOK AT YOU! ALL INDEPENDENT ALREADY!
YOU'D *NEVER* SPEAK TO ME LIKE THAT AT *HOME.*
DON'T FORGET WHO YOU'RE TALKING TO, VEY'EL.
I HAVE NOT FORGOTTEN.
I JUST DO NOT *CARE.*
YOU KNOW WHAT?
I DON'T THINK YOU *DO* AT THAT.

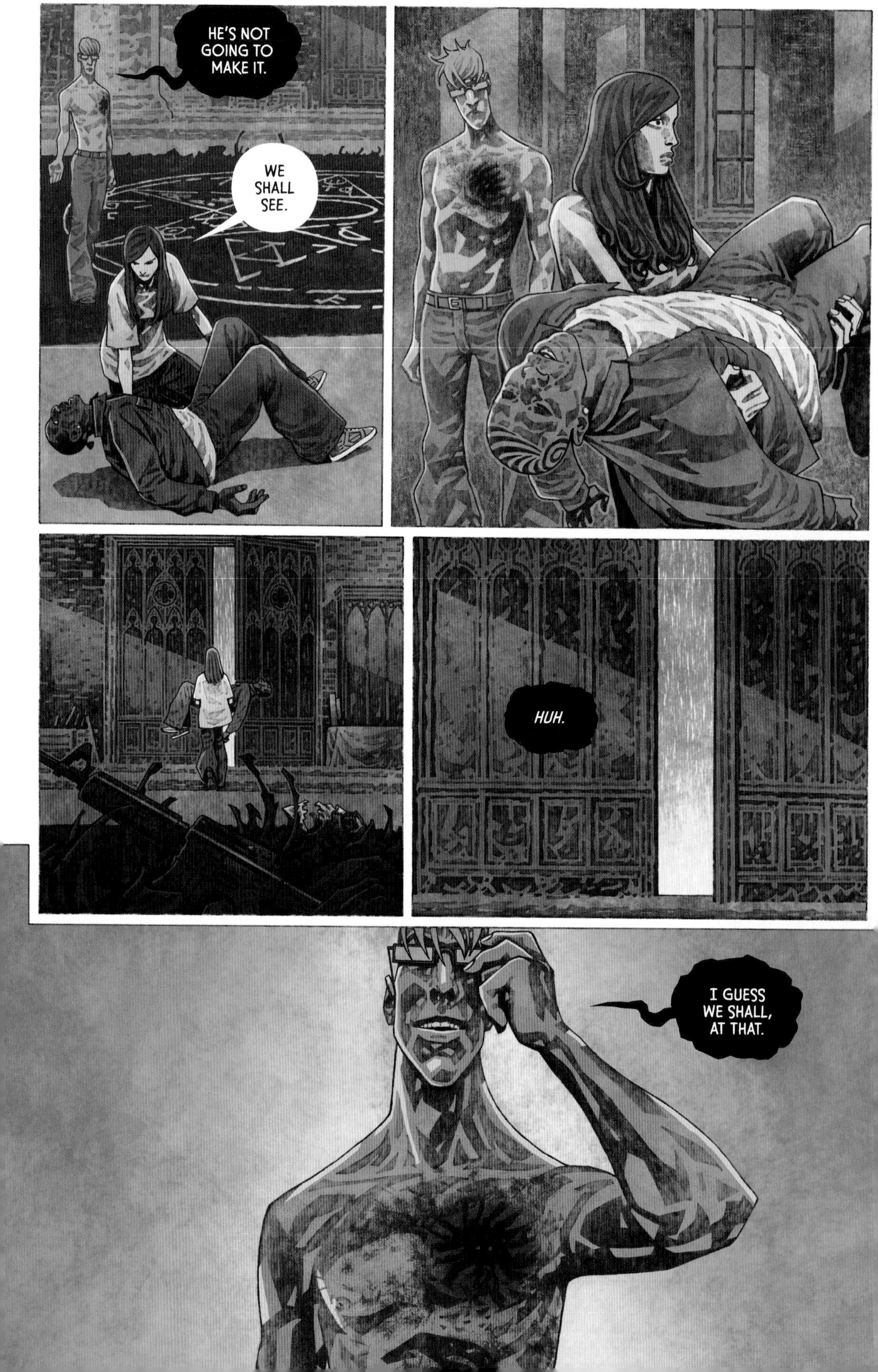
HE'S NOT GOING TO MAKE IT.
WE SHALL SEE.
HUH.
I GUESS WE SHALL, AT THAT.

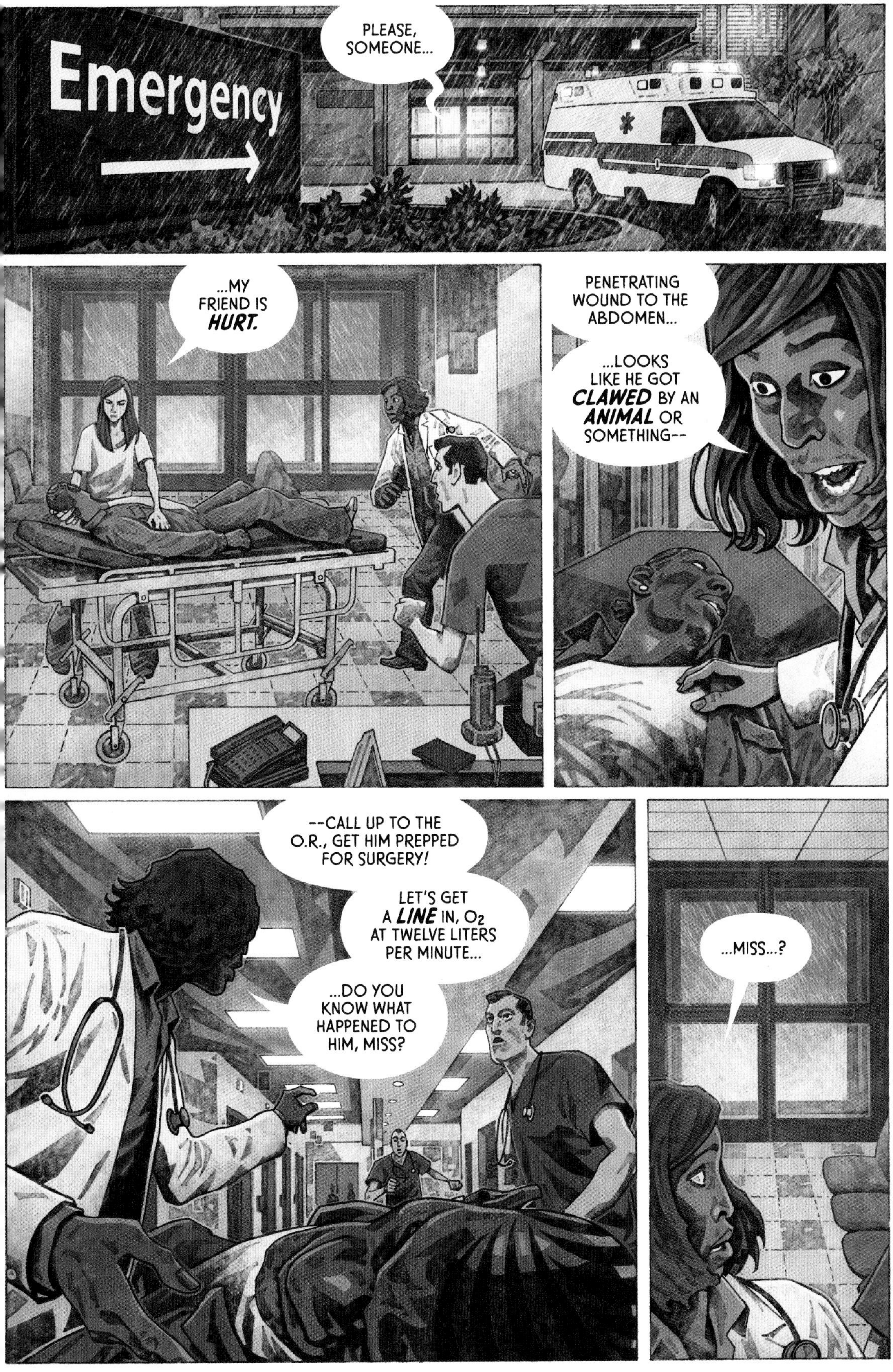
Emergency
PLEASE, SOMEONE...
...MY FRIEND IS *HURT.*
PENETRATING WOUND TO THE ABDOMEN...
...LOOKS LIKE HE GOT *CLAWED* BY AN *ANIMAL* OR SOMETHING--
--CALL UP TO THE O.R., GET HIM PREPPED FOR SURGERY!
LET'S GET A *LINE* IN, O_2 AT TWELVE LITERS PER MINUTE...
...DO YOU KNOW WHAT HAPPENED TO HIM, MISS?
...MISS...?

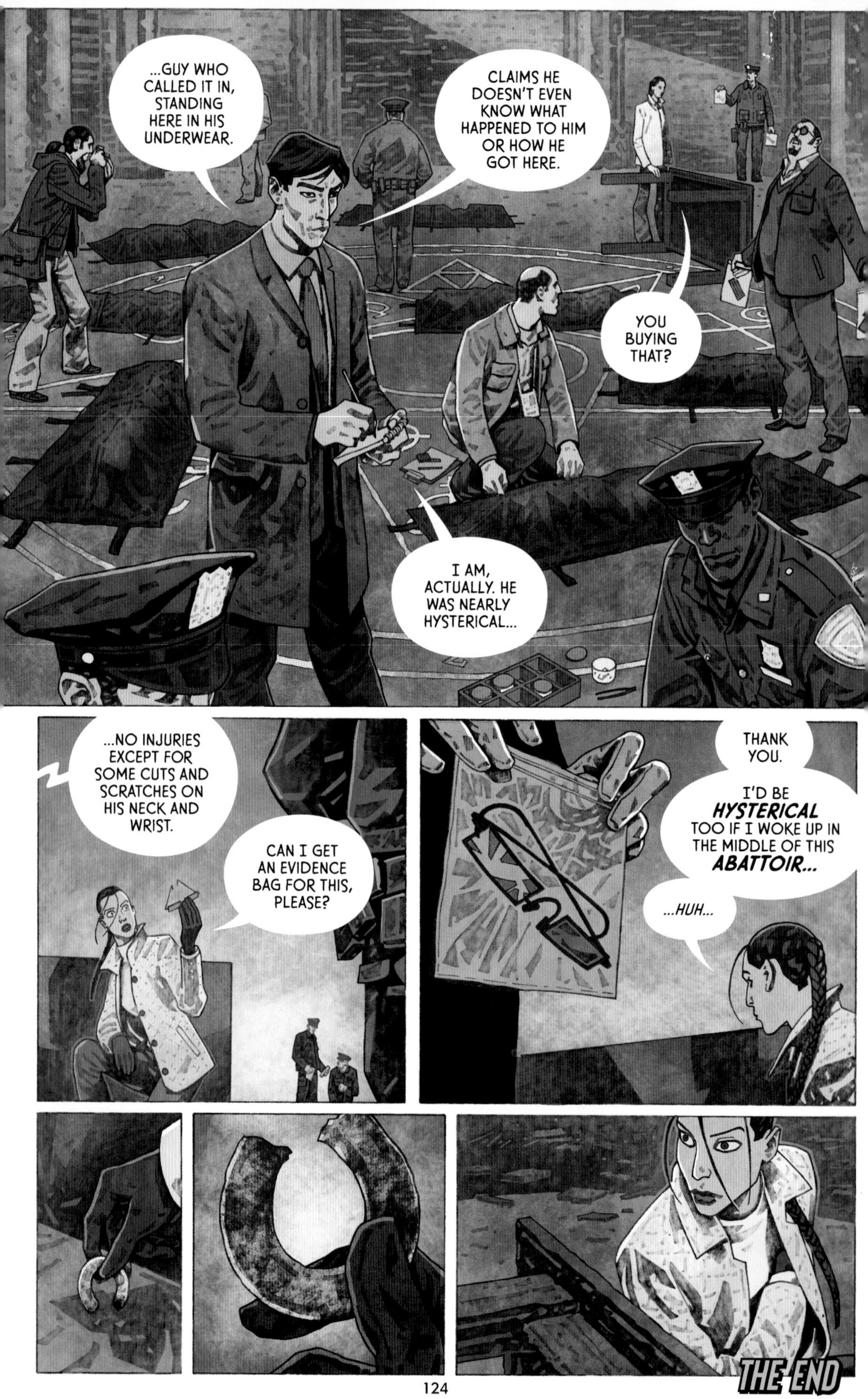
...GUY WHO CALLED IT IN, STANDING HERE IN HIS UNDERWEAR.
CLAIMS HE DOESN'T EVEN KNOW WHAT HAPPENED TO HIM OR HOW HE GOT HERE.
YOU BUYING THAT?
I AM, ACTUALLY. HE WAS NEARLY HYSTERICAL...
...NO INJURIES EXCEPT FOR SOME CUTS AND SCRATCHES ON HIS NECK AND WRIST.
CAN I GET AN EVIDENCE BAG FOR THIS, PLEASE?
THANK YOU.
I'D BE **HYSTERICAL** TOO IF I WOKE UP IN THE MIDDLE OF THIS **ABATTOIR...**
...HUH...
THE END

VEIL SKETCHBOOK

ART *by* TONI FEJZULA

NOTES *by* SCOTT ALLIE

The design for Veil was the most important part of getting this book right. The world around her sexualizes Veil, but Greg and Toni had to be careful about how they portrayed that themselves. The character would ultimately have three forms, which in his scripts Greg referred to as the woman, the succubus, and the demon. The drawing below is the seventh draft of the succubus form. Rather than conventional model sheets or sketches, Toni's preliminaries tended to be in the form of tightly penciled pinups, suggesting the mood and feeling of an idea more than just the details.

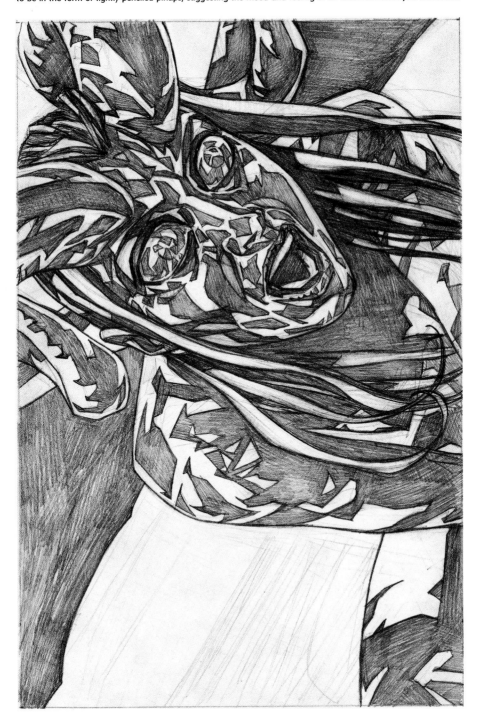

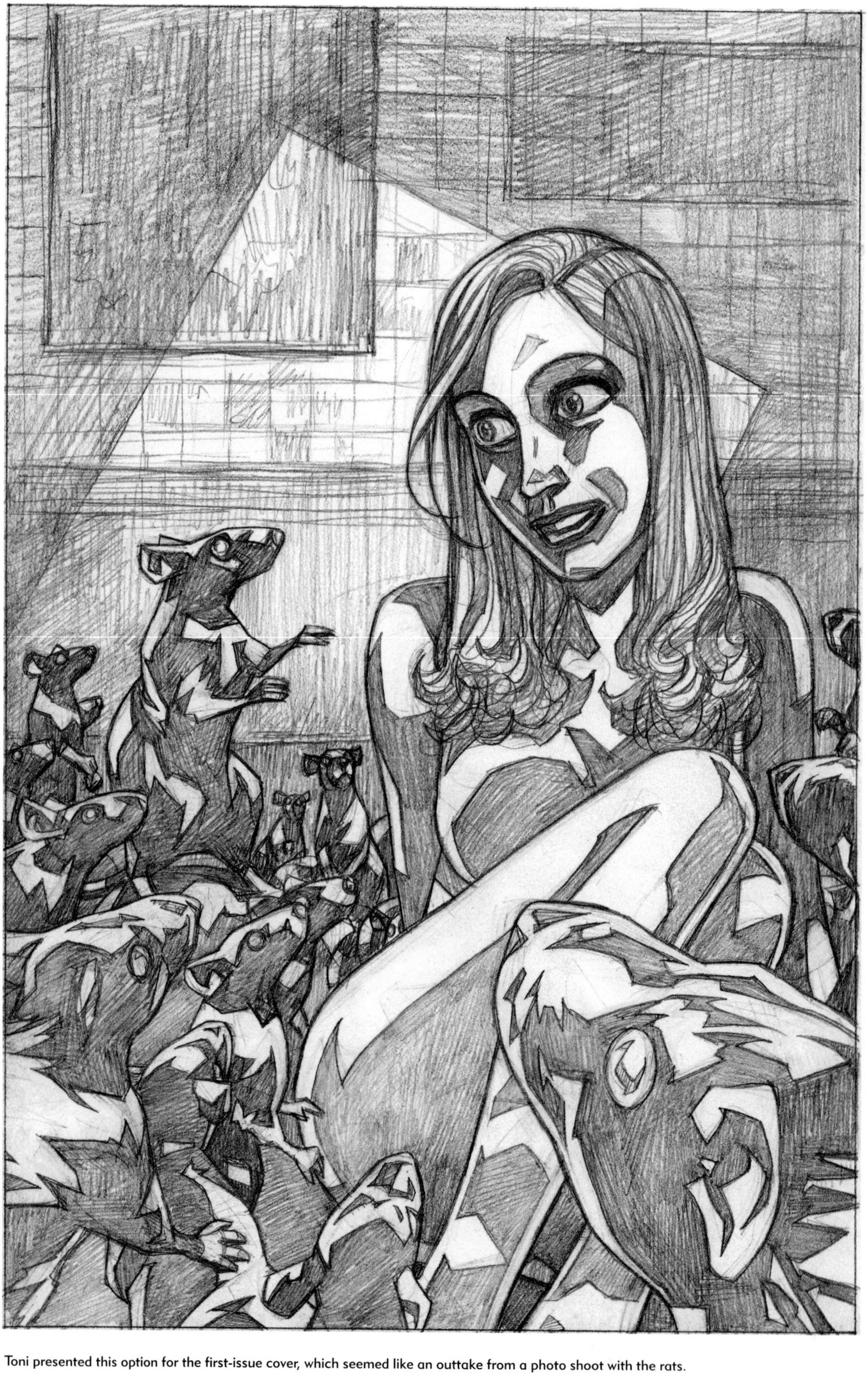

Toni presented this option for the first-issue cover, which seemed like an outtake from a photo shoot with the rats.

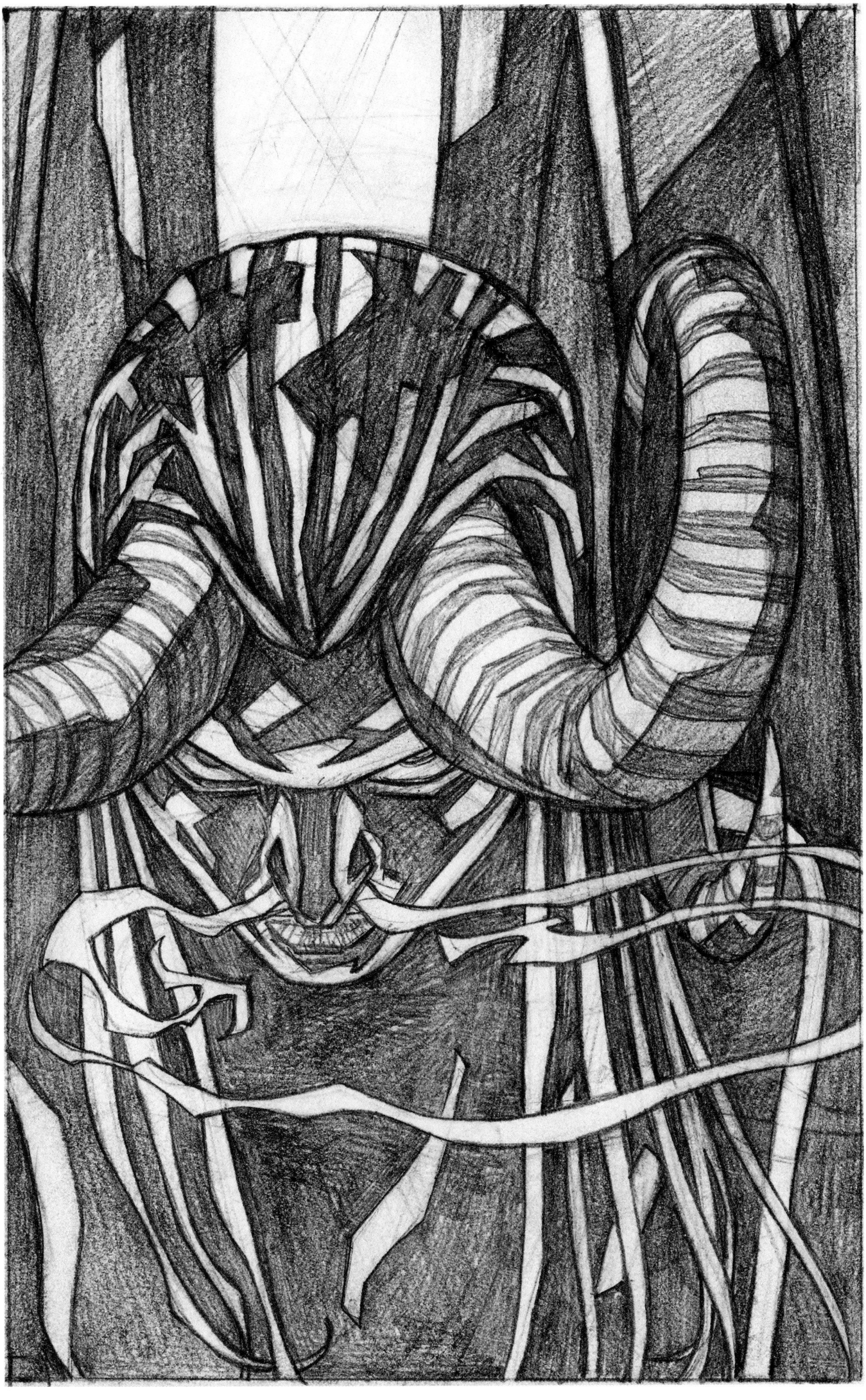

More development work on the succubus. We liked the form, but in this case the sketch didn't really tell us what she looked like.

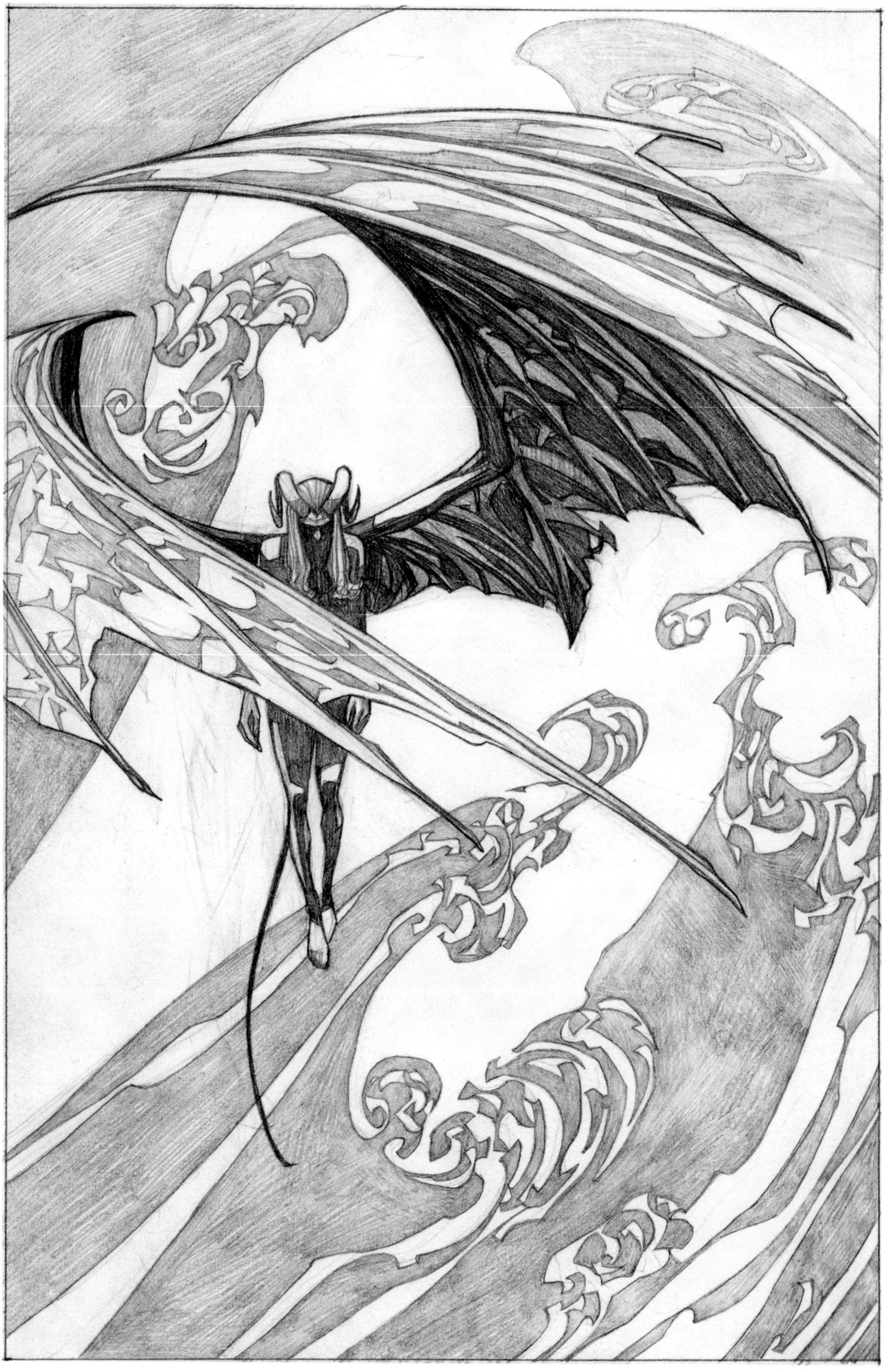

Toni works out the concept of the wings.

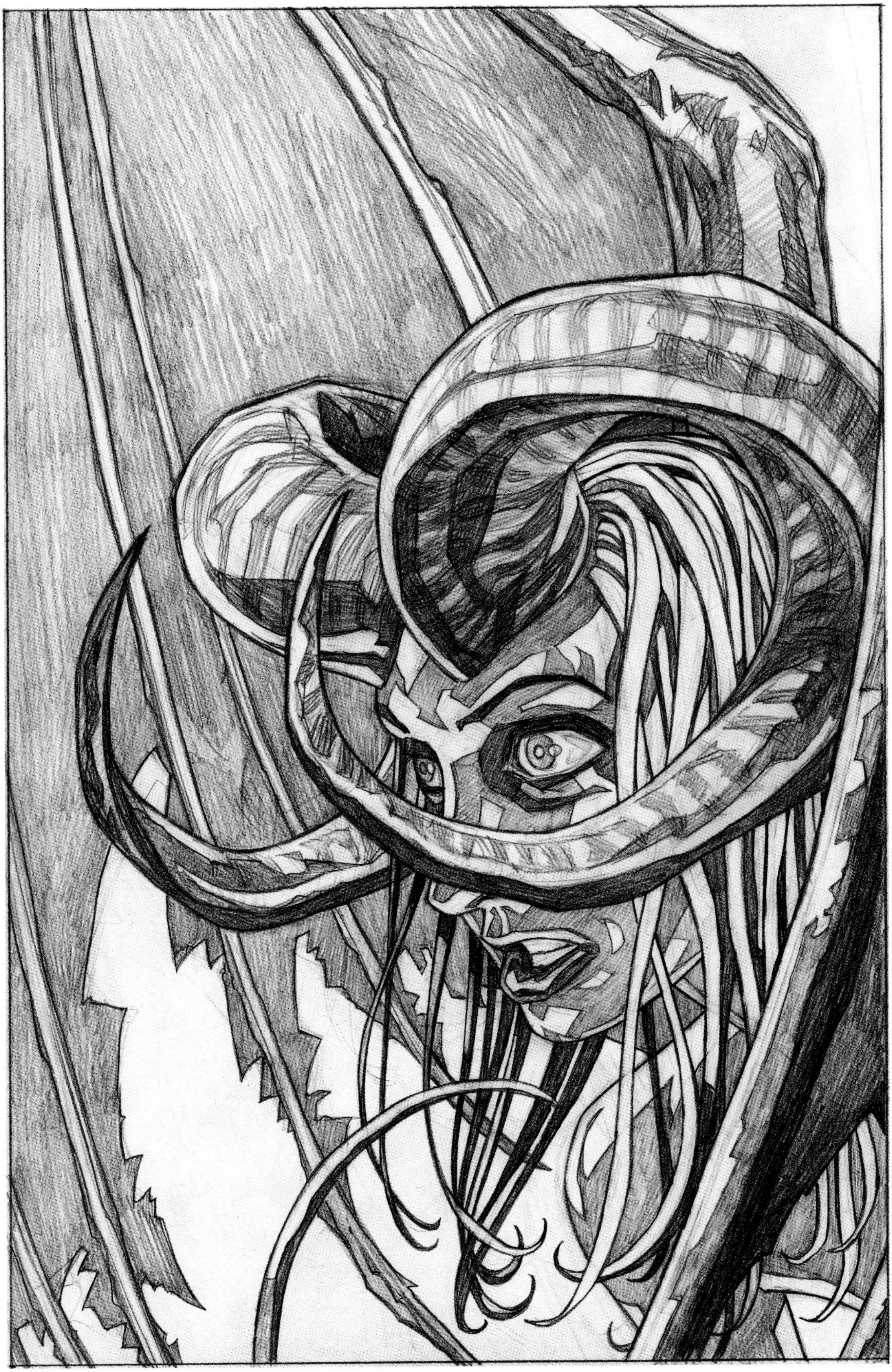

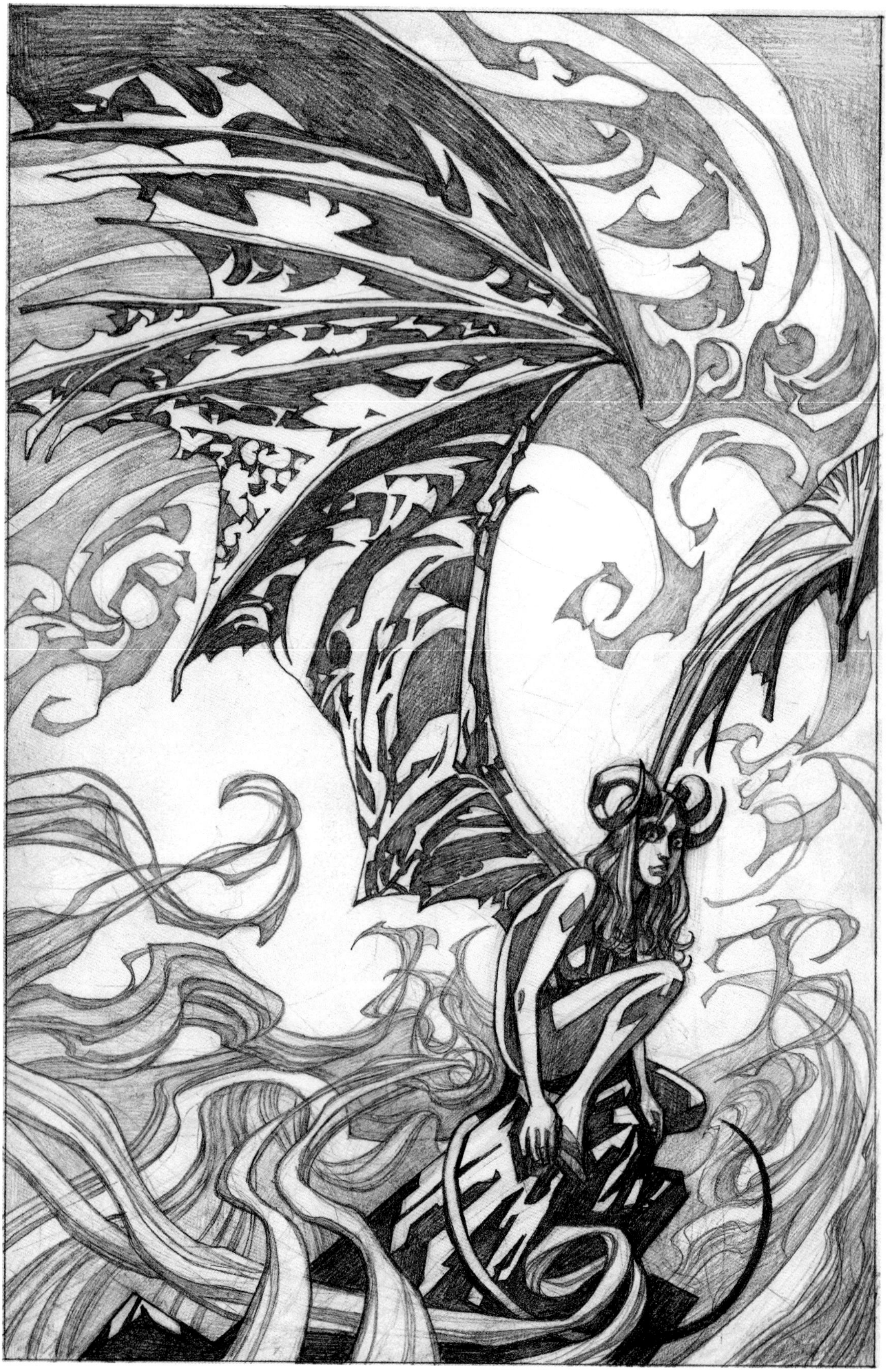

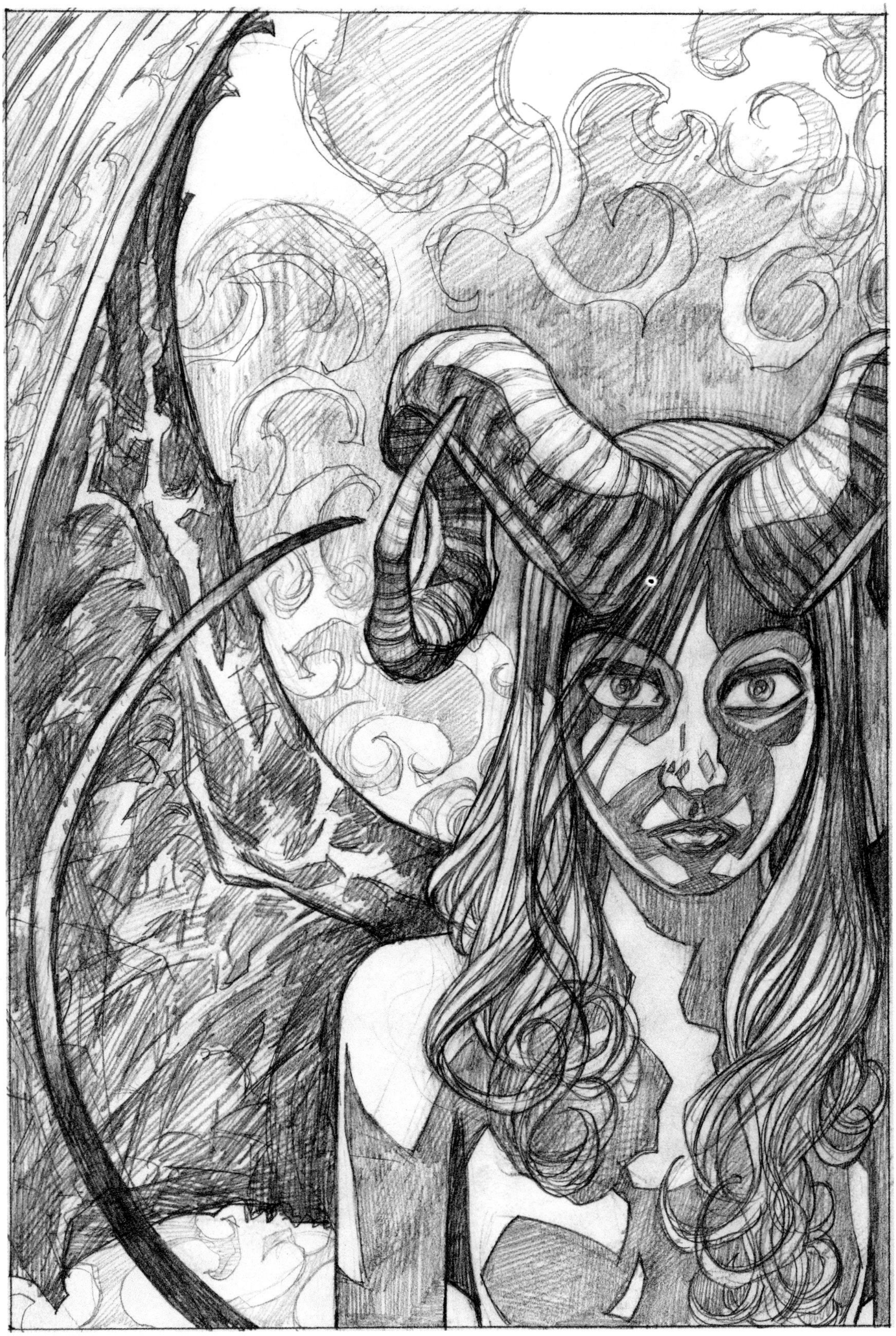

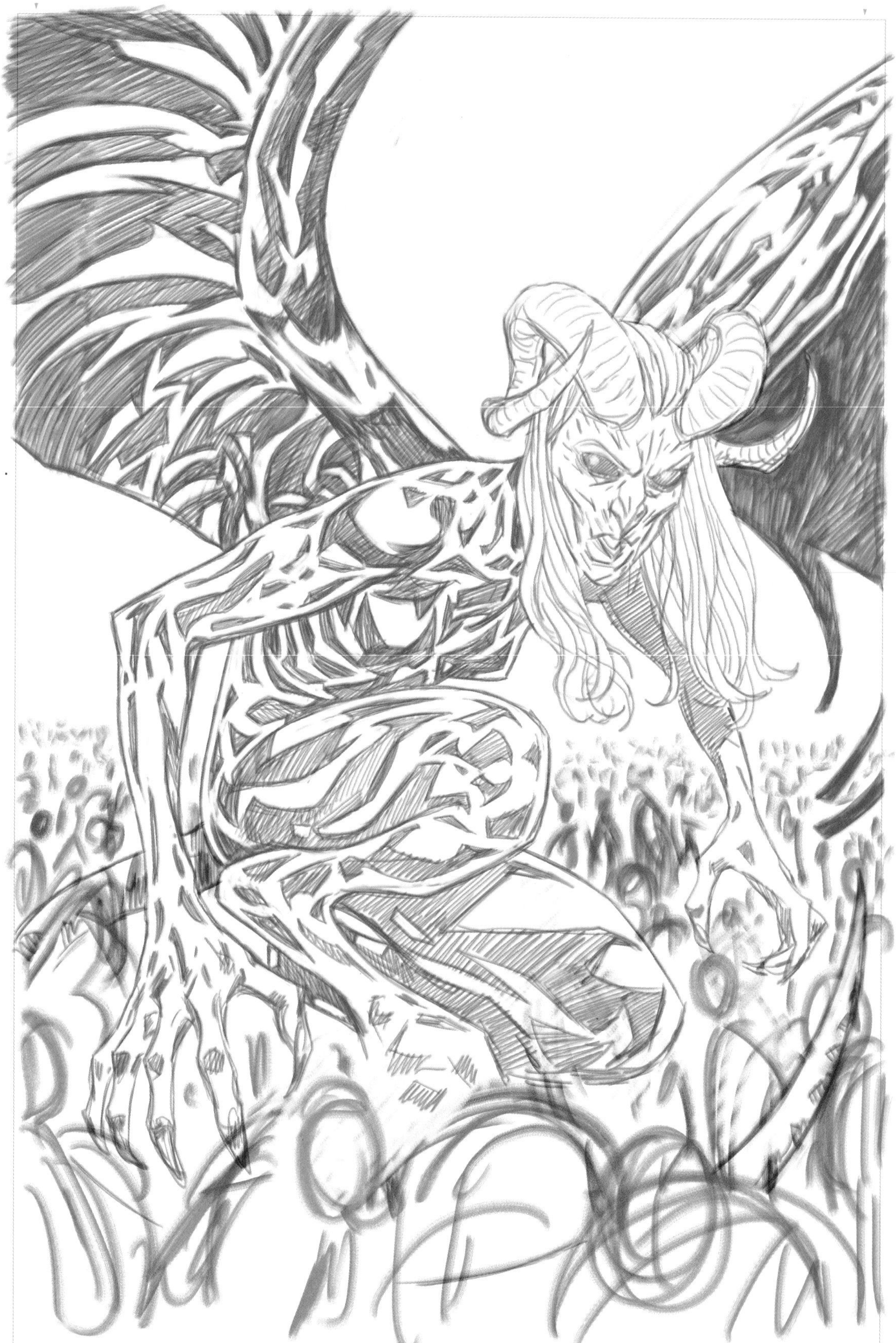

Since covers are shown so early in the promotional process, we wanted a fifth cover that would conceal the fact that Veil was a demon. This sketch gave too much away.

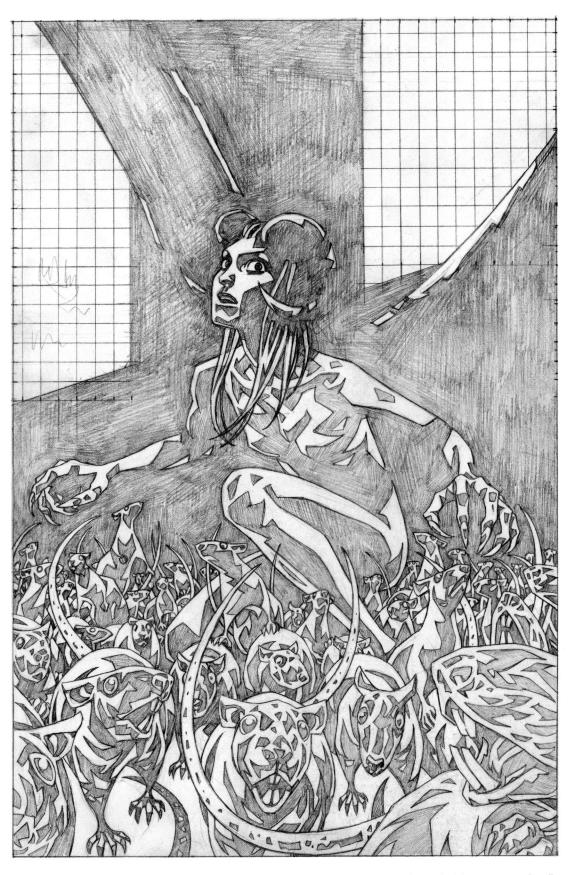

Even this showed it a little too clearly. Greg wanted to echo the first-issue cover, and we pushed that concept very literally.

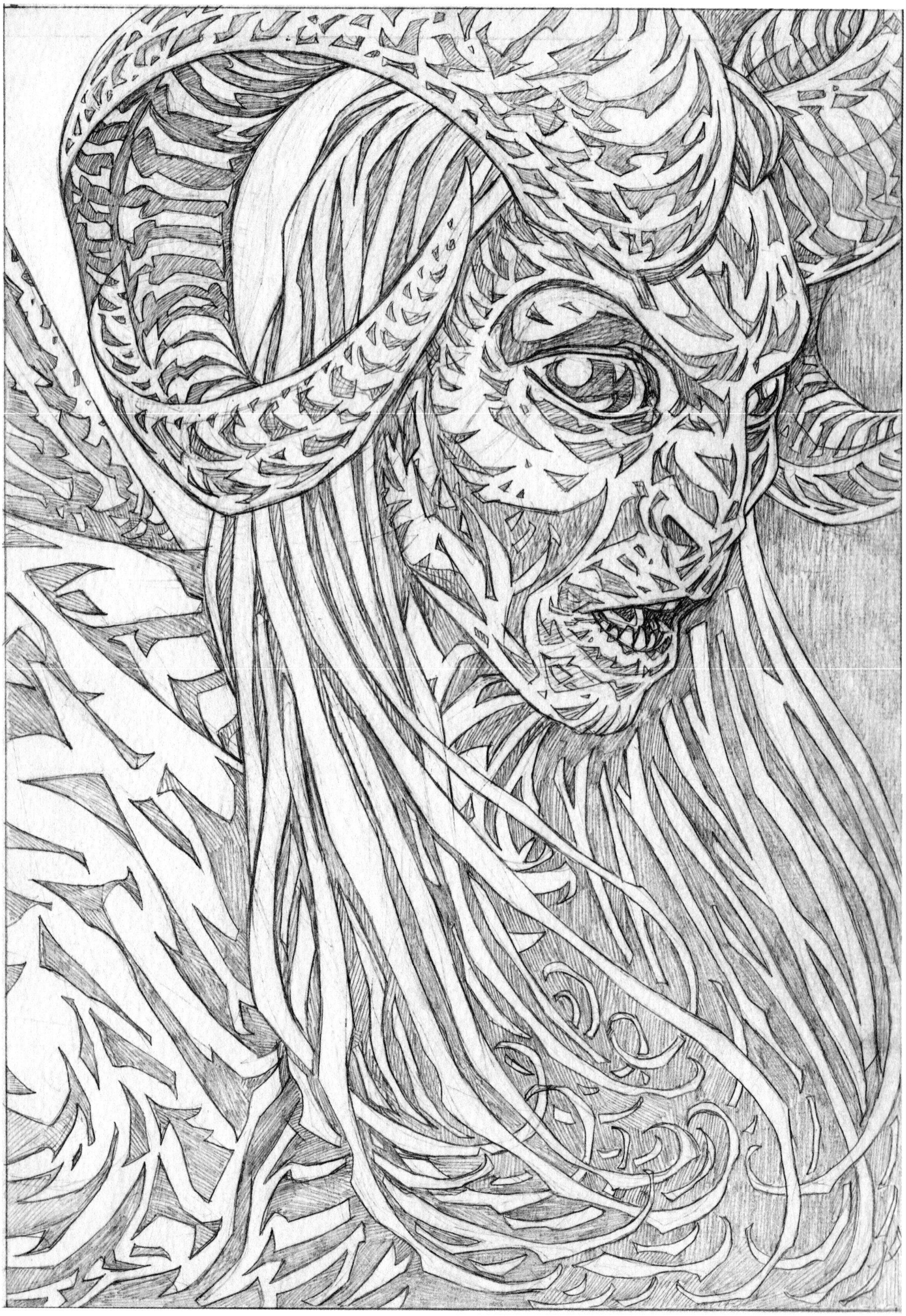

Refining Veil in her demon form.

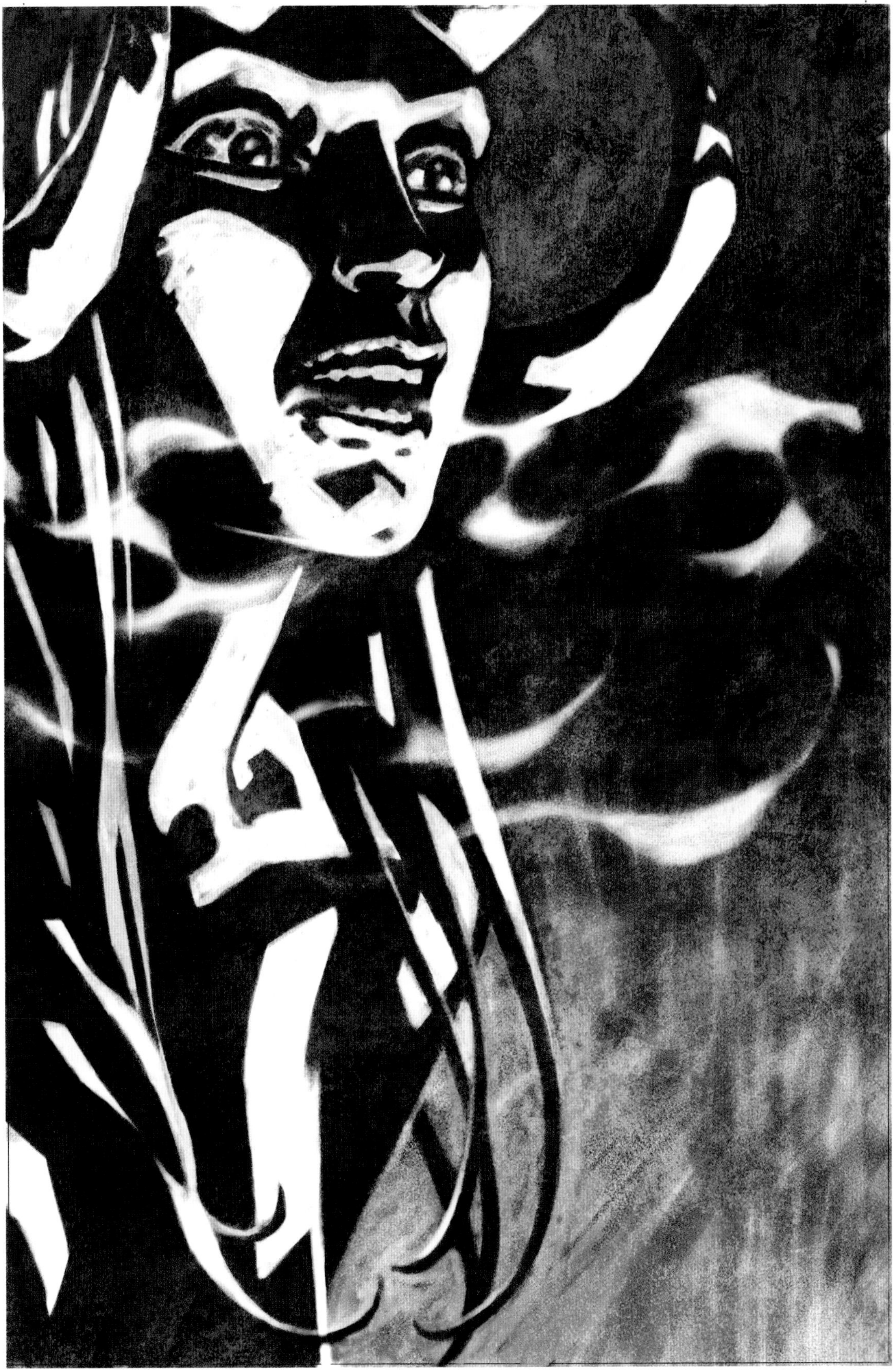

Toni only used this style in a few of the concept drawings, this time finalizing the succubus design.

drawing on your nightmares

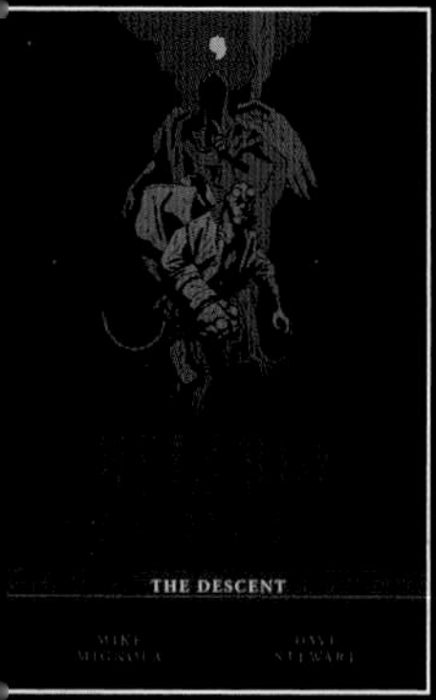
THE DESCENT

HELLBOY IN HELL VOLUME 1: THE DESCENT

Mike Mignola

Mike Mignola returns to draw Hellboy's ongoing story for the first time since *Conqueror Worm*. It's a story only Mignola could tell, as more of Hellboy's secrets are at last revealed, in the most bizarre depiction of Hell you've ever seen.

ISBN 978-1-61655-444-6 | $17.99

THE AUTHENTIC ACCOUNTS OF BILLY THE KID'S OLD TIMEY ODDITIES

Eric Powell, Kyle Hotz

The world believes the notorious outlaw Billy the Kid was killed by Pat Garrett, but in reality the Kid is very much alive, the hired gun of a traveling spectacle of biological curiosities—or "freaks," as Billy calls them. Follow Billy and this crew of oddities, presented in one gunslingin' omnibus!

ISBN 978-1-61655-470-5 | $24.99

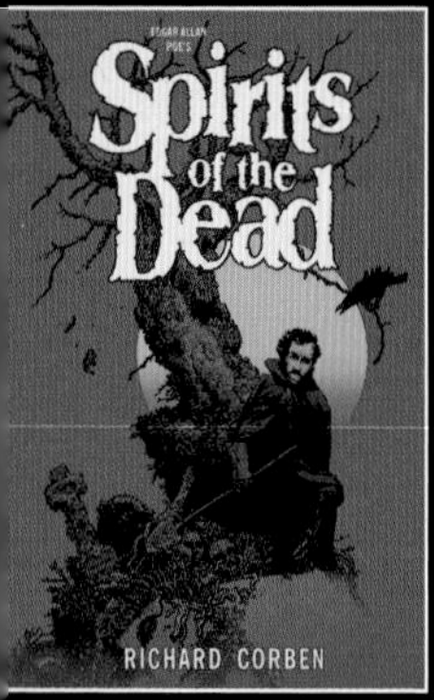
Spirits of the Dead
RICHARD CORBEN

EDGAR ALLAN POE'S SPIRITS OF THE DEAD

Richard Corben

The complete collection of Poe classics adapted by master horror comics artist and Eisner Hall of Fame inductee Richard Corben. Collects *The Conqueror Worm*, *The Fall of the House of Usher*, *The Raven and the Red Death*, *Morella and the Murders in the Rue Morgue*, and more.

ISBN 978-1-61655-356-2 | $24.99

COLDER VOLUME 1

Paul Tobin, Juan Ferreyra

Declan Thomas's body temperature is dropping. An ex-inmate of an insane asylum that was destroyed in a fire, he has the strange ability to step inside a person's madness and sometimes cure it. He hopes to one day cure his own, but time is running out, because when his temperature reaches zero . . . it's over.

ISBN 978-1-61655-136-0 | $17.99

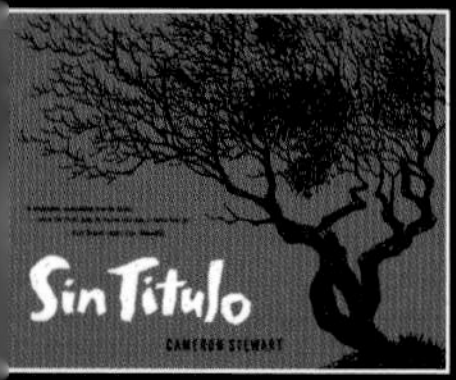
Sin Titulo
CAMERON STEWART

SIN TITULO

Cameron Stewart

Following the death of his grandfather, young Alex Mackay discovers a mysterious photograph in the old man's belongings that sets him on an adventure where dreams and reality merge, family secrets are laid bare, and lives are irrevocably altered.

ISBN 978-1-61655-248-0 | $19.99

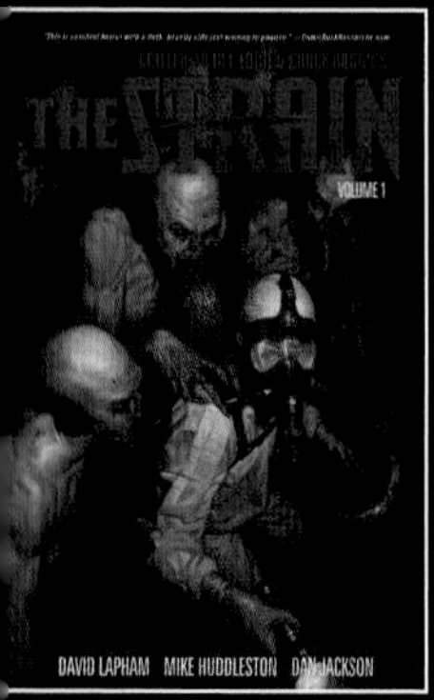
THE STRAIN
VOLUME 1
DAVID LAPHAM MIKE HUDDLESTON DAN JACKSON

GRINDHOUSE: DOORS OPEN AT MIDNIGHT DOUBLE FEATURE VOLUME 1

Alex de Campi, Chris Peterson, Simon Fraser

Literature: overrated. Morality: expendable. Midnight is right for some over-the-top sex and violence, and this *Grindhouse* double feature is packing the aisles with blood 'n' guts and T 'n' A! Gasp as insatiable alien insects overtake a Southern town with only a one-eyed deputy to stop them in "Bee Vixens from Mars"! Shudder as the sexy lady convicts of Block E revolt against an insane warden in "Prison Ship Antares"! Tremble in anticipation at the gallery of shocking "coming attractions"!

ISBN 978-1-61655-377-7 | $17.99

GUILLERMO DEL TORO AND CHUCK HOGAN'S THE STRAIN VOLUME 1

David Lapham, Mike Huddleston

When a Boeing 777 lands and goes dark on the JFK runway, the Centers for Disease Control, fearing a terrorist attack, calls in a team of expert biological-threat first responders. Only an elderly pawnbroker from Spanish Harlem suspects a darker purpose behind the event—an undead threat intent on covering mankind in darkness.

ISBN 978-1-61655-032-5 | $19.99